OLD NEW WORLDS

OLD
NEW
WORLDS

A TALE OF TWO IMMIGRANTS

JUDITH KRUMMECK

GREEN WRITERS PRESS | *Brattleboro, Vermont*

Old New Worlds is a work of nonfiction. Apart from the actual historic figures, events, and locales that provide background for the narrative, some of the names, characters, places, and incidents are products of the author's imagination or are used fictitiously to bring the historical narrative alive.

Green Writers Press is a Vermont-based publisher whose mission is to spread a message of hope and renewal through the words and images we publish. Throughout we will adhere to our commitment to preserving and protecting the natural resources of the earth. To that end, a percentage of our proceeds will be donated to environmental activist groups and The Southern Poverty Law Foundation. Green Writers Press gratefully acknowledges support from individual donors, friends, and readers to help support the environment and our publishing initiative. Green Place Books curates books that tell literary and compelling stories with a focus on writing about place—these books are more personal stories, memoir, and biographies.

GREEN PLACE BOOKS   GReen writers press

Giving Voice to Writers & Artists Who Will Make the World a Better Place
Green Writers Press | Brattleboro, Vermont
www.greenwriterspress.com

ISBN: 978-1-9505840-9-3

COVER DESIGN: Dede Cummings & Rachael Peretic
BOOK DESIGN: Dede Cummings
ARTWORK: Joan Krummeck

PRINTED ON PAPER WITH PULP THAT COMES FROM FSC-CERTIFIED FORESTS, MANAGED FORESTS THAT GUARANTEE RESPONSIBLE ENVIRONMENTAL, SOCIAL, AND ECONOMIC PRACTICES BY PRINTOPIA.

"Fiction is the history of the obscure."

—JILL LEPORE,
*Book of Ages: The Life and
Opinions of Jane Franklin*

Contents

PART ONE

THEOPOLIS, SOUTH AFRICA

DECEMBER 20, 1836

THE RAUCOUS CALL of hadeda ibis overhead was followed immediately by a low, growling roll of thunder, as if the birds had shaken loose the storm. For one beat, two beats, everything was utterly still and silent, then a downpour set up a percussive rhythm on the parched ground, and the pungent smell released by the rain drifted in at the open window. As the storm picked up momentum, the wind caught at the flimsy curtain, sucking it out through the window. A woman rushed to pull the casement shut.

"No, leave it!" said Sarah.

The woman stopped and turned toward the bed. Sarah's voice was almost inaudible against the noise of the drumming rain, but its urgency carried. The woman waited, unsure. The storm had given the room a lurid color, and the wind whipped the curtain in and out, in and out, at the window, the jagged rhythm mirroring Sarah's breathing. The strange light picked up a sheen of perspiration on Sarah's face and the silhouette of her pregnant belly.

The storm was directly overhead by this time, and a simultaneous flash of lightening and a sharp crack of thunder were the prelude to torrential rain. Under cover of the noise, Sarah gave a wrenching, guttural groan. The woman tentatively approached the bed. Sarah's dark hair clung to her wet face, and a long strand was plastered across her throat like a gash.

"It's all right. . . ," she said, but the end of the word was twisted in a cry. "Go and call Reverend Barker!"

The woman, relieved to have something concrete to do, ran from the room.

Sarah listened to her bare feet padding away down the passage. The wind swirling through the room felt blessedly cool across her damp face. As the grip of pain began to subside she listened, still for a moment, to the rain pounding the earth outside the window.

When the cycle of pain began again, it was a clutching cramping that brought with it an overpowering urge to bear down. She felt a gush of warmth between her legs. She thought, at first, that it was her water breaking . . . but the warmth kept seeping and spreading. She lifted her head and looked down the length of her body, sprawled at an angle across the bed where she had fallen when the pain first hit, and she watched as the first stains bled through her dress. Her head fell back again as her consciousness shrank to a scarlet circle of pain.

The storm began to subside as quickly as it had come. The rain turned to drips, and the sodden curtain hung limply at the open window. The light in the room slowly changed as the late-afternoon sun broke through again. The strange call of a red-chested cuckoo drifted into the silent room, *Piet-my-vrou . . . Piet-my-vrou . . . Piet-my-vrou . . .*

Chapter One

I DON'T KNOW if this is what happened. But, as I started to feel my way towards Sarah's story, and based on the few scattered facts I knew about her, I imagined that this is how it *might* have been.

I know the date; it was the eve of the summer solstice in the Southern Hemisphere. It would have been hot, and it's possible there was one of those thunderstorms that cool things off on a late-summer afternoon in South Africa's Eastern Cape. Perhaps the simple room at the mission station in Theopolis was redolent of earth, heat, dust, sweat, and the metallic, cloying smell of blood. This would have been Sarah's sixteenth pregnancy.

I also know for a fact that Sarah Barker née Williams sailed from Portsmouth, England, aboard the tall ship *Alfred* on March 2, 1815, bound for the Cape of Good Hope at the southern tip of Africa. One hundred and eighty-two years later, on July 18, 1997, my life intersected with Sarah's when I leaned forward in my window seat to watch Cape Town dropping away below me as the plane took off. I etched the moment in my mind's eye, storing it away for all the times I knew I would need to take it out and relive it. It was the first step of my immigration to America—a process that was taking me away from the country where Sarah had planted me, and that would ultimately take me on a long, looping search for her story.

I don't remember a time when I didn't know the history of my ancestors who emigrated from England to become missionaries in South Africa's Eastern Cape. My mother, Joan née Barker, was a compelling storyteller, and her low voice, with its trace of the Eastern Cape accent, wove its way into my imagination and memory. She kept a double portrait of her great-grandparents by her front door, and I could see in George Barker's high forehead, deep-set eyes, straight mouth, and large, flat ears a likeness to my mother, and also to my grandfather, my uncle, and my brother. My cousin, Elspeth née Barker, who looks nothing like the rest of us, is Sarah's *doppelgänger* with her periwinkle-blue eyes, softly-rounded cheeks, dark, wavy hair, and full, curvaceous mouth.

The portrait was my first clue to Sarah. My second was her slanting signature with its beautiful "W" where she signed her maiden name, Sarah Williams, as a witness on the marriage certificate of Elizabeth Rogers and Joseph Williams on January 16, 1815. At first, it was tempting to think that Joseph Williams was Sarah's brother—but no, he was George's fellow student when they trained to be missionaries at the Gosport Academy near Portsmouth. Sarah and Elizabeth were both natives of Shropshire and worked together as servants for the Rev. Mr. Waters and his wife on Kingsland Road in London's present-day Hackney.

George's signature appears underneath Sarah's on Elizabeth and Joseph's marriage certificate, and I've experimented with several scenarios as I've puzzled over whether Sarah and George first met on their friends' wedding day, or if the four of them had been in each other's company beforehand. In any event, exactly one week after Elizabeth and Joseph's wedding, George informed the London Missionary Society's Committee of Examiners that he wished to marry Sarah Williams.

But she wasn't his first choice. Seven weeks earlier, George had advised the L.M.S. Committee of Examination that he wished to marry a young woman who was a member of a Mr. Kemp's church at Terling in Essex. Five days later, he'd sent a letter to the committee announcing that he had failed in his application to the young woman at Terling and expressing, apparently "in the most suitable Terms," his desire to "acquiesce in the Will of God and go to Africa in the single State."

A cold chill of empathy runs over my skin at the thought of Sarah being George's second choice. Did he think that the young woman from Terling was the love of his life? Was he on the rebound? Had he simply been desperate to have a wife—any wife—to accompany him on his mission work, as St. John Rivers had been when he proposed a loveless marriage to Jane Eyre in the book that Charlotte Brontë had yet to write? Nobody wants to be someone else's backup plan. I was haunted by the thought that perhaps Sarah knew, and felt she had to try to measure up.

But she appeared before the committee on the very same day that George informed them that he wished to marry her and, according to the minutes, "gave satisfactory answers to the Questions proposed to her." My twenty-first century hackles rise at the thought of these pompous old men passing judgment on her in this way. But, their judgment was evidently favorable because, three days later, George was granted permission to marry Sarah.

Journal
Feby. 4th, 1815

This day I entered into the solemn engagement of marriage previous to my departure from my native land the Lord having provided Sarah Williams a native of Shropshire to be my companion in the arduous undertaking before me. Lord give us wisdom and prudence so to conduct ourselves in this new station in life.

When you climb the three curved steps to St. Mary's Church in Islington on the busy thoroughfare of Upper Street in north London and close the double-glass doors behind you, it becomes suddenly hushed and secluded. Light reaches in through immensely tall windows to lie across the cork flooring, carving out a shadow of the marble baptismal font on the right, and then stretching towards the shallow steps where Sarah and George would have stood before the Rev. Joseph Rose.

Standing where she stood, I tried to inhabit her life as she might have lived and thought and felt it. In my mind's eye, she keeps her gaze fixed on the minister's mouth as it forms the words, "We are gathered together here in the sight of God, and in the face of this Congregation, to join together this man and this woman." It's as if she's looking at herself from the outside, as though this is all happening to someone else. A carriage passes in the street, the jingle of the horse's bells muffled by a clammy winter fog. It is still cold enough for the Thames to be frozen, but she feels flushed, and her heart beats in her ears.

"George. Wilt thou have this woman to be thy wedded wife . . . ?"

Sarah senses George shifting on her right and slides her eyes under lowered lids to study the hem of his frockcoat as she waits for the minister to complete his charge.

"I will," says George.

"Sarah." She lifts her eyes and fixes them again on Rev. Rose's mouth. "Wilt thou have this man to thy wedded husband, to live together after God's ordinance in the holy estate of Matrimony? Wilt thou obey him, and serve him, love, honor, and keep him in sickness and in health; and, forsaking all other, keep thee only unto him, so long as ye both shall live?"

"I—" But no sound comes. She swallows. "I will."

George takes her hand when it's time for the ring. The dry, cool roughness of his skin triggers the memory of him taking both her hands in his when he'd asked her to come with him to Africa—the sudden, astounding surprise of it. How she'd opened the door to him at the Waters' house on Kingsland Road where she was working as a servant and had been nonplussed to find him standing on the doorstep. She couldn't imagine what he was doing there—unless it was on business with the Rev. Mr. Waters. But after she ushered him into the parlor, he had taken her hands and said, "Miss Williams . . ." standing so close that his face swam out of focus above her. Then he'd done the most perplexing thing; keeping a firm grip on her hands, he'd knelt down on one knee so that she was now looking down into his face, and said, "Sarah, would you do me the honor of accompanying me to South Africa as my wife?"

She'd stared down into his gray eyes, astounded, bombarded by half thoughts. What had she to keep her here, she wondered? When her father died, she'd been sent as a young girl to live with relatives in a neighboring Shropshire county, but she'd rarely seen them since she came to London. There was her brother, John, but although they corresponded regularly, she seldom saw him either. She thought of Elizabeth, who had befriended her when she felt abandoned as a child, and how she was dreading saying goodbye to her when she sailed for South Africa with Joseph. She thought about her dreary life in service. She tried to envision Africa, a new life there. She searched the vulnerable face of this near stranger. She was silent for so long, simply staring down at him, that he began to speak again, and their words collided into each other.

"Perhaps you need more time..."

"I will ... yes, yes ... I will!"

That had been only two weeks before, but it seems both longer and shorter at the same time. Now, when George slides the wedding ring over the bump of her knuckle, I imagine Sarah rubbing the tip of her left thumb across the thin band, exploring the strangeness of it where it separates the base of her finger from her palm.

When Rev. Rose says, "I pronounce that they be man and wife together," she glances up into George's face and finds his eyes fixed on her. His straight mouth is tilting up at one corner, and quite suddenly she can't breathe properly.

With the ceremony over, the minister leads the way to an alcove behind the pulpit for the signing of the marriage register, and when George puts his hand under her elbow to guide her up the shallow marble steps, she feels his touch like a warm current shooting through her. Rev. Rose sits at the small table, picks up the quill, which he's evidently had the forethought to sharpen beforehand, dips it in the inkwell, and carefully scratches out the letters. *St Mary, Islington, Middlesex, 1815. The Reverend George Barker of this Parish. Sarah Williams of the Parish of St Olave, Silver Street, London. Spinster. Fourth February.* In the space after the words *In the Year One Thousand Eight Hundred and—* he writes *Fifteen,* and signs *J.P. Rose, Minister.*

Then he lays down the quill, scrapes the chair back, and holds it for George, who takes his seat, and in the space after *This Marriage was solemnized between us* he writes *George Barker.* When it is Sarah's turn, she has the sense that there is too much bobbing up and down and scraping of chairs, so she just leans over the table and carefully writes *Sarah Williams* directly under George's neat signature. Then, because it is the last time she will sign her name this way, she makes a little line under the "W."

When I saw a copy of their marriage certificate online for the first time around two hundred years later, sitting in my writing studio in America, the little line she made under the "W" was like a whispered greeting.

Chapter Two

I NEVER REALLY MET MY HUSBAND. I had seen him
playing French horn in various South African orchestras,
and he'd heard me hosting an arts program on the SAfm
radio station. We passed each other in the corridors of the
South African Broadcasting Corporation in Johannesburg.
We got into the elevator together one day en route to our
respective gigs and we made small talk. The talk was so
small that I can't remember what it was about, but there was
enough of it for me to hear that he had an American accent.
We got to know each other by a process of osmosis. I learned
that his name was Douglas Blackstone.

After an orchestra function one evening, he kissed my
hand and said, "We should meet for coffee sometime," in a
way that made me think, "Oh, *I* see!" It took a while, but we
eventually arranged to meet at the coffee shop in the foyer
of the SABC's monolithic office building. It was closed. As
I was dithering about, not quite sure how to proceed, he
popped out of an elevator.

"Oh!" I said, "I thought we would miss each other."

"I would have found you," he said.

We ended up in the very unromantic workers' canteen. There was no cashier—or anyone else, for that matter—and so we just helped ourselves, and he left a twenty rand note balanced on its edge on the counter.

He was droll and vulnerable and out of the ordinary. He was passionate about musical note grouping and nineteenth-century painting and Somerset Maugham.

But it was complicated. He was married to someone else, and so was I, even though my marriage had reached the final stages with a death rattle so excruciating that I felt stripped, not knowing who I was anymore, but sure that I would never risk putting myself through anything like that ever again.

When Douglas, newly unmarried, asked me to marry him, and I said no, and he had to ask me again, it wasn't only because I was feeling traumatized about marriage in general. It was also because I was waging a fierce battle with myself. For years I had been searching all which-ways to leave South Africa. I found the geographical and cultural isolation, exacerbated by the pall of apartheid, cloying and stultifying. But as a fifth-generation South African, I didn't have the right to citizenship in any other country. Here was a man offering me a gift-wrapped chance at American citizenship, and I had to keep testing myself to be absolutely certain that I wouldn't be marrying him just to get a green card. He said I was like Elizabeth Bennet refusing Mr. Darcy.

Halfway between Johannesburg and the Kruger National Park in the northeastern region of South Africa, there's a place where the mists roll in over the hills, where the air is unalloyed, where you can easily imagine yourself in the Scottish Highlands. It is, in fact, the highlands of Mpumalanga, "the place where the sun rises." At 6,811 feet above sea level, it is home to the country's highest railway station, to South Africa's premier fly-fishing region, and to a farm called Millstream, which is Douglas's favorite place in all the world. When too much time has elapsed since his last visit, he begins to get restless and a little haunted, and we have to start making plans.

Every time we've gone there is like a bookmark or a corner folded down on a page to remember the passage. We've experienced every season there from drought to snow, it's where we went when we were first lovers—and it's where we were married in a cabin redolent of tuber roses, surrounded by the small group of irreplaceable friends who had travelled the journey of our on-again, off-again courtship with us. When it was all signed and sealed, maverick that he was, Douglas went out in his wedding clothes to cast a fly-fishing line into the dam below our cabin.

Six months later, on July 18, 1997, I emigrated. For Sarah, the time lapse from marriage to emigration is just twenty-six days.

CHAPTER THREE

Tuesday February 7th, 1815

Took leave of the friends in London and came to Portsmouth in order to embark for this place assigned me by providence as the scene of my future labours (Lattakoo) in South Africa.

FEBRUARY 7, 1815 was George's twenty-ninth birthday. I picture Sarah and him taking the stagecoach from London to Portsmouth along the same road where, just the year before, the Duke of Wellington, Tsar Alexander of Russia, and the King of Prussia had paraded to celebrate the capture of Napoleon.

I imagine the coach jolting over the London cobbles on a cold and foggy winter morning, Sarah feeling grateful that George has been able to secure a place for them inside, even though the man next to her has pungent halitosis and she and George must travel with their backs to the coachmen so that the scenery slides past the windows like an afterthought. George murmurs a prayer for safe travel, and Sarah leans her shoulder against her husband of three days as she settles in for the nine-hour journey.

"Tell me something of the other missionaries," she says in a low voice, creating a little space of private conversation between them in the crowded coach.

"Well," George responds in kind, "Joseph and Elizabeth you know. Robert Hamilton is a millwright by trade, and since I am a blacksmith, the committee recommended that he and I should be associated to establish the mission at Lattakoo together. Brother Robert is a reserved man, some-what older than we are—nearly forty, I believe. The fourth missionary is John Evans, from Wales. God has bestowed on him the gift of writing, and he was of great assistance to me at the Gosport Academy in that regard. He has a wife named Mary, with whom I am not yet acquainted. You will meet them all soon enough."

She nods, and lets the conversation rest. She feels less strange with him now and silences no longer hang awkwardly, so she is content for the quiet to settle between them as she jostles against his body with the swaying of the stagecoach. The malodorous travelling companion on the other side of her has fallen into a wheezing sleep, and the others inside the coach stare vacantly, their minds clearly absorbed elsewhere.

George slips a hand under her cloak and finds hers. She feels a tug of sexuality. Of all the astonishing things that have taken place over the past month, this is the most unexpected of all. The clutching anxiety about what she had regarded as her conjugal duty had dissolved into an intimacy she hadn't even guessed was possible. And even more than the plea-sure they learned from each other's bodies was the feeling of belonging that the intimacy gave her. She had to think back to her earliest childhood to remember such a sense of affinity. The relatives who had taken her in after her father died were kind in every way, but the kindness was given consciously, with intent, not instinctively in the way that they gave to their own children. She had always been the outsider. This feeling of being part of someone, and he of her, makes her thrum with contentment. She rubs her thumb over his knuckle, and feels a returning pressure.

They stop at an inn at Guildford to change the horses. George helps Sarah down from the coach—she is still getting used to the novelty of these courtesies—and she goes in search of the privy while he gives a shilling to the coachman for the first stage. It's curious to be going about the countryside like married folk, paying their way as if they were gentry. Or, at least, so it seems, compared to the quiet, hidden life she's led in service.

The last staging post, eight miles north of Porstmouth, is the village of Horndean. From there, the stagecoach climbs up the long chalk ridge of Portsdown Hill. As they crest it, George urges Sarah to lean forward and look back so that she can see out the window. Dusk is falling, but she can make out the glinting water beyond the downs and the etched silhouettes of the masts and rigging of the tall ships in the harbour.

"That's Portsmouth Harbour to the south," says George, "and the bulge to the west across the harbour is Gosport, where the missionary academy is. You might not be able to see it clearly now, but the land mass beyond Gosport is the Isle of Wight."

"Oh my!" Her expression is rapt.

"Have you ever seen the sea before?"

"Never."

When they disembark, Elizabeth and Joseph are there to greet them. Elizabeth is two years older than Sarah and has always seemed to be two steps ahead. She had gone first to London and found the position at the Rev. Mr. Waters' house, she had married first, and she had come down to Portsmouth soon after her marriage. She holds fast onto Sarah's hands now, looking deep into her eyes. She is not a beautiful woman—her brow is low and her features heavily drawn—but her nose is delicate and her eyes are a striking ice blue.

"Aren't you a one to be full of surprises?" she says.

"Oh, Beth," says Sarah, "I would never have had the courage to change my life's course so dramatically were it not for you."

A week later, George writes in his journal:

Went on board the ship Alfred (Captain Grainger) bound to the Cape of Good Hope.

From the vantage point of the deck, they can clearly see the HMS *Victory* moored in the harbor.

"She was badly damaged in the Battle of Trafalgar," Captain Grainger explains, "and her career ended a little over two years ago."

He turns to a large uniformed man on his left, whose nose, cheeks, and chin are all the same notable shade of pink, and says, "This is Mr. Higgs, our third mate. He will show you your quarters below deck."

They are to be quartered in the rear of the ship below the poop deck, where the large open space is divided into makeshift "cabins" by canvas screens set up between gun portholes. Each cabin has a cot, barely wide enough for two, suspended like a hammock.

"These partitions can be quickly cleared away if the *Alfred* comes under attack," the third mate says matter-of-factly. "Napoleon may be on Elba for now, but we don't know for how long. And there are Barbary pirates, and the like." He registers the stricken faces around him, and adds, "But don't worry! We'll have an escorting fleet." He turns back towards the stairs. "I'll leave you to get settled. It may look close here, but it's better than the crew's quarters on the berth deck below. The men are crammed in cheek by jowl down there, and it's like a baker's oven in the summer."

Once he has taken his big personality with him, the place seems even darker. Sarah and Elizabeth, without a look or a word needing to pass between them, slip quietly into two cabins next to each other. If they and their husbands are going to have next to no privacy for the next two months, at least they can share an adjoining screen.

On their first night at sea, Sarah wakes to the sound of violent retching. She makes to get up, but George holds her still. He puts his mouth to her ear and whispers, "It's Brother Joseph. He has seasickness." Sarah hears the soft, soothing voice of Elizabeth, but it seems to do nothing to ease her husband's extreme discomfort, and his bouts of heaving are interspersed with low groans of complete wretchedness. The close, dank air of their shared sleeping quarters is redolent of vomit, and Sarah feels her own mouth fill with watery saliva as if she might succumb to sickness herself. George pulls her head onto his shoulder, and she presses her face into the folds of his nightshirt, inhaling the comforting smell of his now-familiar scent.

As the *Alfred* leaves the calm waters of the English Channel and ventures into the Atlantic Ocean at the notoriously treacherous Bay of Biscay, they are battered by gales and heavy seas. The sea runs mountain high, and great waves beat on deck. The ship is in such violent motion that it is impossible to stand, the sailors are drenched, everything rolling about. The tension on the ship matches the insidious wind that howls around them. A squall is so ferocious at one point that the escorting fleet scatters and disappears, and

Captain Grainger makes no secret of his grave concern in light of the lingering threat of the Napoleonic wars.

Gradually, they drift into calmer waters past the Spanish mainland, and George points out a small village nestled there. Portuguese fishermen hail them from their boats and climb aboard to share their catch—mostly in sign language, since only one of the sailors can speak any Portuguese.

At one o'clock on the morning of March 20, the alarm is given that a stranger sail is bearing down on them from the south. All are in consternation, and preparations are made for an engagement. In various states of dress, the missionaries clamber above deck as the canvas screens between their makeshift sleeping cabins are thrust aside, the portholes opened, matches lighted, guns primed with powder horns, and cutlasses strapped on in readiness.

"She's hoisted British colors, Captain!" shouts the first mate.

"I will not trust her!" the captain calls back.

When the stranger vessel comes alongside, Captain Grainger raises a trumpet to his mouth and hails her. "What ship?"

"His Britannic Majesty's brig!" echoes the reply over the water.

The ship passes to leeward.

"All females below deck, please!" calls Captain Grainger.

As Sarah climbs back down the wooden ladder to their quarters, her foot slips on a rung and she realizes that her whole body is trembling. It's chaos down below. Her box of possessions has tipped over, a bonnet and a shift spilling out, intimately vulnerable in what is now a male milieu of trampling boots, shouted orders, and grunting maneuvers to man the guns at the portholes.

The three missionary wives, Sarah, Elizabeth, and Mary Evans, stand in a tight circle in the midst of the pandemonium. Sarah sees her own fear in Mary's pinched, taut face. Her heart is thudding. She squeezes her eyes shut. *Dear God*... she starts a silent prayer. Her eyes fly open when a red glow suddenly lights the portholes. A second later, there's a shuddering reverberation underfoot.

"Damn and bloody hell," shouts a sailor, "the bastards are firing at us!"

"Watch your language! There are ladies present."

Another flash of fire; another reverberation.

"Take care of your heads!" Captain Grainger shouts above. "The grapeshot will fly about like hail."

The *Alfred* is moving faster now, and Sarah strains her ears to try to sense what is going on in the melee up above. She thinks she can hear the crack of sails, but it's difficult to distinguish one sound from another in the commotion.

"Sarah!" George's voice comes out of the disorder. She runs to the bottom of the wooden ladder and looks up at him. "We are outsailing them. Brother Robert and I are going to stand on the poop deck. Come!" She bundles her skirt in front of her and climbs the ladder as he reaches down to help her, with Elizabeth and Mary following.

When George and Sarah join Robert Hamilton, their missionary friend says, "It's the opinion of all that it is an American privateer. Evidently, there are still a number of Americans who try to seize British ships as prizes in the aftermath of the British-American War."

As he speaks, the brig turns and twists about, making tall sail to follow the *Alfred*, but it is not as good a sailer and continues to lose ground. It maneuvers sideways and fires a broadside, the deafening sound of the simultaneous firing of all its guns ricocheting across the water. Sarah covers her ears and counts six in all. By this time, the *Alfred* is so far away as to be perfectly out of danger, and Sarah can see, by the illumination of the firing shots, the balls falling into the sea halfway between the two ships. They send up huge fountains of seawater, which arc back down like fireworks in the garish light.

It's the final volley from the privateer. As the *Alfred* continues to outdistance the brig, passengers begin to drift below deck again to try to get some sleep for the remainder of the night. The sailors have restored order—miraculously, it seems to Sarah—and the makeshift sleeping quarters are set up again. But George and Sarah are too taut with nervous energy to sleep. They lie entwined in their narrow cot, reliving the scenes in low voices. They've become practiced at creating their cocoon of intimacy in this way, and these are the moments that Sarah loves most.

Over the next days, the scattered escorting fleet rejoins their convoy one by one. They meet a fleet of British naval vessels, and a captain hails them with the news, "Napoleon's armies are defeated! The war is over!" A huge cheer goes up on the *Alfred*.

The farther south they sail, the brighter the sun and the warmer the weather. They round the bulge of Africa, and the heat grows stultifying as they near the equator. Each morning, the four missionaries take turns reading prayers on the deck for whoever wishes to attend, and one morning the heat is so intense that George takes the unprecedented step of reading the prayers in his shirtsleeves under an awning. When they cross the equator, the missionaries join the sailors in the traditional ceremony of shaving off their beards.

Sarah finds the soft, naked skin on George's cheeks touching and that night, lying entwined in their narrow cot, she runs her fingers over his newly smooth face, speaking close to his ear in a voice so low that only he can hear.

"I feel almost certain that I am carrying our child."

When he doesn't immediately respond, she draws back slightly to look at him in the dim light, and sees that his eyes are brimming over. She watches a tear make its way over the bridge of his nose and plop onto the makeshift pillow. He pulls her close.

In early May, the *Alfred* reaches the last leg of its voyage down the west coast of southern Africa. Conditions are increasingly trying as provisions start to run low, and George frets about Sarah's wellbeing in her newly pregnant state. All are rationed two quarts of water per day. Personal hygiene is a challenge, and George and his companions grow their beards again. The days and nights drag on, each a monotonous repetition of the one before. Sarah feels she would give anything to feel solid ground under her feet. The last of their livestock, a pig, is slaughtered on Saturday, May 20. Hardly any wind is blowing, and the *Alfred* moves languorously. A soporific sea weariness hangs over the ship.

Suddenly, "Land, Captain!" comes from the lookout up in the crow's nest.

His words are like a current that galvanizes everyone, sailors and passengers, to rush to find a vantage point. They alternately strain their eyes to try and see land, and look back up towards the poop deck, where Captain Grainger has a spyglass trained directly ahead.

Eventually, he calls out, "I think not."

Rather than his words deflating the atmosphere on the ship, the excitement holds, and all continue to look out anxiously for land. In the afternoon, unmistakably, the flat top of Table Mountain presents itself to their view. The wind, such as it is, moves the *Alfred* very slowly closer, and George goes up the mizzenmast at the rear of the ship for a look.

"I saw two mountains," he reports back to Sarah, his gray eyes alight with excitement. "To the right of Table Mountain, there was a smaller, rounder one, shaped almost like a head."

As the sun sinks over the mountains, the wind picks up briskly, and they can hear it buffeting around the ship when they go below deck for the night. George is too restless to sleep, and he gets up again at two A.M. Sarah watches him adroitly negotiating the steep wooden steps in the dark, with all the familiarity of two months' practice—so different from the time they had all gingerly made their way down the steps when they'd first come on board at Portsmouth.

When he climbs into their cot again, he is cold to the touch, and shivering, whether from cold or excitement Sarah can't tell. He folds himself in next to her, putting his hand on her belly, and she can feel the biting cold of his fingers through her shift.

"The mountains of Africa were in sight," he whispers. "By the light of the moon I could see this land I have long wished to see."

At five A.M., he gives up trying to sleep altogether. By the time Sarah joins him on the deck, the wind has died down and the *Alfred* is in a complete calm on a clear, late-autumn day.

"The scenery is beautiful!" says George as she joins him and slips her hand through his arm.

She sees now that there are, in fact, three mountains: a dramatically angular mountain on the left, the imposing expanse of Table Mountain in the center, and the head-shaped mountain George had described, which slopes down towards a rounded hill on the right.

"I think we're about twenty miles from the foot of Table Mountain where it rises up behind Cape Town," George estimates.

As they lie becalmed throughout the day, there is nothing for it but to look and marvel at the city nestled in the amphitheater of the mountains. Then the wind picks up again at about seven in the evening.

"We should come to anchor by twelve!" calls one sailor.

"I say sooner!" replies another.

"No, it will be later," says the second mate.

The wind isn't in the *Alfred*'s favor. The ship has to make a great many tacks before she can come to anchor opposite Cape Town a little after nine in the morning—to the no small joy of all on board.

CHAPTER FOUR

Our baggage was all on shore by 1 o'clock & before three, the customhouse business all finished & we at our lodgings.

IF ONLY GEORGE had given more than this dry, Spartan description! I long for more details about "the custom-house business." The customs house on Buitenkant Street in Cape Town, complete with its double stairway and the sculptured British coat of arms in the pediment, had been dedicated just the year before they arrived in Table Bay. This was surely where they went to present their equivalent of a passport, which would have been printed on an official document with the British Royal Coat of Arms letterhead, and read something like:

By His Britannic Majesty's
Secretary of State
These are to request and require all those whom it may
concern to allow *Rev. George Barker and his wife Sarah*

Barker, British subjects going to *South Africa*
to pass freely without let or hindrance and to afford them
every Assistance and Protection of which they may stand
in need.
Given at *London*
This 6*th* day of *February* 1815
Signed by The Most Honourable Robert Steward
2nd Marquess of Londonderry
Signature of the Bearer
George Barker

They would have considered themselves British subjects
first and foremost, like the early colonists in America, with
none of the eagerness to take on an adopted nationality that
I had two centuries later.

When the impossibility of my long-dreamed immigration first began to look as if it might turn into a possibility, I
fantasized about going by ship. I envisioned the voyage that
Sarah and George had taken. Vividly, I saw myself sailing
past the Statue of Liberty to Ellis Island like the myriad
immigrants before me. A sea passage—both in the sense of
time and in the sense of journey—would help me transition
from one life to the next, I thought.

Then the shipping company told me that the first port
of call would probably be Houston, Texas, and I would have
to go through my immigration process there. Just like that,
all the romance was sucked from my idea like a deflated bal-
loon, and I had to opt to go by plane after all. The part of
my dream that I hung on to, though, was leaving from Cape
Town, my soul-mate city. It held my family, my most potent
coming-of-age memories, the best parts of my benighted
country. When I'd left Cape Town with a pang thirteen years
before to go and work at the radio station in Johannesburg,

I'd had a sense, born of hope, that the next time I moved on from anywhere, it would be to leave the country altogether. Now that my hope was turning into reality, I wanted Cape Town to be a significant part of that.

Intercontinental air travel is like going to the dark side of the moon. You disappear into a vacuum of suspended time, you give yourself over to the bubble of existence that revolves around the peculiar rhythm of the airlines, and you hold yourself in limbo until you emerge into another world on the other side. A two-hour flight from Cape Town to Johannesburg; an eleven-hour flight from Johannesburg to London; a who-knows-how-long layover in Heathrow; an eight-hour flight from London to Washington, D.C.—all adding up to thirty hours spent in limbo. It felt interminable, and left me travel-smudged and jittery from upended sleep cycles. But it was too short by far for the jump from one life to the next.

I stood waiting in the queue at passport control—my bedraggled jet lag thrown into sharp relief by the fluorescent lighting I am sure—and it was then that I began to feel that fluttering mixture of fear and excitement in my stomach. I was holding tight against my body the officially-sealed immigration package that had been handed to me at the American Embassy in Johannesburg two months before, and which I'd been on edge about misplacing ever since. Inside it were the myriad documents to support my immigrant application. Crucially, the American non-immigrant visa in my South African passport had been stamped *Cancelled Without Prejudice*, so there was no way for me to get into the country if anything went wrong.

When it was my turn, I was too on edge to come up with anything profound and I just blurted out, "I'm immigrating."

"Ah!" said customs control officer. He was young and fresh faced, his uniform and all-American crew cut reminding me of a West Point cadet even though I had never seen such a person in real life.

I didn't know what to expect, but I wasn't prepared for what he did. He didn't take my proffered immigration package, but said, "Please come with me, ma'am," and left his station at passport control. Was this good or bad?

The only sense I had of my surroundings was a blur of stark lighting, white and steel partitions, gray tiled floors. It was just me with my package, walking alongside this courteous young man to goodness knew where. He led me into the cramped secondary inspection immigration office, which was full of the bureaucratic clutter that is universal the world over. A handsome man in his thirties was sitting with his feet up on the desk, reading a newspaper.

My courteous West Point cadet said, "I'll leave you in the capable hands of . . ." He mentioned the immigration officer's name, but I was too nervous to catch it. When he left, he took my hopefulness with him. The handsome man took his feet off the desk and reached for my package. He tore it open without ceremony and began to flip through the contents. Upside down in front of me on his desk was an encapsulation of my life—application forms, fingerprints, photographs, testimonials, financial statements, a criminal background check, and medical reports that included an AIDS test. I waited. He was implacable. It was a snapshot of the chasm between my life-hanging-in-the-balance anxiety and his another-day-another-immigrant indifference.

The instant of my immigration is a sound. It was the mechanical *ca-chung* of the red stamp in my passport:

Processed for [smudge] Evidence [smudge] lawful admission for permanent residence . . . Employment authori [smudge] Admitted Until—and he scrawled with his left hand—CR-1, 18 Jul 99.

He kept all the documentation, but he handed my passport to me. I wanted to fall on his neck in gratitude. He clearly couldn't wait to get back to his newspaper. Right outside the secondary inspection office, I opened my passport again to study the priceless new stamp where it said, *"permanent residence . . . CR-1 . . . 18 Jul 99."* The *"CR"* stood for Conditional Resident. I'd been issued a conditional resident visa since I had been married for less than two years. The "1" meant that the person sponsoring my immigration was my spouse. The date meant that I could apply to have my conditional status removed at that time, with the ominous proviso that if a petition to remove the conditional basis of my status was not filed within the specified period, my conditional permanent residence status would be terminated automatically and I would be subject to deportation from the United States.

The heavy double doors of the Dulles International arrivals hall slowly swung open, and I saw Douglas at the same instant that he saw me. I leaned into him, holding on to his tall, thin frame, inhaling his remembered scent. He felt so familiar, but also strange. It had been two months since he'd come ahead to find us somewhere to live and to interview for jobs. In those pre-Skype and FaceTime days, we'd resorted to almost-daily faxes to keep in touch—an improvement upon the six weeks it took for a letter to go by ship in 1815, to be sure, but hardly an adequate replacement for the smell, the touch, the sound, the finishing of each other's thoughts, and the uniquely forged rituals of a shared life.

He sent his first fax from Reston, Virginia, on May 21, 1997:

Dear Judith,
You mustn't worry about me being upset. It's a good feeling to cry and know how much I feel for you. I was

pensive for a good while until the plane finally left the runway. It was so good to talk to you. We belong together! If I can talk to you every so often, it will be okay. I'm feeling much better about being here this time around. I'm feeling a great sense of first-world relief and a real sense of purpose.

Reston, Virginia, May 28th
I like talking to you. I don't want to hang up. I'm glad of this because we are going to be in each other's pockets. I took the carriage house. It's just too enticing to pass up. I'm sure you'll like it, but it is tiny. I think it will be very exciting, and perhaps now I'll get a job right away.

Carriage House, Alexandria, Virginia, June 16th
My Dear —
<u>So</u> wonderful to talk to you. I feel so much closer, talking to you, and to make it last I'll save your message for a while, so I can listen to your voice from time to time. What a social life you're leading! I hope it will take your mind off the long wait we have, but by next weekend we'll be on the home stretch! It seems like I've been here forever! But it's only been 4 weeks since I left. I've been doing so much running around. This weekend has been somewhat quiet, and I feel somewhat strange being alone. I guess the combination of missing you & missing the society I'm used to. Try to stay cheerful, my love, and I will too.

June 18th
It's 10:45 PM & I'm on the Metro back to Old Town. I heard your message by phoning my answering machine. You sounded quite plaintive, so I want to get this fax to you. I've been out all day as the conference is an all day

& evening affair. It's been a good day. And tomorrow I meet with Wheeling. Wheeling is a small town, but they seemed good folk, and they're very excited about their orchestra. Sorry I missed your call, but it was lovely to hear your voice. Here's my stop!

Carriage House, June 19th
My Dear Wife,
I'm feeling married today & I want you to share in that feeling! I also find it hard to understand why we're apart, but it is better than last time. I just have to cope, and I am coping. When people ask when you're coming they always express how soon it is. I always reply that it doesn't seem so soon to me especially when I tack on the 5 weeks it's been already!

Carriage House, June 30th
My Dearest wife,
I was happy to get your 2 faxes today, and happy to hear of the party on Sunday. I sorely missed being with you all. I've been feeling very much alone lately in our little Carriage House & and missing you badly—sort of aching. Also missing the company of our friends, which took so long to cultivate. That doesn't sound quite right, and I'm not sure how to express it, but for so long I sought the company of friends like Hillary & T, Jan & Julia, Andre & Moira, and it was all sort of coming together. I'm sure it will be different here. The people are different—a lot of rough edges—and they're so loud! I miss your gentle voice. It will be better when we are together. I hope you still want to come! I feel a little stranded here. I'm sure I'm feeling this way because the novelty is beginning to wear off & my time is not so full now. I could be out &

*about more, but I want to save it for when you're here, so
we can discover things together. So I'm just waiting until
you get here, trying to fill up the time.*

Carriage House, July 2nd
*I spoke to T. a while ago, and he reiterated that it was
important for us to just have time together before either of
us actually gets down to working. We have lots to discover
and a relationship to rekindle, and I am sure it will work
out that way. I'm ready now though, as I'm sure you are.*

Carriage House, July 15th
*You mustn't worry that you (we) are leaving our dear
friends & loved ones forever. If this adventure doesn't
work out or isn't right for us, we can always return to
S.A. I know it's unlikely, but we must keep all options
open. It's early days and we will decide what's best for us.
That's why it's so important for us finally to be together.
I know all the reasons for my coming ahead, and they are
valid, but I will not choose to be apart again. I hope you
don't find it too difficult to make space for me again, my
love.*
*So, my dear, are you ready to go? You remember about
terminal 2 & 3? I will be thinking of you on my way
home. You will be well on your way.*
I love you, my love,
Your,
D.

When I materialized out of that limbo of suspended ani-
mation into the arrivals hall of Dulles International Airport,
it was as if all my senses went into high alert to make up for
lost time. Even after I let go of Douglas, I held on tightly

to his arm, feeling the boniness through his shirt. He was my lifeline for the moment. We emerged from the chill air conditioning of the airport into Washington's midsummer, and it clamped on to me like a living thing.

"*Sjoe!*" I said, the South African equivalent of "Whoa!"

I thought I knew all about heat, but it was not this swampy, clinging, blindsiding variety. It made my skin prickle as if thousands of minute sprinklers had been activated at once all over my body. Inside the car, as the air conditioning flip-flopped my body temperature again, I orientated myself to sitting on the driver's side with no steering wheel. Douglas nosed into the traffic, and it was the most disconcerting sensation to have things whizz by so closely on my right, as opposed to my left, in a moving vehicle.

He took the scenic route along the George Washington Memorial Parkway, heading south towards the carriage house he'd rented for us in Alexandria, Virginia—not that I could tell because my sense of direction was nonexistent from a combination of switching hemispheres and being a passenger on the driver's side. I looked where he pointed across the Potomac River—at the spires of Georgetown University, at the Kennedy Center, the Lincoln Memorial, the Washington Monument, the dome of the Capitol, the Jefferson Memorial. I was seeing them with my own eyes, in real time, as I lived and breathed.

CHAPTER FIVE

This cape is the most stately thing and the fairest cape we saw in the whole circumference of the earth.

So said Sir Francis Drake as he rounded the Cape of Good Hope at the southern tip of Africa in 1580. After Sarah and George landed at the Cape two hundred and thirty-five years later, and one hundred and eighty-two years before I emigrated from there, George left a six-week gap in his diary. My guess is that they were all too much in the thrall of Cape Town.

With no diary to guide me, I have decided to have them lodging in the Bo-Kaap, above the Cape, since it's the city's oldest suburb with some of the original Dutch and British architecture dating back to the 1700s. Also, I want to imagine Sarah there becaue when I first moved to Cape Town, I lived in the neighboring area of De Waterkant, the waterfront, and I like to think that she walked along those same cobbled streets on the slopes of Signal Hill in the lee of Table Mountain with a view out to Table Bay.

When I approached Cape Town for the first time, from inland over the Hottentots Holland Mountains, I saw Table

Mountain in profile, and the city revealed her beauty gradually, almost modestly. They say that you are not a true
Capetonian until you have lived there for ten years, but I felt
like one from that very first moment. I fell instantly, hope-
lessly, irrevocably in love.

Every sound and smell triggers a memory. That is the
beach where I tried to gather phosphorus one night; this is
the city hall where I heard my first live symphony concert;
there is the cathedral where we gathered to protest police
brutality. I know my way around as instinctively as I know
my own body. You don't merely live *in* the city, you become
of the city. Your attachment is palpable, and it never grows
any less so. The late South African writer Stephen Watson
wrote, about those of us who have moved away, "There is
something about Cape Town . . . which induces a homesickness the pure force of which is almost intimidating in its
longing."

When the days are still and clear, the light in Cape Town
is so intense that it makes the mountain look like a cutout
against a blue backdrop. And when the fierce Southeaster
blows—this was the setting for the legendary Flying
Dutchman, after all—thick clouds pour over the mountain
like a billowing tablecloth. Umbrella-shaped stone pines
grow at rakish angles, taking the line of least resistance against
the gale-force winds. The granite folds of Table Mountain
loom over the city like a crouching elephant, and behind the
mountain, the whale-backed Constantiaberg runs down to
Cape Point at the tip of the continent, where the cold, blue
currents of the Atlantic meet the warm, green currents of the
Indian Ocean in a clearly demarcated line.

In imagining Sarah in Cape Town, I've tried to strip away
two centuries from this city that I adore. I envision her being
a nineteenth-century tourist—visiting the Dutch East India
Company's seventeenth-century Castle of Good Hope;

walking under the oaks up the avenue to the Company's Garden where they grew the produce to supply vessels sailing around the Cape; worshipping at the Dutch Reformed Groote Kerk or "Great Church." Perhaps she bought muslin or a bonnet or some keepsake from a vendor along the Heerengracht before it became Adderley Street.

The foreshore that was reclaimed from Table Bay in the 1940s was still a beach when the missionaries came ashore, so the Castle of Good Hope stood at the water's edge. I remember the first time I visited the castle and the guard pointed out the desperate fingernail scratchings in the earthen wall where prisoners had tried to find an escape as the sea crashed against the outer wall of the cell. The nearby Groote Kerk was rebuilt a quarter century after Sarah was there, but the original tower was kept, as she would have seen it. The oak-lined Company Avenue is probably not too much changed since she walked along it, although the squirrels, pigeons, and hadeda ibis that populate it have seen many generations.

At the bottom of the avenue stands the South African National Library, which Lord Charles Somerset, the first governor of the Cape Colony, founded in its original iteration just three years after Sarah left. Now, the library houses a photostatted copy of George's diaries and some of his original letters. It was here that I first saw his beautifully-formed copperplate handwriting. I sat at a long wooden table in the quiet of the Special Collections Reading Room, with the light dappling in on my left through the arched sash windows along the oak-lined avenue, holding in my hand a letter that George had touched—that, perhaps, Sarah had touched—and I knew, even as I was living it, that it was an existential, utterly unforgettable and indelible moment.

Next door to the library, diagonally across from the Groote Kerk, is the Anglican Cathedral of St George the Martyr, built almost a hundred years after Sarah and George arrived at the Cape. When I was an undergraduate at the University of Cape Town, a group of students gathered on the steps of the cathedral to mount a sit-in protest against the apartheid government. The South African Police, upholders of the regime, charged them. When the students fled into the inner sanctuary of the cathedral, the police chased after them and bludgeoned them with batons on the altar.

In the weeks following, as I crowded with thousands in the cathedral, and at the city hall, and on the campus of the university in protest, the kernel of the idea began to form that I would one day emigrate from my country. But it took me twenty years to achieve what Sarah had accomplished in a matter of months.

CHAPTER SIX

July 12th, 1815
We took leave of the friends at Cape Town & about 12
o'clock began our journey accompanied by Brother Pacalt
& a number of Hottentots who had come to conduct us to
Hooge-Kraal the place of his residence.

GIVEN WHAT I KNOW about the damp, chill Cape winters, I imagine it's such a day when Sarah sets off from their Cape Town lodgings toward Greenmarket Square where she is met by a great din. Just at that moment, I imagine, a flock of African hadeda ibis flies overhead with their all-enveloping "haa-haa-haa-de-dah" cry. The Khoikhoi herders are yelling as they yoke the oxen; about fifty ragtag bystanders are calling out their sixpence worth of advice; and the animals themselves are adding their own grunting and stamping to the commotion. The air is redolent of dung and sweat, and Sarah hangs back, daunted by the chaotic scene. She scans the crowd for a sight of George, but can't see him. Then the Rev. Carl Pacalt shoulders his way through the crowd to come and greet her, shouting out a welcome above the commotion.

"We'll be ready to leave about noon," he tells her.

Brother Pacalt had trained first in Germany and then at Gosport, where George and his three companions had studied. In 1813, the London Missionary Society had sent him to start a new mission station at Hooge-Kraal in the Western Cape, but, before that, he'd been stationed at Bethelsdorp in the Eastern Cape, where the missionaries are now headed. He radiates an openhearted generosity, which has taken the very practical form of his coming to guide the missionaries on the early part of their journey.

All five wagons—Brother Pacalt's two and three new ones, looking strangely naked and vulnerable since they don't yet have their tent covers—are now stocked, packed, and lined up in a convoy, ready for the long trek. Sarah has learned a Dutch word during the saga of the wagon building: *kakebeenwa*. George followed every detail of the wagon building, and he explained to her that the word was a literal translation for "jawbone wagon," so named because of the aesthetically-pleasing slant of the siding of the Cape Wagon—higher at the back and tapering down towards the front—suggesting a jawline. Each of the four missionaries and Brother Pacalt has their own *kakebeenwa*, large enough to accommodate a family for long-distance travel.

When Sarah approaches their wagon, she finds George taking a keen interest in the complicated process of how to inspan and outspan a team of oxen—the terms, meaning "yoke" and "unyoke," borrowed from the Cape Dutch *inspan* and *uitspan*. Because they will have to cross the precipitous Hottentots Holland Mountains, each of the five wagons drawn up on Greenmarket Square must have sixteen spanned oxen. It's not surprising that there is such pandemonium.

By noon, as Brother Pacalt had predicted, everything is ready for departure, and with George's help, Sarah climbs up into their wagon. They settle down just behind the box where their assigned Khoikhoi driver is already sitting.

She tries out her fledgling Dutch on him, "Goede dag."

She is rewarded by a flash of white teeth against his almond skin as he grins back at her and returns the greeting, "Goeie dag, miesies."

He watches to make sure that Sarah and George are safely seated, then he casts back a whip more than twenty feet long and cracks it in the air over the backs of the oxen with a piercing, "Hah!" The commotion reaches a fever pitch as whips crack all around them, herders call, the crowd of bystanders shouts out their goodbyes, and the wagons gradually creak into motion. They settle into a slow, walking pace as they begin to head east out of the city towards the Hottentots Holland Mountains and the hinterland.

As they plod away from the city bowl towards the Cape Flats, Sarah looks out through the back of their open *kakebeenwa* toward the receding mountains. It is overcast, and the granite mountain etches a dark outline against the light gray of the sky. From this angle, Devil's Peak appears to have become part of Table Mountain, as George had first seen it, with the Lion's Head silhouetted on the right. An outcrop of trees makes it look as if the lion has eyelashes, and the more the road curves around, the more Lion's Head appears in profile until it looks like a creature in repose, sloping gently down through the saddle and up again to the rump of Signal Hill near the Bo-Kaap suburb where they had lodged.

Towards evening, it begins to drizzle. George pulls up his coat collar, and Sarah covers her head with her shawl.

"We should *never* have come away without tents for the wagons!" George explodes.

Sarah, a little taken aback at his vehemence, puts her hand on his knee. "Perhaps it will clear up as we get closer to the mountains," she says.

But no amount of wishful thinking is going to have an effect on the Cape winter weather. The drizzle turns into a steady, soaking rain, and an upturned collar and a shawl are no match for the trickles that slide down Sarah's neck and drip off the brim of George's hat. Sarah senses George's tension next to her as he tries to keep his irritation in check.

The light begins to fade and the herders, with a good deal of hollering back and forth, decide to stop for the night and outspan the oxen.

"*Maak 'n kraal.*" calls Brother Pacalt, and as the herders begin to circle the wagons to keep the oxen fenced in, Sarah guesses that a *kraal* means an animal enclosure.

The missionaries have adequate provisions with them to last a week, but it is impossible to light a fire in the damp, and a cooked meal is out of the question. They have to make do with curried green beans from the Cape, *mieliemeal* bread, and *droëwors*—a kind of cured, spiced sausage, which Sarah learns is an acquired taste. After curtailed evening prayers, they settle down for their first night on the road, the men in one of Brother Pacalt's covered wagons, the women in another, and the herders taking shelter underneath the other three *kakebeenwaens*. Sarah loves nothing better than lying entwined with George at the end of the day, and she finds it difficult to fall asleep now without him there. She is chilled to the bone in her damp, clammy clothes, and the musty smell of wet wool only adds to her discomfort. She lies listening to the murmuring voices of the men and the relentless rain drumming on the tent cover.

The day dawns bright and fresh, as if the sodden day before had never been. They inspan the oxen and begin to travel through wine country, stopping at the farm of Mr. Roos, a wine *boer*, where they buy some Cape brandy and arrange for tent covers to be made for the new wagons. After another three days, they come to the foot of the Hottentots Holland Mountains where they outspan to rest up for the ordeal of crossing over the precipitous mountain *kloof* the next day.

It is only because of the Khoikhoi herders and drivers that the missionaries are able to make the crossing over the pass at all. Since time immemorial, their ancestors have used it as a stock route. The Khoikhoi name for the treacherous Hottentots Holland Kloof is *Gantouw*, their word for the *eland*—the antelope—that they hunt here. The story goes that it came to be called "Hottentots Holland" because the Khoikhoi tried to explain to the Dutch that the land was as precious to them as Holland was to the settlers, and so the name was a conflation of misunderstanding. What makes it worse is that Hottentot was the Dutch exonym for the Khoikhoi people, mimicking the sound of their speech, and I cringe every time I see George refer to Khoikhoi as "Hottentot" or to black Africans as "Caffres," the Arabic word for "an unbeliever." Even though I understand, intellectually, that these words were the accepted terms of that time, I still can't help overlaying them with my present-day emotional baggage of apartheid.

The missionaries' crossing over the so-named Hottentots Holland Kloof begins at daylight on July 15, a cold but dry Saturday. At first, the slope is gradual, but they have been amply warned about what is to come. Sure enough, as the inclination becomes more and more sheer, the wheels of the wagon begin to churn and spin in the ground, trying to gain purchase.

"We should get down," says George, "to lessen the weight." He jumps off and reaches up to lift Sarah down. They walk alongside as the spanned oxen lower their heads, groaning and straining to pull the wagon as it jolts over the ruts in the steep path. The wagon sticks fast, and it looks as if it will roll backwards towards the precipice. The herder brings the whip sharply down across the backs of the oxen to urge them forward.

"No!" cries Sarah, flinching as the beasts are whipped.

"He must, Sarah," says George. "It would be worse if the wagon went over the edge and pulled them all to their death. By the help of God we will make it safely over."

They finally reach the summit at eleven o'clock that morning.

The deep ruts that were made on the sheer path of the Hottentots Holland Kloof by scores of wagon wheels like theirs were declared a national monument one hundred and forty-three years later. Almost a quarter of the ox wagons that tried to make the crossing every year were damaged or lost. The new, less-perilous Sir Lowry's Pass was built thirteen years after the missionaries made their ascent, but even now the crossing can be treacherous. Someone I knew once drove over the pass when a thick fog overcame him so suddenly that he was trapped. He had no option but to open the door of his Mini Minor and drive by the guidance of the painted line in the center of the road, trusting to blind faith that it wouldn't lead him over the edge of the precipice.

Two hundred and two years after the missionaries crossed the Hottentots Holland Mountains, almost to the day, in one of a series of serendipities that began to pop up like little miracles as I became more and more intrigued by Sarah's story, I walked into the Rondebosch United Church in Cape Town one wintry Sunday and stopped in my tracks on the doorstep, staring. Both my mother and my brother were buried from this church in 2013, and although I have a complicated relationship with religion, it is a church I had walked into countless times before. This time, though, with my mind and heart full of Sarah and George from my time spent poring over records at the National Library in Cape Town, as well as at the Cory Library in Grahamstown, and at the School of Oriental and African Studies in London, my eyes suddenly fell on the plaque hanging in the vestibule, which I had never read before.

Here lies the Dust of a Faithful Zealous
and Learned Missionary of
Jesus Christ
the Rev^d
Johannes Theodorus Vanderkemp
M.D.
who died the 19th December 1811
aged 64 years.
He studied at the Universities
of
Leyden and Edinburgh
and was the author of some Theological works
in Latin and Dutch.
Dr Vanderkemp was once an infidel but
by the Grace of God became a Christian
and Laboured as a Missionary 12 years
XXXXXXXXXXXXXXXXX and was
a Director of the Missionary Society
established in London in 1795.
April 1816

The XXX represents duct tape that had been stuck onto the plaque to cover the words underneath, "amongst the Hottentots and the Caffres," terms that are now as deeply offensive as the N-word is to a twenty-first-century ear. Given that race relations are still so tender in South Africa's new democracy, the present minister of the church felt it right to cover the words out of sensitivity towards the many people of color who attend Rondebosch United.

Still, the rest of the tribute remains, and what brought me to a sudden stop in front of the plaque—put up just over a year after Sarah and George were in Cape Town—was that I had learned in the time since I last visited the church that the Rev. Johannes Theodorus van der Kemp, M.D. was the missionary who first established the Bethelsdorp mission station, the destination of the missionaries' long overland trek. This small epiphany brought home to me with fresh clarity the extent to which I will always be rooted in Africa, no matter how long I may live elsewhere.

In the United States, I am as old as the number of years I have lived here. That makes me barely old enough to have a driver's license and to vote, whereas in biological years I am, as the French so delicately put it, *une femme d'un certain âge*. I process my life in America, but the extended sweep of my backstory is grounded in Africa. It is only there that I could come across something that creates a link so far back to my personal and familial history. It's why a small, chance moment can be so thrilling because, with hindsight, we can overlay the instance with meaning and significance. Usually, in the instant of living it, we are too busy looking ahead, as I imagine George and Sarah were.

CHAPTER SEVEN

THE DRIVER of Sarah and George's *kakebeenwa* is not named in George's diary, but I didn't want him to be a faceless nonentity, so I have given him the name "Klaas Buys." He would have been descended from the Khoikhoi—their *own* name for themselves meaning, approximately, "men of men." They were the aboriginal hunter-herders who migrated down from the Botswana region into South Africa about two thousand years ago.

When black Africans migrated south from central Africa around the year 300, the Khoikhoi were dispersed into farther, and often more arid, regions of South Africa. There was some intermingling of the groups, the distinctive clicks of the Khoikhoi language being one of the shared features, but the Khoikhoi remained their own distinct folk for the next thirteen hundred years.

Then, in 1652, Jan van Riebeeck was sent by the Dutch East India Company to set up a refreshment station at the Cape to supply the crew of the Company's passing trade ships with fresh water, meat, fruit and vegetables, and medical assistance. He was under strict instructions not to colonize the region, but within five years, nine of the Company's servants were given permits to farm along the river that they named after the small Liesbeek River in the Netherlands. In so doing, they encroached on the nomadic pastoral lifestyle of the Khoikhoi. Slowly, but inexorably, as the Khoikhoi were driven off their land by greater numbers of Dutch farmers, and as the smallpox they contracted from the Europeans drastically depleted their numbers, their social structure was broken down. Many resorted to working as bond servants on the colonists' farms.

The more the colony expanded, the more labor was needed, and the Dutch began to import slaves from their East Indian settlements. These groups of Cape Malay, largely from present day Indonesia and other regions of Southeast Asia, brought Islam to South Africa and an exotic cuisine of subtle spices, bright colors, and a blend of savory-sweet flavors. They formed a new language, a pidgin Dutch, in order to make themselves understood to their Dutch masters and amongst each other. This Cape Dutch was the fledgling Afrikaans, and it spread to become the language, too, of the Khoikhoi across the Western and Eastern Cape.

Cape Dutch would have been the mother tongue of the Khoikhoi herder whom I have named Klaas Buys. Because he grew up in Cape Town, he can speak some English, and, two days after their grueling crossing over the Hottentots Holland Kloof, he addresses Sarah for the first time without her having initiated the conversation.

"Does *miesies* know about the baths at Caledon?"

"No, but I hope you'll tell me," she says, wanting to encourage this new development.

"The Dutch call it *'Bad agter de Berg.'*"

"What does that mean?"

"Bath behind the mountain."

"Oh yes?"

"There's six hot springs and one cold one. They all just come up out of the mountain."

"There is a city like that in England, named Bath."

"My people called this place */gam-sa //gam-i* when they herded sheep and cows around there before the Dutch came."

Sarah tries the name, "*/gam-sa //gam-i,*" but she can't get her tongue around the Khoikhoi clicks. "Do people still bathe there?"

"Oh yes. It makes them get better."

"What does it feel like?"

"I don't know," said Klaas. "We are not allowed."

"But you said your people have known about these springs since before the Dutch came."

"We are not allowed," he repeats with a finality that makes Sarah feel it is better to let the matter drop.

Feeling her lack, Sarah tries to learn Cape Dutch from the notes that George gives her, but it makes her bilious when she reads in the lurching wagon, and the language proves elusive—especially the back-to-front way that the verbs come at the end of a sentence. George reads to her sometimes, and she studies the strange country passing by their slow convoy day after day. The rolling hills are green and lush from the winter rainfall, and the blue-gray mountains in the distance are often shrouded in mist, so the landscape has a look of England. But her senses tell her that she is in another country. The air smells different— earthier, more pungent—and the sounds, over and above the creaking, plodding convoy that has become the constant background of their lives, are full of unfamiliar bird-calls and a beating hum of insect life.

All along their journey, they meet great kindness, thanks in large part to the goodwill of Brother Pacalt. At one place, a group of Khoikhoi bring new oxen to help the travellers on their way, and the old oxen are sent forward to graze.

"It's like the posting station at Guildford," says Sarah, "when we changed horses between London and Plymouth."

At another place, they take shelter from the rain at a *boer*'s farm, spending the Sabbath there and using the opportunity to bake bread.

"They appeared to have no Bible," says George as they drive away, "so I gave one to the mistress of the family."

"She begged a loaf of bread from us," says Sarah. "I'm glad we could repay them for their hospitality."

Their next stop is the house of a preaching farmer called Mr. de Jager. At midday on Saturday, members of the congregation start arriving on horseback, others making a day's journey by wagon.

"This is a large assembly!" says George.

"Yes," says Mr. de Jager. "And this is after their usual custom—it isn't because they knew you would all be here."

"Are the Hottentots and slaves permitted to hear the word of God with you?" asks Joseph.

"Oh yes!"

"I am glad of it. I have learned it is a custom not very common in Africa for the natives to be allowed to go into your churches."

"We don't worship separately here," says Mr. de Jager. "But your Hottentots greatly augment the number of those who usually attend, so this time I think it will be better if we divide white and black. One room could not contain us all."

"I will preach to the Hottentot group in the morning," says Brother Pacalt, "if you will preach to the others, Brother Joseph."

"With pleasure. And in the afternoon, we will reverse it."

After being on the road for three weeks and five days by George's calculation, and just as the shadows of the winter evening are beginning to lengthen, they arrive at Hooge-Kraal on August 5. Here, they settle in to rest for a time. The mission station is on the outskirts of a town called George, and the name delights Sarah, even though she knows full well that it has been named for the King, and not for her husband.

"I will accompany you on your forward journey as far as Lange Kloof, the long ravine northeast of George," says Brother Pacalt. "A group of men is newly arrived from Bethelsdorp, and they will then convey you the rest of the way there."

By now, their travel has become a way of life, and George, who had been an anxious traveller at the beginning, allows himself more time to read. As they begin the last leg of their trek, he settles down in the back of the wagon to continue with *Travels in South Africa, Undertaken at the Request of the Missionary Society*, newly published by the Scottish minister John Campbell. Sarah is into the sixth month of her pregnancy and is beginning to feel a little ache in the small of her back. She stretches to ease the discomfort and at that exact moment, the wheels of the wagon slip, sending a scuttle of rocks and pebbles down the slope. The wagon begins to tilt, teetering and hanging suspended for a moment. Then the weight of it shifts inexorably and it flips over on its side with clamorous creaking and groaning until it comes to a grinding halt with its wheels turning uselessly in the air. For a moment, there is echoing silence.

"Sarah!" George scrambles up from where he's been thrown, reaching for her. She lies inert, curled on her side, her arms cradling her belly.

"Oh my God! Sarah!"

"I think I'm all right," she whispers.

Klaas had managed to jump clear as the wagon toppled, and people from the other wagons now come running. As a group, they hold the precariously balanced wagon steady while Klaas and Brother Pacalt reach in and pull out first

Sarah and then George. With the two of them safe, the men all set to work, with grunts and calls and slip-sliding feet, to right the overturned wagon.

The all-purpose remedy of strong tea and the no-nonsense "it-could-have-been-worse" comfort of Elizabeth gradually ease Sarah out of her fright. But she is now dreading the pass through Duiwelskop in the Outeniqua Mountains. Klaas has explained that *outeniqua* is the Khoikhoi word for "man loaded with honey" because in the summer the lush green slopes hum with bees. But he also told them that *duiwelskop* means "Devil's Head," and the difficult crossing over the pass is much spoken of. Evidently, though, the experience of the overturned wagon has made everyone especially vigilant, and they make it safely through, with George proclaiming it, "Not worse than some other places between the town of George and Lange Kloof."

They stop over at a farmhouse for two days to bake bread for their onward journey, and it is here that they must finally part with Brother Pacalt and his herdsmen. In the melee of departure, Sarah seeks out Klaas Buys.

"*Dankie vir alles,*" she says in her awkward Dutch, trying to thank him for everything.

He pulls his hat off his head and twists it around and around in his hands. "*Alles van die beste,*" he says, wishing her well.

Sarah and George are both very much affected at parting. As their wagon continues its plodding eastward journey, she rests her temple on his shoulder. George takes his small travel Bible from his pocket and flips through the pages until he finds the passage from John that he is looking for. He reads aloud, "This is my commandment, that you love one another as I have loved you. Greater love has no one than this, that someone lay down his life for his friend."

Their journey trudges on, guided now by their new

Khoikhoi herders who know the route by instinct, just as the Khoikhoi from Brother Pacalt's party knew the Gantouw Pass over the Hottentots Holland Mountains. Two days after parting from Brother Pacalt, George looks up from reading John Campbell's *Travels in Africa* and says, "There's a wagon coming toward us."

Sarah stands up in their swaying wagon to look. The wind is strong, and she has to hold on to the side rung to steady herself. To her right, the low scrub of early spring slopes down toward the coast. In the far distance, coming towards them from the east, she can make out a wagon with a small group of people in tow. The two parties gradually edge closer to each other until they are almost nose to nose.

"Well met!" calls a man riding on horseback alongside the oncoming wagon. "I am the Reverend James Read. I have come to take you the rest of the way to Bethelsdorp."

He could not have wished for more surprise and joy as the missionaries crowd forward to meet him.

"No sooner have we lost one guide than we are provided with another," says George.

Brother James Read is a man in his late thirties, his hairline just starting to recede. "We will reach Bethelsdorp within a week," he predicts.

The following Thursday, about two and a half miles before they come to Bethelsdorp, a large company of the people of that place joins themselves to the convoy and sings the whole way until they arrive at Brother Read's door, the plaintive beauty of the intricate, interweaving harmonies bringing tears to Sarah's eyes.

On September 14, George wrote in his journal, *Reached longed-for Bethelsdorp about half-past five o'clock in the evening.* They had been on the road from Cape Town for two months and two days.

Chapter Eight

FALLING IN LOVE with a country is no different, really, from falling in love with a person. There is the exhilarating tumble of sharing and discovery and the click of finding how alike you are, even as you marvel at how uniquely special he is. And, just as there is also the rather more pragmatic side of learning that he dislikes cucumber, that he doesn't take sugar in his coffee, that he likes his socks folded not rolled, there are the mundane aspects—like applying for a Social Security number and opening a new bank account—of settling into the relationship with your new country. There was no doubt in my mind that I was in love with America; it had been love at first sight.

For the first six weeks, it was difficult for me to shake a feeling of holiday dislocation. Everything was so wondrously novel. *The Washington Post*, only ever known to me before as a faraway instrument in the Watergate saga, was right here in my hands, and the first Sunday edition took me a week to read, because I was so enthralled by all it had to offer. An exhibition of *Picasso, the Early Years*, with its one hundred and fifty-one drawings, paintings, and sculptures at the National Gallery of Art, left me dumbfounded by the sheer marvel of having all of this before me in one place, as did the thought that I could come back and see it again if I wanted to without having to travel halfway around the world to do so. We drove to New York City to meet up with a South African friend in Tribeca, walk through Central Park, and visit the Egyptian Temple Gallery at the Metropolitan Museum of Art.

It was as if I was playing at living in America. My first grocery shop took the better part of an afternoon as I turned over each article, inspecting it, reading it, trying to find an equivalent that might conceivably match something I would have picked up without a moment's thought in a grocery store back home. When I ventured out to mail a batch of introductory letters and résumés to broadcasters, art galleries, and theater groups, I stood for a minute in front of the blue postbox, trying to find the slot to mail the letters, before I tentatively pulled on the handle and it yielded with a complaining creak. Why were all the green dollar bills so confusingly alike, aside from the portraits of famous men I didn't yet recognize, and why was the five-cent nickel bigger than the ten-cent dime?

When Douglas landed the position of executive director at the symphony orchestra in Wheeling, West Virginia, his niece teased, "What's the West Virginia money clip?" and produced a paper clip with a quarter in it. I didn't get the joke. What did I know? True, I had fantasized about being a classical music DJ somewhere on the northeast coast, but we had to start somewhere.

I celebrated my first United States public holiday on Labor Day. Appropriately, Douglas started his new job the day after, and *boom!* the season changed overnight from summer to autumn. How neat and organized this country was in every way, I thought. On that Tuesday, September 2, I drove into town—driving on the right-hand side still just this side of nerve-racking—to run some errands.

We had already explored Wheeling's famous suspension bridge, a forerunner of the Brooklyn Bridge and the largest in the world for a brief moment around 1850, I'd been told. I'd read up about the state of West Virginia being born in Wheeling when it was loyal to the Federal Government during the Civil War. I loved the trees, just starting to turn, and the slowly flowing Ohio River, so massive compared to the often-dry riverbeds in Africa. It was really beautiful up there in the northern panhandle of West Virginia, at the foothills of the Appalachian Mountains, sandwiched between Pennsylvania to the east and Ohio to the west.

But, apart from the orchestra, it was a backwater culturally, and that posed problems for something for me to do. I drifted on and on that Tuesday, feeling restless, aware of how small-town Wheeling was, in both the literal and the metaphorical sense. *This is not what I want*, I thought, followed by, *I know I must try not to prejudge it*, followed by, *Have I turned my life upside down to immigrate and travelled halfway around the world for this?*

I tried valiantly to see if I could cobble together a freelance portfolio by trying to pick up some work at the classical radio station WQED in Pittsburgh, or by setting up a film series at the Oglebay Institute in Wheeling. Simply to fill my days, I resorted to filing the orchestra's music library and received my first American paycheck for my efforts—a princely sum of $130.

All of this was hardly the hoped-for capstone to my broadcasting or former acting careers. I had reveled in the identity of being the arts editor at SAfm, and now being simply the wife of the executive director of the Wheeling Symphony Orchestra made me recoil with something that felt like claustrophobia. What did that say about my sense of self? I wondered, *am I only as good as the outward title I could give myself?* And how dare I feel like this, anyway, when I had migrated by choice and not from necessity as so many others had been forced to do?

Douglas wanted to buy a house to help me feel more settled, and although the prospect of investing in property seemed scary if I was going to be frustrated and unhappy, we ended up buying a gambrel-roofed double story on a hill overlooking the valley. It backed onto a forest, and I stopped in still wonder the first time I saw whitetail deer casually sauntering out from the trees. Our container arrived via Baltimore in mid-October, and I threw myself into unpacking the precious things that would surely make me feel at home—my paternal grandmother's tea set and silver butter cooler; the leather-bound Jane Austens that were a gift for my twenty-first birthday; my childhood copy of Percy FitzPatrick's *Jock of the Bushveld*; the wooden *kist* for storing blankets and the bookcase that were crafted by my grandfather, Reginald Barker.

But I felt like a visitor in our house with its painted woodwork and heavy, floral wallpaper—so different from the traditional white walls and stripped wood of the homes I'd made in Africa. I'd done everything I could do. I'd plodded doggedly through the bureaucracy of immigration; I'd packed up my African home; I'd transported myself to America; I'd unpacked my American home. Now that the dust had settled, had it been worth it?

Chapter Nine

I'VE WONDERED if Sarah experienced a similar was-it-all-worth-it feeling when the tumult of the moving wagons and the singing Khoikhoi came to a stop outside James Read's house, and she sat for a moment on the wagon, taking stock of their surroundings. Bethelsdorp is on a wide, barren plain, with hardly a tree in sight or any semblance of a garden. Marshy lowland stretches between the settlement and Algoa Bay in the far distance.

I envision Sarah scanning the forty or fifty little huts at the mission arranged in half circles, but with gaps where some have fallen down, giving the impression of missing teeth. I see George taking a deep breath, as if to brace himself, then jumping from the wagon and reaching up to lift Sarah down. As the missionaries are milling about, trying to get their bearings, a young woman comes up to them, holding by the hand a boy of about four.

Brother James puts his arm around her shoulders. "This is my wife, Sara," he says, "and our son, little James."

Mother and son share the same cloud of black curls, high cheekbones, huge black eyes, and skin the color of milky coffee. So Brother Read has married a Khoikhoi woman. Sarah had not expected this, and she is momentarily taken aback. But instantly chides herself: *Why wouldn't he?* she thinks.

The only entry in George's journal from the day that the missionaries arrived at Bethelsdorp on September 14, to November 18, in 1815 is: *Neglected to write.* They were probably all too busy learning the business of the station and the London Missionary Society, and preparing for the departure of Brothers Evans and Hamilton to Lattakoo. At this time, with Sarah so near her confinement, George would not be travelling to Lattakoo with them as originally planned. When George does pick up his journal again, it is to record his mixture of sorrow and joy, of fear and hope.

In the small hours of Friday, November 18, Sarah wakes and knows, even before she is fully conscious, that it is beginning. The tug of a contraction brings her sharply awake, and she puts her hands on either side of her belly, waiting for the spasm to pass. There is a half-moon framed in the window, and she focuses on that when she feels the next contraction begin. After it passes, she reaches for George. It still amazes her how he awakes instantly, and he is *compos mentis* right away.

"Is it time?" he whispers.

"Yes, I believe so."

He opens his pocket watch and angles it so that he can read it by the moonlight. "It is four o'clock. Shall I call Elizabeth?"

"No, wait awhile."

She begins to measure her contractions by the position of the moon in the window frame. When it disappears from view, she asks George to fetch Elizabeth, and she comes, herself now six months pregnant with her first child.

Dawn slides into the room, and then full sunlight. The contractions grip and release, grip and release, but the baby does not come. Sarah crushes Elizabeth's hand so tightly that her nails leave half-moons on the skin. Elizabeth goes to the door and speaks in a low voice to George, who is hovering just outside.

"Please, Brother George," she says, "go and ask Sister Sara if she will come and help us."

Sara Read is soothing and steady, assuring Sarah in her low voice, touched by the accent of the Khoikhoi language, "You are doing very well, everything will be all right." But still the baby does not come.

Around lunchtime, the contractions become inexorable, and at half past one, almost ten hours after the first contraction had woken her, Sarah strains with all her might. She feels the hot, moist weight of her baby on her stomach, where Sara Read has placed it, and she looks down her torso at the flailing, uncoordinated limbs of the tiny, slightly mottled creature.

Once everything is clean, Elizabeth calls George into the room, and he stands gravely watching this new life that is now miraculously present in the room with them.

After a while of simply staring, he says, "This day God did great things for me, which I hope never to forget." Then he looks up at his wife. "We will name her Sarah—for you, and for my mother and sister."

Sarah finds her new state of motherhood strangely agricultural in its continual cycle of sleeping, feeding, and excreting. And she has a heartbreaking time trying to learn how to breastfeed her infant. She has an overabundance of milk and little Sarah can't latch on properly to drink enough to empty her breasts, so it becomes a vicious cycle of painfully engorged breasts and a desperately hungry baby. After weeks of trying, Sarah is forced to give up. They have to find a wet nurse, and Sarah has to bind up her throbbing breasts until her milk dries up, aching not only physically but also emotionally at losing this bond with her child.

On the last Sunday in January, three adults are baptized in the small church at Bethelsdorp, and two infants. Even at this early hour, the heat shimmers. The church smells of dust, and motes hang suspended in the shaft of sunlight between Sarah and Brother James.

"Dearly beloved," he says, "you have brought this child here to be baptized, you have prayed that our Lord Jesus Christ would vouchsafe to receive her, to cleanse her, and to sanctify her." With infinite care, he takes the small bundle from George's arms and says, "Name this child."

"Sarah," her parents say in unison.

Her mother looks at the vulnerable head of her namesake where it rests up against the dark linen of Brother James's coat, her downy hair pushed slightly awry. Her bright eyes are open and seem to be fixed intently on the underneath of the minister's chin. For the christening gown, Sarah has taken one of her old shifts, and, lacking lace or any other trimming, she's spent hours embroidering the bodice with a honeycomb smocking stitch, trusting that she would have more children to pass the gown on to, so that her handiwork will have more than just this one outing.

George holds the basin ready for her baptism. "Sarah, I baptize thee in the name of the Father," Brother James pours water carefully over her head, and she gives a start, "and of the Son," he pours water the second time, "and of the Holy Ghost." On the third dousing, she makes a little vocal sound that could go either way—toward a coo or toward a cry—and her mother holds her breath, hoping for the best.

"We receive this child into the congregation of Christ's flock, and do sign her with the sign of the cross. . . ." Brother James makes a cross with his thumb on her forehead, and the gesture prompts the gurgle that her mother has been holding her breath for.

In the evening, Sarah, full of the portent of the day, stands in the room where they are lodging in the Reads' house, watching her sleeping child in the cot that George has built for her. She loves to see the utter abandon of sleep, the way the lashes rest on the rounded cheeks. George comes to stand next to her. "This day I gave over to God what he has given me," he says, "may he take the child at my hands and adopt it into the family of Jesus and give me grace to train her in the fear of the Lord."

Our children are our future. It's the phrase, or one like it, that I hear in so many ways in so many circumstances. When Nelson Mandela said, "Our children are the rock on which our future will be built," he meant that children would be the greatest asset in building a post-apartheid nation. For Sarah, it was the way she planted her children and their offspring in Africa.

At the end of her life, my mother lamented that each of her three children had ended up living on three different continents. The cousins are scattered too. Only three have remained in Africa. Four, like my sister Anne, have made their way back to England. Another, the one who looks just like Sarah, has landed up in New Zealand—with me far-flung in the opposite direction, in America. Still, Sarah planted us all in Africa, and she knew, from her first child onwards, that they would be her future.

When I was growing up, I knew with such unques-tioning certainty that I would have a child that it never even occurred to me to prepare for the alternative. When I couldn't, I tried to shield myself from it by pretending that I didn't particularly like children anyway. What gave the lie to that were my niece and nephew . . . and then my niece's three children. When I held the fragile, birdlike, yet surprising weight of my first great-niece when she was just hours old, I had a breath-holding, limb-dissolving inkling of what motherhood must be like. But though our line will carry on, albeit under another name, my particular branch of our family tree is broken off at my little twig. There is no point in even trying to pretend that my longing to reach back toward Sarah to try and find where I belong in her past doesn't have something to do with my not having a child to be my future.

PART TWO

Chapter Ten

February 17th, 1816, Theopolis
My dearest Sarah,
We reached Theopolis about half past 9 on Friday eve-
ning, and found Brother Ullbricht better, but very weak.
This is the beautifullest country that I have yet seen in
my travels in Africa; the grass is long and thick, and the
ground appears to be very fertile.

After I left you on Tuesday, we reached the Great
Swartkops River about 2 P.M. The river being full, it
was concluded to be best to stop where we were until
morning, but some Hottentots from a Boer's place on the
other side persuaded us to cross it immediately, which
we did. My box was set upon the riemschoen to keep it
dry. When we were through, it rained very hard, and
we spanned out directly; in the evening, I held worship
with Mr. Marais's people and his neighbours. I slept in
Mr. M's house.

On Wednesday night, we outspanned in the evening
after crossing Sundays River, and on Thursday night we
outspanned for the night after crossing Bushman's River.

About 1 o'clock on Friday morning, we spanned in and travelled by moonlight, and reached Assegai-Bush about half-past 6 P.M. where we halted. From thence, we proceeded over a large and beautiful plain where hundreds of quaggas were running in droves. These creatures are half-zebra and half-horse, being striped in the front and brown at the back. This was the longest day's journey I had travelled since I had been in Africa. The surrounding country from Bethelsdorp was much better than from Cape Town to Bethelsdorp.

Yesterday, I rode with Bro. U. to lay out ground for the people to plow. I never saw finer land in England. This morning, I preached my first sermon in Dutch from Peter 1, from 2 to 5 verse. I spoke with some freedom and pleasure. The church is rather small, and was quite full and very warm.

We plan to stay here about two weeks, and will begin our return journey to Bethelsdorp on Saturday, March 2nd. I hope this finds you and our daughter well. It comes from your affectionate husband,
G.B.

Sarah folds the letter and smoothes it on her lap. Then she opens it and reads it again. Saturday the second. He will be home next Wednesday, then. He has gone to visit the ailing Johann Ullbricht, who was sent three years before to set up the Theopolis mission station about sixty miles to the east when Bethelsdorp became too overcrowded.

Sarah has missed George with such a visceral longing that the first night he was away she broke the rules and took their child into the bed with her. She was rewarded by a full night's sleep for the first time since little Sarah was born. Their baby has begun to hold her wobbly head upright and interact with eye contact and gummy smiles. Sarah writes about all of it in a letter to George, hoping it will make him feel closer, and she has read his letter aloud to her namesake, who alternates between avidly sucking her fingers and clutching the corners of the letter in her damp hands.

On Sunday, Sarah is in the Reads' kitchen preparing vegetables for the evening meal, thinking of George on the first day of his journey back home, when she hears the unmistakable commotion of an arrival—horses clopping, jingling, whinnying, and men's voices calling. Curious, she dries her hands on her pinafore and walks over to the window. When she sees George jump down from his horse, she tries to convince herself that it is just her wishful thinking. He left Theopolis only yesterday; he could not possibly have completed the four-day journey in this time. Nevertheless, she runs to open the door—and he is already there, reaching for her.

"How is it possible?" she asks.

"We travelled the whole night. We spanned out only once for refreshment and worship."

He pulls her close, and she molds herself instinctively into the familiar contours of his body. These two weeks are the longest they have been apart since their marriage and were all the proof she needed of how completely he is now bound up with her sense of self. In this strange country, where everything is unfamiliar—from the seasons, to the people, to the language, to the way of life—she has grown into this man's destiny as his wife, lover, helpmeet, friend, in a way she hadn't even known could be possible fourteen months ago.

That night in their room, speaking low so as not to disturb the Read household, Sarah tells him that she is expecting their second child. He stares at her, not speaking, his face blank with surprise. Little Sarah is barely four months old.

"I fear this will delay our departure to Lattakoo still further," she says, filling the silence. "Your designs and desires seem all to be frustrated by the providence of God."

"Yes," he says, "my design was to proceed. My desire is at Lattakoo among the Tswana people. But who am I that I should withstand God? I desire His will should be my will and the place He appoints me be my place of labor."

Within two weeks, George has the answer as to where his place of labor will be. James Read appoints him as the temporal manager at the Theopolis mission in support of the ailing Ullbricht—and this time his family is to go with him.

"Will this be our permanent place of calling, do you suppose?" Sarah asks George.

"My hope is still for Lattakoo, but I shall feel myself useful at Theopolis. It is beautiful country, as you will see, and the Hottentots there are industrious and friendly."

Sarah feels a little as if she is being pulled in all directions. Just over a year ago, she was living a quiet life in service in London. Since then, she had been married, travelled by sea from England to the Cape, trekked overland to Bethelsdorp, given birth to a child, is expecting another, and now they are going to uproot themselves again—possibly for good, possibly not. But she senses a new purpose in George and tries to match her sensibility to his. On the evening of Sunday, March 24, just three weeks after his return from Theopolis, George preaches his farewell sermon at Bethelsdorp.

The following day, the oxen are spanned in for the family's four-day journey, their meager belongings are loaded, little Sarah is safely stowed in her cot, and the Reads and the Williams are gathered to say goodbye. When Sarah turns to Elizabeth, who is cradling two-month-old baby Joseph in her arms, she wavers. She thought she was prepared for this farewell, but she is not. This is the person who befriended her when she was sent away to live with relatives as a girl, in whose footsteps she had followed to London and to Africa. All at once, she feels unmoored, heading off to God knows where and leaving behind the one individual who has been her constant for the greater part of her life.

"Write to me!" she says, her voice coming out in a lurch as she tries to bite back tears.

"Of course I will," Elizabeth soothes her. "I'm sure we will see each other soon. It is not so far."

Sarah envelops both mother and son in an urgent hug. Then she turns blindly, and George helps her climb into the wagon. He says a prayer for safe travel, adding, "We petition you, Lord, for guidance as to my final missionary destination—Lattakoo or Theopolis." When the wagon moves off into its plodding gait, settling into the familiar creaking, jerking rhythm, Sarah looks back. The others in the group begin to drift away, but Elizabeth stands, getting smaller and smaller, watching as the ox wagon lumbers steadily out of sight.

CHAPTER ELEVEN

I STOOD ON THE TOP STEP of the Wheeling house
on Sunday, December 7, 1997, watching the snow
drift down in mesmerizing silence, while I waited for
Douglas to park the car so that I could tell him my news.
We had just driven back from a weekend in Cleveland to
visit the American conductor Louis Lane, whom Douglas
had first met when Louis served as the principal conductor of the National Symphony Orchestra in Johannesburg
in the early 1980s. Louis had been forced to withdraw from
the position after the United Nations General Assembly
adopted the special resolution on a cultural boycott of South
Africa's apartheid government, but we'd been able to renew
our acquaintance after the cultural boycott was lifted in the
early 1990s. Now, at Louis's invitation, we had just heard the
Cleveland Orchestra in the exquisite Art Deco Severance
Hall the night before. Douglas had commented on how good
the tympani player was, and Louis, who served as apprentice
and associate to the legendary George Szell, had responded,
"Ah, but you should have heard the cymbal player, Emil
Sholle. Now there was a true artist."

When Douglas came up the stairs and out of the snow,

he stopped one step below me so his eyes were level with mine. "There's a message on the answering machine," I said. "The classical music radio station in Baltimore wants me to call them."

While we were still living in our rented carriage house in Alexandria, I'd subscribed to a number of different broadcasting publications, *Job Opportunities in Public Radio* being one of them, and I had been scouring them with diminishing hope ever since. Then, in the November 7 issue, there was this:

MARYLAND

WBJC-FM HAS AN OPENING FOR A CLASSICAL
ANNOUNCER/PRODUCER.

I'd read the responsibilities aloud to Douglas: "Program and host classical music broadcasts as required. Produce and host special programs for local broadcast and national syndication as assigned. Conduct and edit interviews with artists and representatives of arts organizations."

"It might as well have been written for you," he said.

I went on, "Operate broadcast console and production equipment." Here I faltered. The technical side of things had always been distinct from production at the SABC, and the buttons and faders on a broadcast console made about as much sense to me as an arcane quantum theory equation. The last listed responsibility was "participate in on-air fundraising activities." I had never fund raised on-air in my life.

I skimmed over the qualifications: *knowledge of classical music recordings . . . professional announcing experience . . . interviewing, editing, and production skills . . . conversational on-air delivery.* Those, at least, I could manage.

All I knew of Baltimore was that the Peabody Institute of music was there, and that when we had driven past the city on I-95 en route from Washington to New York, Douglas had said, "We could do worse." I thought about my far-fetched daydream of working at a classical music station somewhere on the northeast coast. This job posting was, without a doubt, too good to be true. Now I was standing on the top step of our newly bought house in Wheeling, telling Douglas that WBJC wanted me to call them back.

Nine days later, I drove the five hours east from Wheeling to Baltimore for a three-o'clock interview at the WBJC studios. I didn't think I was nervous, but when I opened my mouth to answer the first of the questions put to me by the panel of six, I gagged on my response, and the part of my brain that wasn't answering the question was thinking, *Oh, that's a great way to begin an interview for a job that requires talking for a living!* Still, they took me to dinner afterwards, organized tickets for the Meyerhoff Symphony Hall, and put me up overnight at a B&B in an old brownstone in the Mount Vernon neighborhood.

I caught a curious hodgepodge of impressions of the city. En route to the studios, I drove past drab strip malls along Reisterstown Road that made me think, *Uh-oh!* But then I came across the gorgeous Victorian conservatory when I ventured on to Druid Hill Park to kill time because I was way too early for my interview. When I drove into town after the interview, the marble-stepped row houses made me think of north London, and I was intrigued by the cluster of the Maryland Institute College of Art, the Lyric Opera House, and the oddly shaped Meyerhoff Symphony Hall, all within striking distance of each other in the cultural district.

Both Baltimore and Wheeling fell into a category I had only just learned about—rust belt cities. This one, though, seemed to me more culturally and ethnically diverse. It was bigger in every way, it was on the corridor between

Washington and New York, and it was on the northeast coast where I felt instinctively that I would be able to feel most at home, given that it was the first part of the country to have been settled and still had some of the European overtones that had also drawn me to Cape Town.

There is a parallel between my first alighting in Alexandria, VA, moving to Wheeling, WV, then contemplating a move to Baltimore, MD, and the way that Sarah had experienced Cape Town, Bethelsdorp, and Theopolis in quick succession. I imagine she must have found the contrasts just as sharp, albeit for utterly different reasons. Cape Town, for all the grandeur of her mountains and exoticism of her Malay and Khoikhoi people, would have been close enough to England not to feel too overwhelmingly strange. But Bethelsdorp was on a desolate, marshy, windswept plane, and Theopolis was an isolated mission station built on a hill.

To the south, Theopolis sloped down to a beach where the mouth of the Kasouga River ended in a lagoon. The tree-flanked river ran along the western slope of the station, and the northern boundary was made up of deep ravines and rocky ground. But *oh!*, it was beautiful. It was, as George had described it, *the beautifullest country*. The clean air was pure and rich, the redolent earth a tawny ochre. The trees along the curve of the river were umbrellas of red currant, now fading into autumn, and there were bush violets whose five-leaved blossoms were the color of Sarah's eyes. And there were the *wag-'n-bietjie* bushes.

George is not explicit about their lodging arrangements in Cape Town, Bethelsdorp, or Theopolis, but I'm imagining them living temporarily in a back room of Brother Ullbricht's house at first. Almost as soon as Sarah has set out their few possessions, and while George is off learning the business of the station, I see her wrapping her infant daughter in a shawl to go out and explore. She is suffering horribly from nausea with this second pregnancy, and she hopes that the clean air might help to alleviate her sickness. She walks down the slope across the grassy *veld* towards the trees edging the Kasouga River bank and slips into their quiet shade through an opening that seems to beckon. She follows a natural pathway until she comes to the edge of the riverbed—almost dry now, in the late autumn.

Hesitating for only a moment, she half clambers, half slithers down the riverbank, and steps carefully over the pools of water in the riverbed across to the other side. The opposite riverbank is steeper. After considering it for a few minutes, she takes her shawl and uses it to bind little Sarah close to her body before grasping onto a series of tree roots with both hands to make her way up, the sandy soil covering her sturdy boots as she sinks into it. She is surprised to find herself being such an intrepid explorer, but the adventure is helping to take her mind off the nausea, and she feels drawn to continue. She emerges onto a plateau, dotted with clumps of trees, and is startled by a cow that stands regarding her a few feet away, placid and unafraid.

She rounds one of the taller clumps of trees, and when she glances back toward it, she stops still. Then she steps into the shadow of a glen encircled by trees. The place is hushed, almost sacred, the light dappling through the leaves. Sarah feels utterly at peace, as if she has stepped into a chapel. *I must bring George here,* she thinks.

The next day, she sets off with little Sarah bundled up again to explore in the opposite direction, making her way up the hill toward the southwestern part of the settlement where the air is purest. She turns and looks back to the buildings of the small mission station, clustered halfway down the hill, and beyond them to where the river and the sacred glen lie in secret under the canopy of trees. As she looks, lost in thought, there is a sudden shriek from a flock of hadeda ibis overhead that makes her start and turn. In the turn, her skirts brush a shrub, and the fabric catches on a thorn. She stoops, holding little Sarah cradled in her left arm, and tries to pull free, but she is stuck fast. The more she tries, the more the thorns catch at her until she is quite bound.

"*Verskoon my . . .*"

Sarah turns at the voice, a little startled to see a lean young man blocking out the sun.

"*Kan ek U help?*" Sarah understands the word "help" and nods with relief.

He kneels, and, with infinite patience, disengages each curved thorn one by one. When she is free, he stands and looks down at her, his black eyes direct and curious. "*Mevrou Barker?*"

She nods again.

"*Ek is* Willem Valentyn," he says, indicating himself.

"I am glad to meet you." She puts her hand on her heart, hoping that will convey her meaning.

"*Dis 'n wag-'n-bietjie bos,*" he says, indicating the bush.

Wag-'n-bietjie—what could that mean? she wonders. He registers her blank look and kneels again, pointing and explaining with his hands as he speaks in Cape Dutch. He shows her how the young twigs are zigzag and how two thorns at the nodes face in opposite directions. Through his careful pantomime, which includes an enactment of how she had become more entangled the more she had tried to pull free, it dawns on her that *wag-'n-bietjie* must mean "wait a bit." She laughs, and his face lights up in response. *How like life*, she thinks, *which is not always straightforward*; one thorn facing backwards, showing where we've come from, and one facing forward, indicting where we're going, while the thorns hold you fast, telling you to take your time. And so she resolves to try to take her time and accept each strange new day as it comes.

They have been in Theopolis about six weeks when Brother Read stops by from Grahamstown on his way to Bethelsdorp. He is en route back from an exploratory visit beyond the frontier where Joseph Williams has been chosen to serve as missionary to the Xhosa. Brother James has also brought news that John Evans and Robert Hamilton have arrived safely in Lattakoo to begin their mission work up north. All three of George's missionary companions have found their calling while circumstances dictate that he must still bide his time as temporal manager to Brother Ullbricht.

Sarah is by now three months pregnant, and, following another bout of vomiting, she is curled up on the bed in their small room as George and Brother James's voices filter through the thin wattle and daub walls.

"I received a letter from Robert Hamilton by return of the wagoner to Bethelsdorp," she hears George say, "in which he charges me with forsaking him and the Lattakoo Mission."

"Have you quite resolved not to go?" asks James Read.

"My heart is yet at Lattakoo, but I have almost given up all hope of ever seeing that place. I returned to Brother Robert for answer that if we undertake the journey, it will be attended with no small inconvenience. In the first, we cannot take so young a child as little Sarah from the breast. We must then, in the second place, take with us the woman we brought from Bethelsdorp who suckles the little one since my wife is unable to do so. I would also have to take the woman's two children. These would make four, which I must, of course, consider as my own family—three of whom are not able to walk."

"Have you asked the woman if she would go with you to take the charge of the little one?"

"Yes, and we received for answer, 'Not so long a journey as that I will not.' Had it been for a week or two I should have considered it my duty to have made the attempt, but to set out on a journey of *two months*?"

"You might reconsider once your child is weaned."

"Nor does it yet appear it will be possible. My wife is again in the family way, and, not being able to give them suck, it is not very likely to be better but worse."

"Well then, I think it best if we agree that you should remain in this place."

"I can assure you that it has been as great a disappointment to myself as it is possible to anyone beside, and Providence still appears to hedge in the way. What the Lord will do with me, I cannot tell. I beseech Him to give me wisdom and understanding to speak to these people here all the words of truth."

The moment that Brother James leaves for his homeward journey to Bethelsdorp, George goes straight to the site where a new smith's shop is being built, without stopping in to say anything to Sarah. She pushes herself up and sits on the edge of the bed, waiting to see if another wave of nausea overtakes her. Her heart is thumping, and it is not only because she is physically weak. She feels hollowed out with remorse that she is the reason George cannot fulfill his long-held dream of ministering to the Tswana in Lattakoo as has been the plan from the very beginning, even before they left England.

She looks over at the cot. It is jiggling, and a small, bare foot appears over the edge. Little Sarah has a way of waking silently and amusing herself with a range of maneuvers that usually involve kicking off at least one bootie. Sarah scoops up her baby, changes her nappy, and goes to the kitchen to brew a mug of tea for George.

She carries the tea out to the smithy, where she finds George pouring his pent-up emotions into the precision of laying the brickwork for the chimney. He has planned the shop so that it will mirror, as closely as possible, the old smithy in Wimbish, Essex where he learned his trade as a boy. He looks up when he hears her and stands still.

"I overheard your conversation with Brother James," she says. "I am sorry."

George wipes his hands on the seat of his trousers and takes the mug from her. "I consider this as the beginning of days," he says.

"You had set your heart on Lattakoo from the beginning. I know full well how disappointed you are."

"It appears to be the will of God I should remain at this place." He takes a deep swallow of tea. "I will invite the people to assist me in building a small house."

CHAPTER TWELVE

DOUGLAS was all packed up and ready to leave for the five-hour drive back west to Wheeling. I stood on the pavement—I hadn't quite mastered calling it a sidewalk yet—and I couldn't hold back the tears. It was the perfect storm of saying goodbye to him again, of the strangeness of everything in my new life, and my panicky stage fright at the thought of going live on WBJC for the first time the next day.

"Just get on the air," said Douglas, hugging me close. "You know how to do that. Just get on the air, and the rest will follow."

He was right—it was the arcane buttons and faders on the broadcast console that were making me panic. But it was also that we were embarking on another three-month stint of living apart. He had urged me to accept the position at WBJC with a generosity I'm not at all sure I could have mustered, and the plan was that he would see out the season at the Wheeling Symphony Orchestra and then join me in Baltimore in May.

We'd spent the week before urgently trying to find somewhere for me to live, and we literally walked off the street into the Tudor-Gothic designed Ambassador Apartments just north of the Johns Hopkins University campus. All they had available at the time was a studio apartment, but the nine-foot high ceiling and oversized walk-in closet made it seem much more spacious. Add to that the hardwood floors and huge windows and I was happy to make this the twenty-fourth home of my nomadic lifetime.

Douglas had driven over from Wheeling with a U-Haul of basic furnishings for me, and now I was standing outside the Ambassador Apartments wanting, with all my heart, for him to stay. At least this time, by dint of one of us driving or flying one way or the other, we would manage to see each other every weekend until—on his birthday, May second— he could join me in Baltimore for good.

Crossovers between Sarah's life and mine present themselves to me like little coincidental gifts. She and George began their migration from London to Portsmouth on his birthday in 1815, and Douglas and I began our life together in Baltimore on his in 1998. There is another, darker parallel. Although my daydream of working as a classical music DJ somewhere on the northeast coast had fallen miraculously and astonishingly into my lap, George's thwarted dreams of Lattakoo were mirrored in Douglas's struggle to find something even remotely fulfilling to do in Baltimore.

When we moved from the studio to a two-room apartment that had become available in the Ambassador, Douglas was arranging things in the solarium with the great care and fastidiousness that is typical of him. Somehow, the glass carafe he was handling slipped from his fingers and smashed on the floor. In that moment, all his frustration and unhappiness erupted to the surface in the encapsulation of one idea.

"I want to go back to South Africa," he said. "Everything I disliked about America is still the same as when I left more than twenty years ago—worse, in fact. I miss the lifestyle in South Africa. I miss the climate. I miss our friends."

Douglas had found his way to South Africa by chance. He'd gone to study French horn in Germany, and, with each audition he took, he improved, getting closer and closer to winning a position with a symphony orchestra. The position that he was finally offered was a three-year contract with the orchestra attached to the South African Broadcasting Corporation in Johannesburg, and he decided to take it for a lark, to learn the symphonic repertoire. And when the three-year contract was up, he returned to America. But something about Africa had caught at him. When, two years later, he was offered a position in the Cape Town Symphony Orchestra, he jumped at it—and ended up playing in various South African orchestras for twenty years.

Having come of age during the Vietnam War, Douglas shared a disenchantment with America that many of his generation felt. He didn't pine for America when he left to go to Europe and then to Africa. In South Africa, he responded to the slower pace—the afternoon teas, the sense of taking time to find pleasure in more than material things. And since he had not grown up during apartheid, he didn't carry the burden of conscience about it in the way that I did. In fact, he felt he could make a difference.

All this made him more homesick for South Africa, ironically, than I was once we came to America, and I felt a clammy chill of horror at the idea of going back. Almost as long ago as Douglas had left America, I had begun to feel the claustrophobic pull to leave South Africa. This was my dream—this living in a first-world country, without the close proximity of apartheid to haunt me. And so began the quiet tussle that became a minor chord in the background to our lives: whether to stay in America or go back to South Africa.

George, for his part, talked no more of the decision to stay at Theopolis, but when he preached the following Sunday morning, he chose a text from 2 Corinthians, about Paul's devoted ministry to his communities of converts. George was very much overcome, and, at the last, he was scarcely able to speak. I imagine Sarah feeling the flush of empathetic adrenaline that races though us when we realize that someone we love is overwhelmed with emotion.

Having made the decision, though, George spends the next five weeks hard at work to build the smith shop and their house, moving quickly to get it done because the busy time of plowing is getting near. Sarah has never seen a house built from scratch, and she stops by often, her seven month old baby propped on her hip, fascinated to watch it take shape. This will be their first true home together, and the anticipation of sharing her first home with George helps to take her mind off the sickness that has yet to let go of its grip on her.

Up until now, they have simply lodged where they could in London, Portsmouth, and Cape Town, with James and Sara Read in Bethelsdorp, and now in the small back room in the house of Johann and Elizabeth Ullbricht. Sarah keeps trying to remind herself of the medieval saying "beggars can't be choosers," but this setup in Theopolis is far from ideal. The three Ullbricht boys, Johannes, Jacobus, and Petrus, ranging in age from one to five, are boisterous and lusty, which makes little Sarah fractious in their cramped quarters.

The building of the new house begins on Monday, May 20, with much thudding and shouting as a group of men from the mission, led by the capable Cobus Boezak, dig holes and plant posts about eight feet apart to make up the basic framework. It is a crisp autumn day, and Boezak, who assumes the role of foreman, handpicks a group of young-sters whose sole responsibility will be to keep up the steady supply of bundles of reeds, which will be needed to make the woven wall frames between the posts and to thatch the roofs.

The kitchen is to be a separate building and, like the smith's shop, will be built from brick to safeguard against the destruction of fires. While the early preparations are going on at the house, another group is working to finish the smithy. They complete the brickwork, thatch the roof with bundles of reeds held together with cords of woven rushes, and George puts down the anvil block. By the end of the week, he is able to stoke a fire in the new smith's shop for the first time, and his most pressing order of business is to make nails for the house.

Sarah has never seen him work at his old trade before, and she goes to sit with him for a while to watch, mesmer-ized by the blaze and the heat and the clang and the speed of it all. Once George has finished the nails, he begins fash-ioning a tool. At first, Sarah thinks it's going to be an axe, but then he shapes the blade at a right angle to the wooden handle.

"What is that?" she asks, projecting her voice above the clamor.

George comes over to her with the tool in his hand. "It's an adze. I need it to square the beams. Then we'll fasten the beams from end to end and across the building to make a framework for the roof before we attach the rafters. I'll have Boezak bring another load of wood for beams and spars on Saturday."

Each Sabbath, naturally, they rest.

At the start of a new week, George gets the house ready for thatching while Boezak goes out with a group to cut more wood for the doorframes. A commotion in the late morning brings Sarah to the window, and she sees a haphazard group struggling under the weight of Cobus Boezak as they carry him to Brother Ullbricht's house. Elizabeth Ullbricht is away from home and Sarah goes to see if she can be of any help.

The front room of Brother Ullbricht's house is over-crowded. Boezak is bellowing in pain, voices cut across each other in anxiety, and the air is pungent with tension. Brother Ullbricht stands in the center—bulky, intense, his bald head gleaming in the dim light—trying to restore some order. He is speaking Cape Dutch to the men, but when he catches sight of Sarah, he switches to his accented English.

"A tree which they cut down fell upon Boezak and lamed him."

"Does he have broken bones?"

"I can't say. He won't let me near."

"Shall I try?"

"By all means!"

Sarah approaches the table where the men have lain Cobus Boezak down. His eyes are wild and bloodshot, and he is drenched in sweat, despite the cool autumn day. Sarah has no nursing experience whatsoever, and she can only hope that her maternal instincts will help her.

"Cobus," she says, speaking in a low voice and laying a cool hand on his forehead, which is slick with perspiration, "I'm going to look at your leg to see what damage has been done. I will be very careful not to hurt you further."

He doesn't have much English, but her intent communicates itself to him. "*Ja!*" The sound is squeezed out between his clenched teeth.

She moves down the table. There is no doubt which leg is injured; the blood has oozed through the fabric of his trousers and is matted into a rip in the cloth. She feels dismayed and overwhelmed, and is aware of a hush now in the room, as all eyes are fixed on her.

"We will need scissors to cut away the trouser leg," she says to Brother Ullbricht, "and also a basin of warm water and some cloths. And, please, could someone call my baby's wet nurse? Little Sarah will wake from her nap soon."

For the next hour, she works slowly and methodically to cut away the trouser leg and clean the wound, while Boezak, evidently calmed by her still focus, only moans occasionally, or sucks the air sharply between his teeth. After a while, she asks for more clean water. Later, she asks for honey and lavender—otherwise, she works in silence.

When she is done, she speaks to Cobus again in a low voice, using her hands to try to explain her meaning. "The wound is bad and deep. I have applied a compress of honey and lavender and bound up your leg with a bandage. I could not see any broken bones although it is possible that your thighbone was crushed. We must pray to God that you will heal."

When she turns away from him, she is surprised to see the men who had carried him still gathered, some standing, some sitting on the floor. They silently make way for her as she goes from the room.

She walks to the bedroom she shares with her small family, thanks the wet nurse, and sends her on her way. She unbuttons her pinafore and wraps it inside out so that Cobus Boezak's blood will not stain anything else. She goes over to the washstand and pours water from the ewer into the basin, rinsing her hands over and over, trying to wash away all traces of the gruesome ordeal.

Only then does she go to the crib where their daughter lies. She runs her hand over the fragile bones, the silky skin. She is so small and vulnerable and utterly dependent on her parents for her life. But Cobus, big and strong as he is, is vulnerable, too, in this raw, unyielding place. She sits with her hand resting on her child, acutely aware of their mortality, and this is how George finds her.

"That was a fine thing you did," he says.

"It was very bad, but he is strong. We must pray that he will heal."

"It was a mercy he did not receive more injury."

"Yes."

He stands looking down at her, his face tender and focused. "What you did today made me think it would be a good thing if you could be more involved in our mission work here," he says. "I have sought a nurse for little Sarah to free up some of your time. Lena Williams promised to do it."

"Williams!" exclaims Sarah.

"Yes, indeed," George smiles. "But you can be assured she is no relation of either you or Brother Joseph. She is entirely indigenous to South Africa."

"Can we afford to have her?"

"We will find a way."

George is a reserved man, and he can sometimes come across as austere and exacting. But Sarah is learning to read him better, and she takes his suggestion as a sign of his approbation.

"If I am going to become more involved, I must learn to be more fluent in Dutch," she says. "What would you think if I were to ask Cobus Boezak to help me while he is recuperating?"

George considers this. "I think it might serve a double purpose very well," he says. "Boezak is a man who likes to be doing, and I think this forced inactivity will weigh on him. He may welcome the occupation."

The hut that Cobus Boezak shares with his family is so humble as to make Sarah ashamed that she had grumbled to herself about their cramped lodgings in Brother Ullbricht's house. The reed-built structure consists of just one room with an earthen floor, and everything must take place in this single room—cooking, eating, sleeping, washing. Cobus shares the cramped space with his wife, Marta, who is as timid as he is gregarious, and with their two children, his father, and Marta's aunt.

Sarah has asked George to teach her the phrase she will need to ask Cobus to help her learn his language, and as she stands just inside the doorway feeling like an awkward intruder, she carefully recites, "*Kan jy my help om jou taal te praat?*"

"*Natuurlik!*" is his immediate and whole-hearted response.

Cobus turns out to be an instinctive teacher, and he helps Sarah to piece together his language like a patchwork quilt, to the growing curiosity and delight of his small boys. As the weeks pass, she begins to feel less the intruder. The musky darkness of the hut offers a welcome of sorts, and she is glad to accept the mug of fragrant *rooibos* tea that Marta offers her each time she comes.

Sarah tries out her new language skills on Lena Williams, who instantly endears herself to both Sarahs with her deep, infectious laugh, and her spontaneous affection. She is small and wiry, and she looks ageless, with her black eyes and tightly packed dark hair, although Sarah guesses she is close to forty. In the process of getting to know Lena and her story, Sarah learns a number of new Cape Dutch words. Lena has two daughters—*dogters*—both in their late teens. She lost her husband—her *man*, one word sufficing for both "man" and "husband"—when he took a bad fall from a horse—'*n perd*.

Soon, Lena is filling a role that is more than simply little Sarah's nurse. By now, Sarah is five months pregnant, and Lena, without being asked, takes on some of the heavy-duty cleaning and washing. This is a novel experience for Sarah.

It had always been *she* who was in service to others, and to have the roles reversed makes her feel self-conscious—even as Lena's easy manner makes light of it.

Cobus Boezak's injury is a setback. Still, George continues to press on with the house, making the window frames and putting them in. The reeds for the walls are put up between the posts, and the people begin to thatch the roof. The third week sees the sawing and planing of the doorframes, and the laying of the dung floors with a mixture of broken-down anthills—which give a good adhesive quality—along with local lime, manure, and ox-blood, pounded down to make a smooth surface. Once the floors are dry, Sarah and Lena set about waxing them. They are rewarded for their knee-bruising work when the floors come up as shiny as mahogany, and just as durable.

By mid-June, it has turned bitterly cold, but George and his builders push on, racing to beat the start of the plowing season. The next step is the first plaistering of the house with a mixture of dung and clay. The house is plaistered a second time, then a third. Using lime that the people burn from seashells gathered along the beach between the Kasouga and the Kariega rivers, George whitewashes their new home, both inside and out. He makes a window shutter, he planes and puts together a door. At the start of the fifth week, George hangs the door, and—on June 25— they move into their new house.

It is cold. In place of a glass windowpane—one of the few materials that the environment here doesn't yield— George has put together a frame and covered it with sheepskin. Sarah, thanks to the infant growing inside her, has her own internal hot water bottle, but she bundles little Sarah up tightly, and she entwines with George in the bed to share her warmth with him when they sleep in their new home that night for the first time.

CHAPTER THIRTEEN

O N HALLOWEEN, eight months after I'd moved to Baltimore and five months after Douglas joined me there, we drove up to the little borough of Mount Gretna in central Pennsylvania, set in wooded mountains by a lake. Mount Gretna had been founded in the 1890s by the Pennsylvania Chautauqua, an offshoot of the Chautauqua Institute on the banks of Lake Chautauqua in New York State. Douglas and I were there for him to interview for the executive directorship of a little jewel of a chamber music series that presented summer concerts in the conical-roofed, open-air Playhouse that was originally built by the Pennsylvania Chautauqua as its centerpiece in 1892.

Like so much about America, names and words had found their way into my consciousness long before I immigrated, and I took them at face value, accepting what they stood for without ever wondering about their origin, like driving a car without knowing how it works. It was only when I got here that I began to learn how many of these words are rooted in Native American language and culture.

I had heard of the Chautauqua Institute as a meeting place for learning in New York State. Now I learned that Chautauqua came from an Iroquois word meaning either "a bag tied in the middle" or "two moccasins tied together," which had nothing to do with education but everything to do with the peculiar shape of Chautauqua Lake. I found out that Manhattan, the epitome of American progress with its skyline of skyscrapers, was based on an Algonquian word meaning "isolated thing in water." I learned that Algonquin, which I'd only ever associated with writers and wits like Dorothy Parker who met at a round table in the hotel of that name, was the language spoken by its peoples across a swath of land stretching from Canada to Virginia; and that Chicago was Algonquian for "garlic field." The Ohio River, whose slowly moving expanse of water I'd loved in Wheeling, was from an Iroquoian word meaning "great river." Tennessee—where my niece Yvette, an American by accident of birth, was an undergraduate at a liberal arts college—was based on the Cherokee name for that region. I found out that the Chesapeake Bay, on which I now lived, was named for the Algonquian word *chesepiooc*, a village "at a big river." And into the bay flowed rivers with names like Susquehanna, the Lenape word for "oyster river"; Patapsco, Algonquian for "tide covered with froth"; Patuxent, for the Algonquian-speaking tribe that lived along the western shore of the bay; Potomac, Algonquian for "river of swans." Suddenly these places came alive with ancient meaning and beauty.

Douglas walked out of a screening of *Dances with Wolves* in Johannesburg when the film first came out. "It was horrendous how the soldiers and white men slaughtered the Native Americans and drove them out of their own lands," he said to me after we became close. "It was no different than Nazi Germany or South Africa or anything like that. The white man in the West was out to annihilate the Native Americans, and he did. Even today, they are discriminated against; they live in their own 'homelands.'" He paced up and down for a while, then added, "You can't say America is the land of the free and the home of the brave if they annihilated the Native Americans and pushed them out of their lands. It just made me sick. I had to leave. I was so embarrassed."

The annihilation of Southern Africa's aboriginal KhoiSan peoples was not as systematic, but it was no less destructive. The San—the first nation of Southern Africa thousands of generations ago—were amongst the oldest humans on earth, with their rock art and archeological artifacts dating back to the Stone Age. The Khoikhoi were newcomers by comparison, going back about five thousand years and migrating down into South Africa about three thousand years later. Then, around AD 300, tribes of black Africans moved southward from Central Africa, and, in the seventeenth century, European colonists began their expansion into the interior from the Cape. The KhoiSan tribes were caught in the middle of these two encroaching groups, and the delicate balance of their hunter-gatherer society was eviscerated. Ultimately, many members of the fractured Khoikhoi populations found protection, in the early 1800s, on the mission stations where Sarah and George ministered.

The parallels in the decimation of Native American and KhoiSan tribes struck me as glaring and tragic—and yet in all the outcry about ethnic discrimination in both my native and my adopted countries, the aboriginal cases, it seemed to me, were overlooked more often than not. I felt as if I came across Native Americans tangentially. I met a writer who looked to my growing awareness to have Native American blood, which she did, but she seemed to identify as black. It was far more complex than I knew.

"Many Americans—black and white—have Indian heritage," she told me. "Black slaves escaped to Indian territories where they were often taken in; white male pioneers who found themselves alone in Indian regions took up with Indian women. The result is many mixtures."

Add to that the "one drop" rule whereby people were categorized as black by one drop of African blood—the equally egregious mixed-blood law that Nazis applied to Jews comes to mind—and the categories became blurred, even tenuous. Although I didn't fully understand the complexities, and Native Americans appeared to me as marginalized as the KhoiSan tribes in South Africa, still I was finding echoes of their indigenous culture all around me.

This included the little borough of the Chautauqua Society in Mount Gretna, Pennsylvania, where Douglas's interview with Gretna Music, it turned out, went exceptionally well. And so, back in the day when gas prices were still eighty-nine cents a gallon, Douglas began a five-year stint of commuting to this Chautauqua enclave to bring together musicians from Philadelphia and Baltimore, and as far afield as New York and Boston, to make chamber music in an idyllic setting of oaks and evergreens in the foothills of the Appalachians—often to the not-so-distant accompaniment of a throbbing cicada chorus. I would go up, too, for weekends and to hear the Sunday evening concerts, often stopping at an Amish farm stall to pick up preserves or oddly shaped tomatoes, and it became for us like the rustic summer retreat it had been a hundred years before. Best of all, Douglas had found something wondrous to do after five wretched months of job searching.

CHAPTER FOURTEEN

October 13th 1816
This day the Lord in mercy made an addition to our fam-
ily by giving us another daughter, which was born about
one o'clock P.M. Mrs. B had a much better time than the
first. O Lord, give us hearts of gratitude to acknowledge
thy goodness.

THEY CHOSE the name Elizabeth for their second daughter. When she was six weeks old, she was left in the care
of her wet nurse while George, Sarah, and her little namesake, now just over a year old, set off for their first excursion
to Grahamstown.

At that time, it was not much more than a military
outpost, but it was the closest thing to a town nearby. The
story goes that, four years before, Colonel John Graham had
stood by a thorn tree on the deserted loan farm called De
Rietfontein ("the reed fountain") and made the decision to
establish a settlement that was named for him. But the dark
side of the story is that the settlement had come about only
after Graham had implemented the British plan to use "a

proper degree of terror" in forcibly removing twenty thousand Xhosa tribesmen from the district and pushing them back beyond the Fish River. After the fact, there was debate that the British had misread the frontier as it had been laid out in the 1770s and that Graham's actions had been an infraction of the boundary. The Xhosa, not surprisingly, continued to make incursions into the territory.

George had intended that they should set out for Grahamstown on the morning of November 25, but the weather was unfavorable—my mother used to comment that you can get all four seasons in one day in that part of the world—so they left instead in the evening, travelling all night. By light of the half-moon, Willem Valentyn drove their ox wagon the thirty-five miles north into the interior as the track wound steadily higher and higher, and they arrived at Grahamstown in time for breakfast. Once they had settled into their modest lodgings, they picked up their overseas mail and attended an auction where they bought a cask, a tea canister, a table, and two plates. Also, although she didn't know it yet, it was around this time that Sarah conceived her third child.

And so their second year in Africa wound down. In his journal on December 31, 1816, amongst his remarks concerning the Institution of Theopolis, George wrote, *The Lord has crowned the year with his goodness. Much of it has been manifested to me & mine.* But he also berated himself for being ungrateful and lacking missionary zeal, closing the entry with: *Lord lay not the blood of this people to my charge.*

Early in the New Year comes a rupture. On the third Sunday, George is standing before the looking glass in the sleeping room, struggling to tie his cravat, fingers shaking, his face ashen. Without warning, he runs from the room, through the house, to the outhouse. He stays away a long time, and when he returns, a faint odor of diarrhea and vomit clinging to his clothes, he sits on the bed, shivering with fever, and weeps.

Sarah comes to kneel by him, smoothing his disheveled hair back from his clammy forehead. "I will send a message that you cannot go and preach today."

"No, I must go. At the meeting with the people of the church last Wednesday, I exhorted them to duties that I consider to be much neglected. I entreated them to do something to improve the church building, and I mentioned several things, which appeared to me not according to the Christian character. I cannot now renege on my duties as preacher."

"Then I will ask Lena to sit with the girls and come to be with you."

As always, Sarah is awed by the way that George loses himself in his preaching. He is in such a frame that it is as if he has forgotten his pains. He preaches from Isaiah on the holiness of God; about the prophet's cleansing and call, about seeing the Lord's seraphim, each with six wings, and how the Lord said Isaiah should tell the people, "Hear and hear, but do not understand; see and see, but do not perceive."

"What we are hearing," says George, "is God's frustration, once again, that despite telling and showing the people over and over again what is required in order to be in the right relationship with God and one another, they continue to be disobedient. They see but they *don't* see; they hear but they *don't* hear. The people need to be stripped of their human senses in order to be healed."

As soon as the service is over and the adrenaline has left his body, George begins to shudder uncontrollably, and Sarah has no trouble in persuading him to retire to bed immediately. She places a basin and a chamber pot nearby as the extremis of the bilious fever takes hold.

"I hate for you to see me this way," he moans.

"'In sickness and in health,' my dearest," she soothes him.

If they had been in London or Cape Town, she could have sent for a doctor to bleed him, but as it is she can only keep bathing his face in cool water, praying that the fever will leave him. But he gets worse. By the following Sunday, he is delirious and agitated. The bedclothes become a sweaty tangle as he tosses and flails. Sarah is afraid that he will hurt himself, and she doesn't have the physical strength to manage him by herself. She sends for Willem Valentyn and Piet Kampher, and they take it in turns, with other men from the mission, to sit with George and restrain him in the bed.

His mind wanders. His reality becomes mixed up with the passage he had preached from in Isaiah, and in his mind, the men surrounding him become the six-winged seraphim. When Sarah tries to give him something to drink so that he doesn't become dehydrated, he confuses it with a seraphim touching his mouth with a burning coal, and he mumbles, "Behold, this has touched your lips; your guilt is taken away, and your sin forgiven."

The next day, his mind still wandering, he slips into lethargy. Sarah crouches next to the bed, distraught, helpless, imagining the worst in this remote, unknown, unforgiving environment. "Please, George, please, do not leave me!" Her voice comes out in uncoordinated lurches, the way it does when she is overcome. "What will I do without you? You are my life! How will I manage out here on my own with two small infants and another coming? Please rally!" She would never have spoken so if he had he been conscious, but she is desperate to try and reach a corner of his unconscious mind.

That night, wakeful, Sarah watches the waning moon through the bedroom window. In the small hours of the morning, George becomes so still that she puts her ear to his chest to be sure that his heart is still beating. He is sleeping peacefully for the first time in two weeks, and she tries not to move her cramped body so that she won't risk rousing him. It is utterly quiet—no wind, no animals stirring—and she feels alone, frightened, abandoned in this dark, alien place. It is February 4, their second wedding anniversary, but even the passage of time has lost its meaning. As the light slides into the room, she looks over to where George is lying and sees his eyes on her.

"I must talk to Andrew Bogle about the furnishings," he says.

She thinks his mind is still wandering, and says, "What is that, dearest?"

"You know Captain Bogle is going to leave his post at Lombards Fort? I have bespoken some household furnishings of him."

He is perfectly lucid. Sarah lets out a little "oh!" and she goes to embrace him, half-crying, half-laughing that the end of the crisis should have been marked with such a mundane exchange.

The bilious fever leaves George gaunt and weak, but he seems to draw strength from slowly picking up the cycle of life on the mission. When, in March, the mission station receives notification that His Excellency the Governor, Lord Charles Somerset, is travelling from Cape Town to the Eastern Cape to discuss the vexed land issues with the Xhosa Chief, Ngqika, and will pay a visit to Theopolis Mission Station on the nineteenth of the month, George supervises the frenzy of preparation. This will be the governor's first visit to the mission station, and it is essential that he see it to its very best advantage. It would be quite within his power to close it down if he found it lacking, whereas his approbation would make a world of difference to the mission's fulfillment.

The chairs and desks are all taken out of the church and schoolroom, and the dung floors are waxed and polished to a mahogany sheen. The furniture is dusted and oiled, the window frames fitted with new sheepskin. In his smithy, George fashions metal candlesticks for the schoolroom and candelabra for the church, and Sarah makes new candles to replace the old. She walks to the rocky northern boundary to look for early blooming, vibrantly orange aloes, and arranges them in the church.

His Excellency the Governor arrives with his entourage at about one o'clock, attended by the landdrost—the district magistrate—and other officials. Lord Charles is an imposing man of about fifty years, with a long, aristocratic nose, and an overbearing manner. The two missionaries and their families are all on hand to welcome him. Brother Ullbricht presents his Khoikhoi wife and their sons, and Sarah sees a look of something like contempt pass over the governor's face. When George introduces Lord Charles to Sarah, he looks down at her from under his hooded eyes, and she has the distinctly uncomfortable feeling of being scrutinized from her bonnet to the tips of her polished boots, and found wanting. He bows stiffly and turns aside with no further acknowledgement.

The schoolchildren, all washed and combed, are lined up to meet him, and the people of the mission station are gathered in eager clusters to catch a glimpse of this all-important man. The Governor gives a cursory inspection of the school and the church and makes only a few enquiries. He has barely arrived before he is gone, all the preparations barely noticed, all the anticipation deflated.

Sarah has, by now, seen George's irritability bubble to the surface often enough, but she has never seen him so angry.

He picks up his older daughter and starts to stride towards their house. Sarah, cradling Elizabeth, has to run a few steps to catch up.

"He has no idea what hardship we endure out here!" George says in a low voice shaking with fury. "And neither would he care, evidently. I had heard tell that he has very little tact and made many enemies, but I wanted to give him the benefit of the doubt."

"It's true that he was arrogant," Sarah says, starting to breathe hard as she hurries beside him, "but no doubt he has many responsibilities that we can only guess at."

"But those responsibilities include us!"

They reach the house and George flings the door open, slamming it hard behind them. "He is not only presiding over Government House in Cape Town," he says, "he is governor of the whole Cape Colony, including our district here, and it behooves him to offer assistance and guidance—or, at the very least, to show an interest."

Little Sarah is fretful at hearing her father's voice raised and wriggles to get down. He tries to get a grip on his temper, sitting down heavily on a chair.

"Oh, Sarah, I don't know. What are we doing here? What is this all for? Is it worth it?"

Sarah goes to him. "You are still recovering from your illness," she says. "It won't seem so bleak when you regain your proper spirits."

"No. Since the new year all has been very dead and lifeless." He leans his elbows on his knees, his head bowed, his hands gripped together. "Oh Lord, revive thy words in the midst of the years. Grant that we may not continue this year so cold. Let thy Holy Spirit descend and warm our hearts that thy work may flourish among us. Without thee we can do nothing."

"Amen," says Sarah.

"Men!" echoes little Sarah.

George lifts his head and looks at her where she stands, holding on to her mother's knee, and he gives a short laugh. Sarah stands with baby Elizabeth in the crook of one arm, her other hand on George's shoulder, half stroking, half patting him, unable to find words that won't sound banal in the face of his despair. She loves this man; she loves his passion, his earnestness. But his distress is so intense that she feels out of her depth in trying to comfort him. He touches her hand where it rests on his shoulder and stands up. He looks down into her face, evidently reading her mixed feelings.

"We will manage," he says.

And somehow they do manage, improvising each new day as it comes along. One evening in mid-May, Sarah is busying herself in the kitchen replenishing their stock of soap. She's finished melting the fat and is dissolving the caustic soda in boiling water to make lye, her hand resting lightly on the five-month swell of her belly. She turns to reach for the melted fat so that she can mix the lye into it. It's a movement she's made countless times, but somehow, this time her sleeve catches the handle of the pot containing the lye, and the boiling, caustic liquid topples over, spilling on to her feet.

The pain is so excruciating and the potential damage of the caustic spill so overwhelming that for a moment Sarah is paralyzed. But only for a moment. She snatches up a pitcher of water and throws it over the spill, hoping it will dilute the worst of it. Then she sits on the kitchen floor to unlace her boots and pull off her stockings. Layers of her skin peel away. She sits looking at her blistering feet and the devastation around her. She thinks of what George had said: *We will manage.* But will they, really? Can they manage in this wild, untamed country so far from the civilization they know?

"Please, God . . ." she begins. But she doesn't know what to pray for.

George bursts into the kitchen. "What is it?" His anxiety makes him speak sharply.

She didn't know she'd screamed, but George must have heard her from the house.

"I spilled the lye."

"Did you get it in your eyes?

"No."

"Thank God!" He sees her scalded feet. "We must irrigate those burns."

He goes to pump water and returns with two buckets. He kneels, and gently positions her feet over the empty bucket. He pours the water from the second bucket in a steady stream over her feet. The cool water is soothing, but even this slight pressure is almost unbearable. When the first bucket is full, George reverses them, continuing to irrigate the wounds this way over and over again. When he is satisfied, he sits back on his heels.

"We need to bind them loosely now," he says. "Where will I find cloths?"

Sarah points to where cloths have been hung to dry over the stove. With infinite tenderness, he binds her feet. Then he pulls her arm around his neck, slides his hands under her knees and shoulders, and lifts her up into his arms to carry her back to the house. They will deal with the mess later. She rests her cheek against his shoulder, and it is only then that she begins to cry.

For a week, Sarah can't walk properly. The burns ooze yellow discharge, and she can't bear anything to touch her feet, even the bedclothes at night. Gradually, her wounds crust over, and once the scabs begin to come off, they expose tender skin, puckered and pale. Sarah is amazed at the body's capacity to heal itself. *May it be so for our souls too*, she thinks.

Chapter Fifteen

O N FEBRUARY 9, 2012, a Wednesday, I saw the subject
heading of an email from my precious friend Posy
in Johannesburg: *Sad news about Stephen Watson.*
My eyes flew over the message: *Oh darling, so sorry to send
you this news. Oh No. I have terrible news about Stephen. He has
cancer. It was diagnosed last week. It's the worst possible news.
The cancer is incurable. . . .*

For a while, perhaps as long as a minute, I sat unrespon-
sive and unmoving, looking out of the window at the slightly
foggy, chilly day, until the shock found its mark. This was how
I learned, sitting in my study on the other side of the world,
that Stephen, beautiful man, gifted poet, lifelong friend, had
months to live. Stephen, whom I had first met when we were
students at the University of Cape Town. Stephen, who had
taken me at my lowest emotional ebb when my first marriage
broke up, to walk in the dappled Cecilia Forest on the lower
eastern slopes of Table Mountain, and shown me how to
drink from a pure, icy, rejuvenating waterfall. Stephen, who
had described his expatriate friends' homesickness for Cape
Town as "almost intimidating in its longing."

It was ten days before I could trust myself to call him. All week I had been oozing tears, like condensation on a glass, and I didn't want to inflict that on him. His voice was frail and tired, but his soul was the same, and he spoke of his illness, and of death, with the frank, exacting insight that is the hallmark of his writing. As I gripped the phone, my only conduit to him, I envisioned him in his home in Cape Town, where he'd told me he watched the whales in False Bay from his bathroom window while he brushed his teeth, and where I had come upon him reading Proust in his sunny front room when we'd last talked together in August. I had never felt so far away.

I draw on these feelings when I think of Sarah out in Africa almost two hundred years earlier. It is an unseasonably cold day on Saturday, September 16, 1817, when Sarah is brought to bed with her third child. Her first contraction comes as she stands up from the luncheon table. It is so sudden and piercing that she cries out, and that sets up corresponding cries in little Sarah and Elizabeth. When the first spasm has passed, Sarah holds her daughters close, trying to soothe them in the few minutes she knows she has before the next contraction comes.

"I'll go and call Lena," George says.

"It's so cold out!"

"I'll be quick."

The door slams behind him, and Sarah feels the next contraction begin. She grips the edge of the table, her knuckles straining white against her skin.

"Breathe with me!" she says to little Sarah, trying to distract her. "Like this—whoo-whoo-whoo."

The girl laughs and mimics, "Whoo-whoo-whoo," in response.

In this fashion, Sarah gets through the time it takes for George to return with Lena.

Lena had helped Sarah to deliver Elizabeth, too, bringing with her the instinct, the intuition, and the eons of childbearing tradition of her people. But this birthing is not like Elizabeth's. It is like the first time, and Sarah feels, as the day turns to night, as if the baby will never come. She is intensely aware of her daughters in the room next door with their father, and as her focus funnels down to her womb with each new contraction, she tries to hold back her sounds behind clenched teeth so as not to distress them again.

When the baby comes, at last, at eleven o'clock that night, she is a listless little thing, and she lies still, fretting and whimpering. When George brings his two older daughters to meet their new sibling the next morning, little Sarah stands on tiptoe to look at the tiny creature in her mother's arms. She puts out a finger and, ever so gently, touches the pallid cheek of her baby sister.

George sits on the bed and nudges his little finger into the baby's palm, watching for the gripping reflex of her small fingers. But it doesn't come.

"Have you thought what you would like to name her?" he asks.

"No. Let's wait." This little creature doesn't seem to be of this world, and Sarah can't envision attaching a name to her yet.

They sit quietly for some minutes, a family of five, and then George quietly shepherds the two older girls from the room. The baby continues inert. As before, Sarah has an overabundance of milk, making her breasts engorged and too full for an infant to latch on to. She teaches herself, through trial and error, how to express her milk into a cup, as Lena has shown her, and she dips a finger in the cup, offering it to the baby to suck, trying to give her some little sustenance.

"Come, little one," she murmurs, "please try." The child seems to focus her navy blue eyes on her mother for a moment, and Sarah takes the chance to offer her more milk—but the baby turns her face away again. "Please, God, show me what to do! I don't know what I can do."

Day follows day like this for three and a half weeks. Sometimes the child will take a little milk, but listlessly, and certainly not enough to thrive. At night, Sarah keeps her in the bed with them so that she can keep watch over her closely.

Sarah wakes at half past six on the morning of October 10, a Thursday. As always, her first thought is the baby, and she cups its tiny head in her hand. The child doesn't respond. Sarah sits up quickly, pulling her infant into her arms. The tiny, veined lids flutter open briefly, but close again.

"George!"

He is instantly awake.

"There's something wrong!" she says.

"I'll go for help." He throws back the covers.

The baby's small chest heaves with a shuddering breath, and is still.

"No!" Sarah's voice comes out on a rasping cry. "No. It is too late. She is dead."

The Khoikhoi bury their dead as soon as the breath departs from the body, and it seems that no sooner has the breath passed out of their child's body than the people of the mission begin to gather outside George and Sarah's house. George goes out to speak with them.

When he returns, he tells Sarah, "I will go now to assist in preparing a coffin. And in the afternoon, she will be buried."

Without knowing how Lena got there, Sarah finds that she is at her side.

"We wrap the body in a mat before we put it in the box," Lena tells Sarah, and she offers her a roughly woven reed mat. Sarah takes it and holds it on her lap, unmoving.

"Come," says Lena, after waiting a while, "do you want me to do it for you?"

"No. I'll do it," she says, but still she sits.

"I'll go make you some rooibos. Then we can do it together."

Once Lena leaves the room and Sarah is alone again, she looks up at her child. Nine months to grow a life, three and a half weeks of a half-life, and now this. The pallid little face is at peace finally. Sarah catches her breath. How can she love so deeply a little soul that has never been fully alive? She reaches and gently holds her hand over the still face. Then she pulls her child into her arms. The small weight feels heavier than when she had been alive, and Sarah rocks and croons as if to lull her. With infinite tenderness, she slowly lies the little creature down on the mat, and begins to fold, over and over, until there is no more infant to be seen. Then she takes the bundle and holds it on her lap. She is sitting like this when Lena returns with the tea.

The coffin is so small that George can carry it by himself. He lays it on the floor at Sarah's feet. She looks down at its gaping cavity.

"Shall I do it?" George asks.

"No, I will." After a moment, she picks up their unnamed child from her lap and kneels at the coffin. She lowers the little bundle into the box, feels the weight release, and she finally lets go.

George says, "Lord, give us resignation to thy divine will. Thou gavest and thou has taken away. Let us be still and know that it is God and say, 'Thy will be done.' It is hard for us but thou, oh Lord, doest all things well."

But Sarah is not resigned. She cannot be resigned to the Lord's will. Why would He give only to take away? She cannot be still. How can she believe that God does all things well when He allows such a senseless thing? It is too hard. She recoils from the pain.

Chapter Sixteen

Give me liberty, or give me death!

THE QUOTATION IS ATTRIBUTED to Patrick Henry in the run-up to the American Revolutionary War, and I know this is because it was one of the questions I studied, and was asked, for my citizenship test. Although Patrick Henry is supposed to have spoken the words in 1775, the quotation wasn't published until 1816, and again in 1817, right around the point that I have reached in Sarah's story. About one hundred and eighty-five years later, I applied to become a naturalized American.

When I think of my friend who spent thousands of dollars on lawyers' fees and went back and forth across the borders to try to keep her visa status in order, and who eventually just had to admit defeat and return to South Africa; when I think of the countless migrants who risk their lives to cram on to barely seaworthy boats or into the backs of airless trucks to try to make it to America; when I think of children being torn from their parents by U.S. Immigration and Customs Enforcement agents at the borders; when I think of these myriad would-be immigrants, I know with excruciating clarity how lucky I am. The only glitch on my road to citizenship—if you can even call it a glitch—was that, after two years, I had to request to have the conditional basis of my permanent resident status removed by submitting tax returns to prove that I was still married to the person I said I was when I immigrated. One year later, by virtue of being married to an American, I could apply for citizenship.

My American friends joked that I knew more about U.S. history and government than they did when I was swatting up for the citizenship exam. Apart from the Patrick Henry quote, there was: What is the Constitution? How many Senators are there in Congress? Name the highest Judiciary Branch of Government. What is the supreme law of the United States? What was the forty-ninth state added to our Union? When was the Declaration of Independence adopted? What is the highest court in the United States? What group has the power to declare war? Whose rights are guaranteed by the Constitution and the Bill of Rights? In what month do we vote for the President? Those were the questions I was asked during my citizenship interview; there were eighty-six other possibilities, many of which were more difficult and arcane.

On the Ides of March in 2001, I presented myself at the United States Immigration and Naturalization Service in downtown Baltimore, conspicuous as pretty much the only English-speaking Caucasian in the waiting room. When INS Officer Imperant called me into his cubicle, I had to stand, raise my right hand, and swear to tell the truth, the whole truth, and nothing but the truth. In that odd little cramped space, with just the two of us, it felt a bit over-the-top, but I also had a curious jab of something that felt very much like pride.

Again, as with the implacable immigration officer at Dulles International Airport, I saw my life splayed out, upside down, on the desk in front of me. When Officer Imperant launched into the questions, I got the second to last one wrong. I said that it is American citizens' rights that are guaranteed by the Constitution and the Bill of Rights. As he dealt with a question that a lackey had come in to ask him, Officer Imperant told me over his shoulder, "The rights are guaranteed for *all* people living in the United States."

"Oh!" I said, taken aback. "That is comforting."

In order to test my English, he dictated for me write, *America is the land of the free.* Douglas might have another opinion, given his strong feelings about Americans' treatment of Native Americans.

The naturalization interview results are handed to you then and there, printed on the form, N-652. It's an inconspicuous form—and it turned my life around. In red, Officer Imperant marked, *You passed the test of English and the U.S. History and Government,* and, *Congratulations! Your Application has been recommended for approval.*

So on May 4, I returned to downtown Baltimore, this time to present myself at the United States Courthouse to take my oath of allegiance. I'd been told to take my green card, and when they said that I had to hand it in, I wanted to hold it to my heart and wail, "No!" It felt too hard-won. It was a precious milestone. I was so proud of it. But in order to achieve one thing, I had to relinquish another. What a metaphor: in order to become an American, I'd had to uproot myself from everything that was familiar, leave behind family and irreplaceable lifelong friends, and risk not being there for profound life events.

With most of the officials I'd dealt with along the way—the implacable immigration officer at Dulles, a bossy woman at the Social Security Administration, the INS officer who conducted my citizenship interview—I was very aware that I was just a chore, one more thing to be got through during their work day before they could go home to their families at five o'clock. But for the judge who presided over my citizenship ceremony, it was his last day before he retired, and he teared up as he told us that swearing in new American citizens had been one of the best parts of his job.

"This is a land of immigrants," he told us. "Even as you become new citizens of these United States, you must never lose the unique cultures that you have brought from your countries. They contribute to the rich tapestry that is America."

Is it any wonder that I was thrumming with the auspiciousness of it all? And then, when my United States passport arrived a couple of months later—in an unsealed envelope!—is it any wonder than I hugged it to my chest with a cry of sheer, unadulterated pride and joy?

My passport was issued on June 19, 2001. Then came September 11.

We all have our 9/11 stories. Mine is that I was home on that sunny Tuesday morning when Douglas called me from the road on his way up to Mount Gretna.

"Two planes have hit the World Trade Center in New York," he said.

It sounded terrible, but the true significance of it didn't immediately hit me.

"Turn on the television!" he said.

With him still on the line, I did as he said. I saw the first tower come down.

"I'm very upset," he said, his voice shaking. And he repeated, more vehemently, "I'm *very* upset."

I couldn't grasp the enormity of it. I couldn't fathom the

implications. Maybe because he is more left-brained, maybe because he is a native-born American, he knew immediately, instinctively what this meant.

When I drove to work at the radio station, I got there without knowing how, just taking the familiar route with my mind glued to the events unfolding in New York— and, by now we knew, also at the Pentagon and at a field in Pennsylvania. This was one of those times when you walk and eat and go through the motions of living while another part of you exists on a different level altogether. I ran my eye over the playlist that I'd programmed the day before and substituted a few pieces of music that were now inappropriate in these inconceivable circumstances. At three o'clock, I went on the air.

Typically, there may be five or six high-priority news bulletins that come down the Associated Press wires during the course of my five-hour air shift. On that day, there were five or six per minute. Instead of reading five distinct newscasts, each music break turned into a mini newscast as I frantically sifted through the continuous stream of late-breaking stories from the AP, trying to pluck out the most salient and vital facts. In between, I played beautiful music. And listeners called in tears to say "thank you" because they could no longer bear being saturated with the constant barrage of horror and the repeating visuals of the towers falling on television. Each story I read caught in my throat, but that was so utterly insignificant in the scheme of things. I just had to keep on doing it because this was all I could do; it was all I could contribute.

Two days later, I interviewed the pianist Emanuel Ax, who was playing the season opening concert with the Baltimore Symphony Orchestra. He put it the best when he said, "It's the one thing we can do, you know. I'm not a doctor, I'm not a rescue worker. All I can do is provide something for people to hold on to."

When my air shifts began to settle down into their familiar rhythm again, my delayed reaction set in like a hollow echo. I fought it because I had no right to it. It was not my city; I didn't know anyone who had been directly affected. But I was disorientated, and waves of depression would swamp me out of nowhere. Gradually, I began to understand what my grieving was about: America—my country of four months and one week—had received a body blow, and in the process, she had lost the openness, the kind of guileless candor that had made me fall in love with her. I began to understand what Douglas had grasped instinctively: something had shifted fundamentally, and it would never be the same.

There was also an insistent question crowding out my thoughts, and eventually I had to force myself to ask it. What was it that had stirred up enough hatred to impel a group of people to attack so profoundly this country that was now my own? Was it an element of smugness and brashness, born out of the confidence of superior strength and security? I didn't want to believe it.

Chapter Seventeen

O NE EVENING IN LATE AUGUST, 1818, Sarah is putting the girls to bed when she hears a disjointed jumble of voices approaching the house, and then a banging on the front door. The children start up in fright, but she soothes them, settles them again, and then goes to see what the commotion is. When she walks into the front room, George turns to her, his face drained of color.

"What?" she asks in alarm.

When he speaks, his lips are stiff, and he has trouble forming the words. "This man . . . This is Jan Neukor. . . . He has come from Kat River. . ." He can't continue. He hands her a letter.

Dear Brother George,
I do not know how I shall write these words: my beloved
husband is dead. I beg you to come to me at Kat River.
Your affectionate but grieving friend,
Elizabeth Williams

Sarah gropes for the chair next to her and sits down. She reads the words over and over. *My beloved husband is dead . . . My beloved husband is dead . . .* Joseph . . . dead? Just snatched away? She looks up at George. She thinks of their two daughters in the room next door, of Elizabeth alone with her two boys and not a single person with her from the colony; nobody there to protect her from the worst that could happen to a human life . . . the worst that has already happened.

George says, "Tomorrow morning, if God spares me, I will set off for Kat River. I'll take with me Jan Neukor as guide, and three or four of our own people."

No! Sarah thinks for a moment that she had said it out loud. But it is only in her mind, every part of her rebelling against the thought of George going to where Joseph has died—has perhaps been killed. But she knows she must keep silent. He *has* to go to Elizabeth. She will have to trust to God that he will be safe and can bring Elizabeth and her two sons out safely.

George rouses Willem Valentyn and four other men from the mission so that they can prepare the oxen and the horses for the journey. Then George sits down to write with haste and brevity to the London Missionary Society, informing them of the terrible news. While George is at his writing desk, Sarah sorts food provisions into a box. She has no idea how long George will be away, but she packs clean linens and some other items of clothing.

Soon after daybreak, they are gone. Sarah watches them ride off, three men on horseback, three on oxen, and she starts to count the days. They will have to ride by way of Grahamstown to get permission to travel beyond the frontier. If the early spring weather remains good, the journey to Kat River will take two days, so they could get there by the Sabbath. They will rest there for two more days and, more encumbered, will probably take three days for the journey home. She can expect them back in the middle of next week.

She begins to ready the house for Elizabeth and her two boys. She asks Cobus Boezak to help her move the girls' cots into the sleeping room she shares with George, and he finds an extra bed, which he carries to the house and sets up in what will be Elizabeth's room. He still has the strength of an ox, despite the injury that Sarah tended when he was felled by a tree. Sarah makes candles and soap—especially mindful after the caustic spill. Lena helps her to wash and air the bed linens.

Sarah wonders if the *vlei* lilies will be blooming near the river yet, and takes the girls out for a walk. It is the first day of September, the beginning of spring, and walking through what George once called "the beautifullest country" with her girls, and another growing in her belly, gives her hope that this wretched time will soften. She finds the lilies just coming into bloom and picks an armful for Elizabeth's room. By Wednesday, all is in readiness.

The lilies have begun to lose their bloom by the weekend, and still no one has come. By Monday, it is more and more difficult for Sarah to stop herself from imagining the worst. She sends Cobus part of the way to see if he can find them on the road. He returns with no sign of them. The girls keep asking when their father will return, and Sarah does her best to come up with perfectly plausible reasons why he is delayed. But she can't convince herself. She discards the spoiled lilies. She bakes breads, she makes soups and stews, she does everything she can think of to keep herself—and her mind—occupied during the day. But at night, when she is able to fall into an exhausted sleep, she dreams of monsters and fires, and George calling out to her, and she not able to reach him.

It isn't until the following Thursday—a week after she'd been expecting them—that word comes of the travellers on the road, and Sarah runs out to wait for the commotion of their arrival. Elizabeth climbs stiffly from the wagon and stands looking about her, as if lost, holding little Joseph by the hand, and John, still a toddler, on her hip. Lena coaxes the two boys to come with her and little Sarah and Elizabeth, while Sarah takes her friend by the arm and leads her into the quiet of the house. In the room she has prepared for her, she sits her down on the bed, and kneels in front of her, looking into her face. She doesn't know how to ask the question that is burning in her mind, but Elizabeth reads it in her eyes.

"He died from fever," she says, her voice flat and life-less. "He was working on a building in the hot sun, and he was stricken down." She sits quite still, and Sarah holds tightly on to her hands, not moving—waiting. After some moments, Elizabeth begins to speak again. "At first, I did not apprehend that his illness was unto death, but by the fourth day, the fever had much increased. He got out of bed, quite wild—but, through weakness, was obliged to lie down again. The next day was the Sabbath. Little Joseph was standing near the foot of the bed. He beckoned for him, and I brought him to his father; but he could not speak to him. I asked him if he knew the children and me. He looked at us with much concern, but could not speak. He did not sleep the whole night, and his breathing grew more and more difficult. He took nothing but water."

Elizabeth's eyes are vacant, as if she is in some other place. "One week exactly after the fever struck, just as day began to break, his happy spirit took flight to be forever with the Lord." The expression on her face doesn't change, but her eyes well up, and the tears spill down her cheeks. Sarah feels her own tears come. "As soon as I was able," Elizabeth goes on in the same flat voice, "I dispatched the messenger to George. When this was done, I was obliged, in consequence of the heat of the climate, to instruct the people to make the coffin and dig the grave. I appointed four young men to put the body into the coffin. I then took my fatherless infants by the hand and followed the remains of my beloved husband to the grave, accompanied by the whole of the people and the children."

Elizabeth pulls her hands from Sarah's and wipes her wet cheeks. Her skin is blotchy and has a grayish tinge. Her hair lies limp and dull. But it is her eyes that break Sarah's heart. They look as if they have been pressed into her hollow face with a dirty thumb.

"I haven't been able to sleep."

"Sleep now. You are safe. We will have tea later. But sleep now." Sarah unlaces Elizabeth's boots and guides her down onto the bed, pulling a cover over her. She kneels again and puts her hand on Elizabeth's forehead. She stays like this, wiping away the tears now and then when they slide across Elizabeth's temples.

"The following Sabbath," says Elizabeth, staring up at the ceiling, "when I had assembled the people for prayer, Mr. Hart arrived." Sarah does not know who Mr. Hart is, but she lets it pass. "I was much affected, and he did his best to console me. After I was a little recovered, he said that he thought it would be best to let his men prepare the wagon and begin to pack, as time was very pressing with him. But oh, Sarah," Elizabeth turns her eyes to her, "I was in great distress of mind. To leave the people and the place where I had been living so happily, and where now the body of my dear husband lay, was like tearing my heart out." She turns then, and sits up, her body heaving, her raw crying catching in her throat like a scream while Sarah cradles and rocks her. At last, her crying spent, Elizabeth subsides onto the bed again, and Sarah kneels, her face on the pillow next to her. When Elizabeth finally falls asleep, Sarah withdraws from her and the room in absolute silence, and eases the door closed behind her.

George has begun to go over all the letters and papers that have piled up in the front room during his absence. Sarah longs to bombard him with questions, but she can read the tension in his body, so she just goes to him and puts a hand on his shoulder. He reaches up to cover her hand with his. Before him is his London Missionary Society diary, which he has been bringing up-to-date.

"Who is Mr. Hart?" she asks.

"He is a superintendent of the government. He was dispatched by the commanding officer in Grahamstown to render every assistance with wagons and men that might be found necessary to remove Sister Elizabeth from Kat River."

"Elizabeth is heartbroken at having had to leave it and the people."

"I can only say that if I had been there, I would not have removed her in this way on account of my connection with the Mission Society. But Mr. Hart did it from the best of motives. The people at Kat River had offered no violence to her, nor had they attempted to take anything from her, but nevertheless it would have been improper to have left her there alone."

He stands and picks out a copy of the London Missionary Society rules and regulations from the bookshelf. "I must settle my mind on one score. My advice to Sister Elizabeth is to return to England, but she has an idea that if she returns, the directors will only provide a passage home, yet if she remains at one of the stations here in Africa, the Society will maintain her. I hope the idea is wrong. If I was on my death-bed, I should be very unhappy if I thought my dear children and widow would not be provided for at home."

"Oh please, George! Let us have no more talk of dying."

He looks at her, closes the book, and returns it to the shelf. He speaks in a softer voice. "Well, Elizabeth will remain with us until she hears from the directors, and I will start to prepare a house for her."

CHAPTER EIGHTEEN

SARAH HAD CONCEIVED her fourth child around the time of their third wedding anniversary—I like to think *on* their wedding anniversary, although George never once mentions the significance of February 4 after their wedding day. Now, I imagine Sarah on the morning of November 8, fourteen months after she had buried her unnamed child, walking the few steps to the house that George had prepared for Elizabeth.

"It is time?" Elizabeth asks, taking one look at her.

"Yes."

"Come! I will ask Lena to take care of the children, and you and I will do this together."

It has been a good pregnancy, and, since this is now her fourth time and she is, at 28, becoming a veteran at childbearing, Sarah is hopeful that it will be a good delivery. As the sun sets, the inexorable contractions take over, lengthening with each onset, until her focus is narrowed to one continuous peak of intense pain. The darkened room contracts and expands around her, funneling down with accelerating speed to a pinpoint in the center of her body as she loses consciousness.

There is an infant's cry pushed to the very last expulsion of its breath . . . there is a halo of muted light . . . and, emerging out of the gloom, there are faces looking down at her, with the light making an unsteady aura around their outlines.

"Oh gracious God!" It is George's voice.

"Sarah?" says Elizabeth. "Sarah, can you hear me?"

Sarah nods her head against the pillow.

"Here is your daughter. She needs you."

Elizabeth places a small weight on Sarah's chest, and the infant's cries falter.

"You've had a sharp time," says George, smoothing her damp hair from her forehead. "You were brought so weak as to alarm us, and the weakness affected your head."

The baby starts to whimper and fret again with increasing volume.

"Are you able to sit up?" asks Elizabeth.

"I think so."

Elizabeth bends towards Sarah, with George on the other side, and they raise her against the pillows. Elizabeth puts the child to Sarah's breast.

"I cannot suckle my babies," Sarah murmurs.

Elizabeth turns to George. "Please, Brother George, will you leave us?" George looks at Sarah, his face naked with uncertainty. She nods. He squeezes her hand, cups the miniscule head of his hungry daughter, and walks from the sleeping room. When the door clicks shut, Elizabeth takes Sarah's hands in her warm, firm ones, and shows her how to draw the milk down from her full breasts. After some initial fumbling, the baby latches on, and there is a vacuum of sound where the volume of her cries had been. Sarah looks down, hardly daring to believe it, at her suckling infant. She is lightheaded with the aftermath of pain, mingled now with radiant relief.

On December 6, they baptize their little girl with the name of Ann. A week later, Sarah is breastfeeding her in their sleeping room when she hears a wagon returning from Bethelsdorp. The commotion of arrival has died down and Ann is asleep in her cot before George comes to the room, standing silhouetted in the doorway. Even though Sarah can't clearly see his face, she can tell by the way he is holding his body that something is wrong.

"The wagon returned from Bethelsdorp and brought the affecting news of the death of our dear Brother Pacalt at Hooge Kraal," he says.

"Oh!" The word catches in Sarah's throat. She goes to George and leans her forehead against his shoulder.

"Eternal rest grant unto our Brother, O Lord," he says, holding her, "and let perpetual light shine upon him. May his soul and the souls of all the faithful departed, through the mercy of God, rest in peace. Amen."

They stand in silence, and Sarah sees in her mind's eye the open, smiling face of Brother Pacalt as he greeted her on the town square in Cape Town, thinking of his many acts of kindness on the first leg of their journey to Bethelsdorp.

"They plan to rename Hooge Kraal 'Pacaltdorp' in his honor," says George.

He leads Sarah to the chair in the room and sits down on the bed, facing her. "This may affect us more deeply even than in our sadness at the loss of a dear Brother," he says, speaking carefully. "The wagon also brought the news that the assistant missionary at Bethelsdorp has been requested to go and head the mission of our departed Brother, and he has resolved to go." He hesitates. "With Brother James also gone from Bethelsdorp now, the question has been put to me whether I would go and reside there as the head missionary."

She stares at him through her tears. "Will you go?"

"If you believe we can make our home there again, I should have no objection to going."

Sarah presses the heels of her hands against her wet eyes and takes a deep breath. She thinks of this beautiful Theopolis mission station on a hill; of Lena and Cobus, whom she has come to love; of her home—her first true home—here. She thinks of the bleak, windy mission station at Bethelsdorp; of George's thwarted hope for Lattakoo; of this opportunity for him, now, to be the head of a mission station. In all her jumble of thoughts, one thing stands out.

"I will make a home with you, wherever you choose to make it," she says.

CHAPTER NINETEEN

"I MISSED MY CALLING," is one of Douglas's favorite refrains. He has a tendency toward grass-is-greener second thoughts. Even though he had a fulfilling career playing French horn in various orchestras, he often says he missed his calling as a conductor. Another refrain was that he'd missed his calling to be a lawyer.

"Well, go to law school," I said, after the umpteenth time he said it.

"I'm too old."

I looked at his thin frame, his slightly graying hair, his alert eyes. "Nonsense. If you want to be a lawyer"—and I thought he'd make a good one—"go and study the law!"

After five years of working at Gretna Music, the three-hour daily commute had become too onerous—to say nothing of the fact that the gas prices had trebled—so Douglas had taken a new position as executive director of the Baltimore Choral Arts Society. The University of Baltimore was within walking distance of his office there, so he took the LSAT, applied to UB Law School, and embarked on four years of night school.

My niece Yvette, who happened to be born in California, grew up in Cape Town, and picked up her American life again when she was offered an academic scholarship at a liberal arts college in Tennessee, was embarking on a master's degree around this time, and was planning to follow that up with a PhD. With Douglas's JD being added to the mix of advanced academic degrees amongst my American relatives, I was beginning to feel out of my league with only a BA, and so I enrolled in an MFA program in Creative Writing & Publishing Arts at the University of Baltimore. In truth, though, it was rather more profound than that.

I had always been in awe of writers. My late poet friend, Stephen Watson—whose death had made me feel so terribly far away from home—had been told once that, when he was in the throes of writing, he hummed unconsciously as he went into that deep place of creativity. It seemed otherworldly to me to create something out of nothing in that way. As a broadcaster, and before that as an actor fresh out of drama school in Cape Town, I was a *re*-creator, and I simply didn't feel that I had it in me to be creative on that raw and elemental level.

Then I immigrated. And the experience was so profoundly life changing that I *had* to write about it. It forced its way out of me and wouldn't be bottled up. I wrote copious letters and emails back home, but that wasn't enough. I kept a journal. *That* wasn't enough. I even tried to collate it all together into a book. But I didn't have a clue how to go about it. I was carrying around this huge load of overwhelming, unwieldy experience, and I had no idea how to make sense of it.

Then I discovered this wonderful thing called creative nonfiction, grounded in fact but making use of the tools of fiction—character, dialogue, scenes, narrative arc—to give the facts life. I was still frightened of the raw creativity of poetry and fiction, but creative nonfiction? I thought perhaps I might be able to manage that. And I believed that the creative writing program at UB could teach me to do it.

The first time I had to share my words when I started the MFA program, I wanted to climb right back inside myself from sheer awkwardness and embarrassment. But, like a beginner learning scales at the piano, I started to experiment with marrying words to each other to make a phrase, a sentence, a paragraph, an essay. And I just practiced away at my scales until I could begin to tell my story. I hadn't known I was missing it, but it seemed I had found my calling. In the process, I also found Sarah.

George is a moderately well-known personage. His original diaries are housed in the Cory Library at Rhodes University in Grahamstown. *The History of Theopolis Mission,* 1814–1851, drawing mainly from George's diaries, was the thesis of a master's degree awarded by Rhodes University in 1983. There's a collection of some of his personal letters at the National Library of South Africa in Cape Town. An online search for George Barker yields seventy-five results in the London Missionary Society archives at the School of Oriental and African Studies at the University of London. His name appears regularly in the index of texts from around that period.

But it was Sarah who seemed to whisper to me from George's diary. She was elusive and fascinating as she slipped in and out of his pages—like a fleeting leitmotif—as "Mrs. B." Who was this ethereal woman who played such a vital role in the life she shared with George? I wanted to learn more about her, the way you want to meet up for coffee with someone you've brushed up against who seems to share your sensibility. I was curious, as an immigrant myself, to learn about her immigrant experience. I needed to find out how, exactly, her bloodline had been passed down to me through my mother. I found that I was longing to get to know her and to try to flesh out her story. I just didn't know where to begin.

My starting point had to be George's diary and the master's thesis from Rhodes University upon which it was based. The journal can be dry and sometimes even dull—entry after entry of planting beans or painting fences—but it is immersive and fascinating as an account of pioneering missionary life, and I combed through it for references to Sarah to glean what I could about her life through the conduit of his. Each glancing mention of her was like a seedling that I tried to plant and nurture and bring to life.

The facts of George's life quite quickly fell into place. He was born on February 7, 1789, and he was the oldest son of Nathaniel Buttress Barker, a smithy and innkeeper of The White Stag Inn in the county of Essex, in England. George trained in the family smithy and was schooled in Cambridgeshire. He was first "awakened," as the committee members of the London Missionary Society put it, at the age of twenty-one when a friend put into his hands to read the book by the Congregationalist minister, Dr. Philip Doddridge, titled *The Rise and Progress of Religion in the Soul*. Soon after, he heard a Mr. Thomas of Chillesford preach on the words that Jesus spoke to his disciples: "The harvest is plentiful, but the workers are few. Ask the Lord of the harvest, therefore, to send out workers into His harvest." George was led by what he described as "a powerful impression of the words" to think of becoming a missionary, and he was admitted to study at the Gosport Academy with the nonconformist preacher Rev. Dr. David Bogue, in January, 1814.

The White Stag Inn where George's father was the pro-prietor still stands, and one late October day in 2013, friends and I went there for a pub lunch, to the curious delight of the present-day innkeeper when she learned of my connection. It was newly renovated—its character nothing like the way that George would have known it—but even so, I had the uncanny sense of occupying the same space that he had once occupied.

It was an unusually mild day for an English autumn, and I wanted to visit All Saints Church in Saffron Walden where George had worshipped as a boy, so we drove along the country road that winds there from the family inn and ends up at a low stone wall, punctuated by a Medieval tur-reted pillar. In the graveyard, the autumn trees just turning, I crouched to read the names on the gravestones of the cen-turies of Barkers buried there; some of the headstones that had fallen over time were propped up from behind by others. It was intensely moving to trace that familial connection so far back—and I urgently wanted to be able to do the same for Sarah.

By this time, I had begun to write tentatively about the connection I felt to Sarah, and when I was catching up with a friend over lunch one day, I mentioned to him in passing that I was trying to find a way to trace how my lineage wove its way back to her. My friend said, "Well, I know a genealo-gist, and I can put you in touch with her if you'd like."

So one spring morning, I made my way to a Bolton Hill coffee shop in Baltimore to meet up with Kristine Smets, who offered me her hand for a firm handshake in that slightly formal European way. She is Belgian, so she was sympathetic to my cross-continental, cross-genera-tional dilemma. She was also gently receptive to my need to try to do as much of the genealogical digging as I could on my own—however inept and amateurish that might be—once she had pointed me in the right direction. When she opened her notebook, flattened the page, and started to make notes in her neat, left-handed script, I felt as if she was taking hold of a part of my life and cupping it gently in her slender hand.

The Dark George's Collection depicted at the 1832 flood

PART THREE

Chapter Twenty

"THE BRETHREN have proposed to me the propriety and the necessity of being fully ordained as a minister should I go to Bethelsdorp," says George.

Sarah has been making soup in the kitchen, and the steam is compounding the summer heat. A tendril of escaped hair clings to her damp neck, and she can feel the clammy warmth in the crook of her arm where Ann lies drowsing. She stirs the soup and knocks the wooden spoon on the side of the pot. "It seems to me that you already serve as a minister in all but ordination," she says.

"I may serve as one, but, strictly speaking, the designation that was conferred on me in London is sufficient only for me to serve as a mechanic missionary. In that capacity, I may offer temporal support, like the preaching, or teaching, or smithy work I have done here, but not spiritual guidance. If I am to be the ruling missionary at Bethelsdorp, I must be fully ordained."

"Will it require much preparation?" She moves away from the heat of the fire and sits down at the table. He pulls out a chair and joins her.

"I believe that I received a sound theological instruction from Dr. Bogue in Gosport," he says, "and that will stand me good stead. But I will have to work very hard to answer the questions in Dutch at my ordination service."

"Are you obliged to have the service in Dutch?"

"No, but I wish it, since it is the language of the people. I want the congregation to be able to understand."

"And when do you think it would take place?"

"The date of January tenth has been proposed for my ordination service."

Sarah eases the weight of their child against her body, trying not to wake her. "Ann would be just two months old."

"Yes. I think it would be too arduous for you to travel so soon with the three children."

Sarah looks across the table at him, feeling torn. He reaches to take her free hand and turns it over, studying it.

"I wish it could be otherwise, but it is probably for the best that you remain here." He looks up into her face again. "I will not commence at Bethelsdorp until the end of the month, and you will all be with me for that." And with that, Sarah has to be content.

When George sets out for Bethelsdorp on December 30 with Brother Ullbricht, Cobus Boezak, and small party from the Theopolis mission station, Elizabeth and her two boys accompany him. That makes it a double loss. Elizabeth has been called to Cape Town to come under the protection of the superintendent of the London Mission Society, and she is making the first leg of the journey to Bethelsdorp to sail from Algoa Bay.

When it is time to say goodbye, Elizabeth hugs Sarah close and whispers, "I will be your ears and eyes and heart at the ordination." Sarah nods, not trusting herself to speak. She has no idea when or if she will ever see Elizabeth again.

George assists Elizabeth into her wagon, then turns and takes Sarah by her shoulders, looking down into her face. She holds on tightly to the lapels of his coat, feeling her eyes sting with tears. He kisses her on the forehead, pulls her into a quick embrace, and, turning blindly, fumbles for the reins before swinging himself up on his horse. With the now familiar piercing "Hah!" from the driver, the ox wagon creaks into motion while the men on horseback settle into a slow gait alongside. Sarah shields her eyes against the summer sun as, once again, she is the one left behind, watching George and Elizabeth and the convoy plod slowly out of sight.

Her heart longs for a letter in the coming days, even though her mind knows that George will be too busy to write. On the morning of the ordination, instead of going to the mission church, she says Sunday prayers with the girls at home, and then she opens up the *Book of Common Prayer* at the place of the Form and Manner of Ordering of Priests.

"Reverend Father in God, I present unto you this person present, to be admitted to the Order of Priesthood," she reads aloud. "Your father will be presented to the ordaining minister in this manner, but only it will be in Dutch." She reads through the order of service in this way, trying to conjure up for them every part of the ordination as it is taking place in Bethelsdorp.

In the afternoon, restless, Sarah ties Ann onto her back with a shawl, as she had seen Xhosa women do with their infants, and she takes little Sarah and Elizabeth out with her into the *veld*, the grass dry underfoot from the summer heat, to harvest prickly pears from the aloes.

"Be very careful not to touch the fruit!" she tells the girls. "The thorns are small, but they'll hurt awfully, like a splinter, if they prick your tender skin. Do you see how I'm using tongs to pull them off the aloes?" Carefully, she drops the prickly pears into the pail she has brought with her.

Back at the house, she spreads out a folded blanket in the corner of the kitchen, puts Ann down on her tummy so that she can practice her newly acquired skill of lifting her head, and sets little Sarah and Elizabeth as guardians, while she turns her attention to her harvest.

Her plan is to try and make juice from the prickly pears, based on what she knows about making jam. With a knife and fork, she tops and tails a prickly pear, then makes a slit along the length of the skin, prying the coarse outer layer away from the densely pitted fruit inside. She dumps her prize into a large stockpot and repeats the exercise until all the fruit is bobbing in boiling water on the stove. While Ann naps and the girls sit up on the table to watch, Sarah strains the cooked fruit through a fine sieve, then squeezes it through cheesecloth into jars. She is up to the elbows in sticky juice by this time, but she luxuriates in a wonderful sense of achievement. If nothing else, the whole process has kept her mind in the present, rather than down in Bethelsdorp, where she most longs to be.

The next day, Cobus Boezak returns to Theopolis, bringing with him the much longed-for letter from George. Cobus is sweating from the hot ride, and Sarah invites him to the kitchen to offer him some of her newly prepared prickly pear juice. His relish is gratifying. There has remained an unspoken bond between them since the time she tended his mangled leg and he taught her his native tongue, and his sadness at their leaving Theopolis touches her.

"We will miss you badly," he says simply. He drains his drink and carefully sets the glass down. "Now you will want to read your letter from Brother Barker." His thoughtfulness is typical of him.

10 Jan. 1819
My dear Sarah,
I write to you as a fully ordained minster.
This morning Brother Messer held the prayer meeting in the old church. At 9 o'clock the service in the new church commenced. I began by reading chapter 8, 1 Kings from 27 to 61 verses, and prayers; Brother Messer preached from 2 Chronicles 7-16, an appropriate discourse on the fire flashing down from heaven following the dedication of the temple by Solomon.

At 11 o'clock the ordination service commenced. Brother Evan Evans, a Welshman who arrived at the Cape two years ago, began by reading the 3rd letter from 1 Timothy, and prayers. Bro. Evans asked the following questions. How do you intend to exercise the office of a minister amongst the people? And what are the doctrines which you believe to be contained in the Holy Scriptures? Which questions I endeavoured to answer in Dutch. Brother Evans gave a very appropriate and affecting charge from Tim: 4-5: "But watch thou in all things, endure afflictions, do the work of an evangelist, make full proof of thy ministry." This sermon was addressed specifically to me, as the ordinand, and then Brother Messer preached to the people.

After the service I baptized, in public, 5 children and administered the Lord's Supper. A most interesting day to me. O Lord give me grace to improve the trust, for the good of those souls given under my charge and for thy Glory. There were many strangers present, from the Drostdy and Algoa Bay. Upwards of 26 Rixdollars were collected at the door for the poor.
With humility I sign myself,
Your affectionate husband,
the Reverend George Barker

With George now fully ordained, the move to Bethelsdorp begins to crystallize into a reality, and Sarah knows she cannot put off packing up the Theopolis household any longer. She asks for Lena's help as the piles of books, letters, clothes, linens, and kitchen utensils seem to mushroom.

"I feel as if we live such a simple, almost meager life here—how is it possible that we have accumulated so much?"

Lena laughs, and Sarah stretches her aching back as she tucks a persistently wayward curl of hair back behind her ear. She sits down on the wooden crate to hold it closed while Lena straps it up with leather thongs. Sarah studies Lena's concentrated face as she pulls tight the strap, and feels a stab at leaving behind this warm and smiling helpmeet. She has become an indelible part of their lives in every way, not least for having helped to bring other lives into their world. Sarah thinks of the places she's left—her family home in Shropshire . . . her relatives' home . . . London . . . Portsmouth . . . England . . . Cape Town . . . Bethelsdorp . . . and now Theopolis. Will she pull up her roots so often that eventually she will have no roots to pull up?

For his farewell sermon at Theopolis, George chooses a verse from Acts: "For I have not shunned to declare unto you all the counsel of God," and on January 21, the family sets off for Bethelsdorp. They all of them part in tears.

Chapter Twenty-One

GEORGE OFFICIALLY took charge of the temporal affairs of the Bethelsdorp missionary institution on February 1, 1819. On the twelfth, he wrote in his journal: *Fixed shelves for my books etc. & prepared my study.* His entry the following day was: *Brought all into the Societies house.*

Then his journal suddenly breaks off for seven months—a blank page follows that last entry. At the top of the next page he wrote: *Having from certain unpleasant circumstances, particularly the receipt of a printed Circular from the Directors of the Missionary Society, and the unsettled state of my mind, neglected to note anything down, the journal of this year is incorrect.*

He drew a line under that note, and then started up the journal again on September 15 with this entry: *Brother Hooper rode to Algoa Bay to procure a passage to Cape Town with a design to return to England.*

Three days later, George's journal entry is: *The Brethren Evans and Hooper left us this morning to go on board the Georgianna bound to Table Bay.*

What on earth was going on during that blank page in George's journal that caused his unsettled state of mind and the departure of the two other missionaries at Bethelsdorp? I'm guessing that the printed circular from the directors he mentioned was probably the new code of regulations for the missions in Africa that the directors issued in October 1818. One of the codes was this:

> *It is a duty which the Directors owe to the great cause of propagating the Gospel among the heathen, no less than to the Society for which they act, to press on the attention of all their missionaries the obligation of finding their support from the people among whom they labour. This principle is of the greatest importance, and the acting upon it in any station will be in itself a security for the progress of the Gospel in that place. But while the principle is kept in view, so long as the circumstances of particular missions shall make it absolutely necessary, the Directors will afford to the missionaries a suitable support.*

My reading of this is that the directors expected the missionaries in the field to be financially and materially self-sufficient. I can only imagine the feeling of abandonment—being stuck at the end of Africa without "suitable support" from the directors who had sent them out there in the first place, and under whose supposed patronage and guidance they worked.

Frankly, I suspect that Frederick Hooper was fed up with the treatment of the London Missionary Society and decided that he'd had enough. The Welsh missionary Evan Evans, who had asked the questions of ordination at George's service, was not leaving the L.M.S. outright, but removing to the mission station at Paarl—the Dutch name for the pearl-shaped mountain looming over the town—forty miles inland from Cape Town.

I think it speaks to George's steadfastness that he decided to stick it out at Bethelsdorp despite the unconscionable directive from the Society, and in the face of being left alone as the sole missionary at the station. But I imagine that, George being George, he probably reacted with a degree of irascible outrage in his response to the directors, which undoubtedly got him off to a rocky start in his new role of head missionary.

This gap in the diary and what it implies—George's hurt and anger, his melancholy—has made me wonder about just what it is that comes down to us through our genes and bloodlines. My niece Yvette maintains that our shared gene pool is evident in the shape of our hands, our breathy laugh, our fastidiousness, discipline, and drive. It's not only that I can see my mother, my uncle, and my brother in George's physical features—it's that I grew up at the receiving end of my mother's quick temper, and I can recognize her in George's responses. I've seen my brother Peter's passionate belief turn into bitterly hurt disillusionment. As I try to listen for an emotional echo, I wonder if I can trace my own tendency toward depression all the way back to George.

George's time and temper were stretched paper-thin at having to manage Bethelsdorp single-handed. There was a simmering undertow of lawlessness, drunkenness, and lewd behavior on the mission, and many of the men were called up to guard against the Xhosa raids, so that there were too few remaining to help with the building repairs so desperately needed at the station.

Trying to fill in the gap in George's diary, I envision the family at breakfast on April 20, when an urgent call comes from the garrison in Grahamstown to send men from the mission. Rumors are rife that the Xhosa prophet-chief, Makhanda "Nxele" ("the left-handed") is leading a force of thousands to attack Grahamstown. The British have only 350 troops stationed there.

"I don't like this," says George gripping the summons in his hand. "We are here to spread the word of God, not to fight."

But George's personal views are moot; he is bound by the administration to send able men when required. He sends thirty men to join up with other Khoikhoi troops from the area. Four days later, the men begin to drift back to Bethelsdorp, with strange stories of a battle.

"Just before we got to Grahamstown, we met up with Cobus Boezak and his men from Theopolis. . ."

". . . when we got to the top of the hill, we looked down, and we couldn't even see the fort."

"There were thousands and thousands of Xhosa as far as you could see."

"And it wasn't only warriors. There were women there also, and children."

"Right there out in the open, in the middle of the day."

"Then Boezak saw an opening on the west side, where the trees joined the hill, and he said, 'If we can just make it to those trees, we can ride down from there and maybe surprise them.'"

"I never thought we'd make it. . . ."

"We got into the fort all *deurmekaar*. . ." —*disorganized*, Sarah translates in her mind.

"There weren't enough English. They couldn't load fast enough . . ."

"But with his troop of buffalo hunters, Boezak opened fire on the Xhosa warriors . . ."

"He turned around the whole battle!"

"Now, we were all shooting too . . ."

". . . and the Xhosa started to fall. . ."

". . . and to fall back."

"It was like water flowing slowly backwards."

"They said Makhanda promised to turn the English bullets into water."

"There were so many bodies on the ground. So much blood."

"A thousand Xhosa died."

"Someone told me two thousand."

Sarah turns away. She has heard enough. *Two thousand dead?* The toll is appalling.

On September 28, word comes that Makhanda has passed by the mission station, under guard, toward the bay. "The government has sentenced him to life imprisonment on Robben Island in Table Bay," George tells Sarah. "The ship sails for Cape Town within days."

Sarah is bottling jam in the kitchen, and she wipes a drip from the side of a jar. "Were you much surprised that he surrendered?"

"From what I've heard, he is an honorable man, and he negotiated his surrender to spare his people." Abstractedly, George moves one of the jam jars to align it with the others that Sarah has filled. "When he was younger, Makhanda heard the gospel message from Johannes van der Kemp. They say Makhanda was a magnetic speaker, combining elements of Christianity with ancient Xhosa beliefs and attracting crowds numbering in the thousands."

"It's no wonder then that they were prepared to follow him to their deaths in Grahamstown. How awful!"

"And I see no end to it," says George. "Although this conflict is over, I have been ordered to furnish twenty-one men for the augmentation of the Cape Corps. It is not right that the administration should have the authority to conscript our men in this way. We are depleted enough as it is as I try to bring order to the mission station."

Sarah begins to stack the jam jars on a shelf.

George says, "When I rode to the Drostdy last week to pay my respects to Colonel Jacob Cuyler, he was kind enough to share with me his correspondence with Lord Charles Somerset respecting a large number of settlers they expect to arrive from England in the early part of next year. He says the governor wishes to consolidate the English-speaking population in the Albany district."

"Where is that?"

"It is an area that includes Theopolis and Grahamstown between the Bushman and Great Fish rivers. Colonel Cuyler named it for his native town of Albany in America's New York State."

"America! How came he to be in Africa?"

"His father, he tells me, sided with the British crown during the American War of Independence, and he was imprisoned and exiled for it. When the British compensated him after the war, he bought commissions for his sons in the British army, and Colonel Cuyler came to the Cape in 1806 with the 59th Regiment of Foot."

The plans for colonizing the Albany district, which Colonel Cuyler had shared with George, came to fruition the following April, and George kept meticulous note of the events in his journal.

April 10th 1820
The Chapman Transport arrived in Algoa Bay with Mr Bailey's party of settlers, the first party.

April 11th
Col. Cuyler rode very early past to the Bay, to see the emigrants.

By the third day, George can contain his own curiosity no longer, and he rides down to the bay to greet the settlers himself, bringing the fresh sea air back with him when he returns to Bethelsdorp in the evening.

"It was fortuitous that I went today," he tells Sarah. "A poor woman died yesterday, and when it became known that I was a minister, I was requested to attend the funeral. Since they were all so newly arrived from Britain, I thought it best to read the Church of England form of burial service, and then I addressed the spectators with a few words."

"How terribly sad to come all this way, only to die almost as soon as landing."

"Even before landing, for some," says George. "There was an epidemic of whooping cough onboard the ship, which resulted in the deaths of five children under the age of two. A five-year-old boy named Daniel Hockly also died aboard the ship—I spoke to his parents. Mr. Daniel Hockly is a silversmith, and his wife, Elizabeth, is a very amiable woman. They have three daughters remaining, whose ages correspond, more or less, to our own. All the settlers were in remarkably high spirits, and they seemed perfectly resigned to everything."

"How many are there?"

"I would guess more than one hundred on this first ship, with as many children besides. They were in tents, two or three families in each, yet rejoicing to have left the *Chapman*. They had been aboard five months, having been quarantined in Cape Town. Almost all of them were from London, I found, and many of them were of good parentage, wealth, and education—men of the first trades in England, half-pay officers, and the like; men who would easily have found good employment were it not for the aftermath of the war against Napoleon."

"How will the settlers proceed now that they have landed?"

"Well, Mr. Hockly mentioned to me that he has been offered employment while at Algoa Bay, and he may be permitted to leave the party. There are a few others in a similar position. For the rest, since the *Chapman* had such a high proportion of skilled tradesmen and professional men, the intention is that they will form village centers in the new Albany district."

The next day, news comes that the *Nautilus* has arrived in the bay, and, the day after, the *Ocean*. Sarah is fairly bursting with curiosity herself by this time, and she is able to have her first experience of these new settlers when Daniel Hockly pays a visit the next Sunday. She guesses him to be in his early thirties, and he looks something of the gentleman, she thinks, with his wavy dark hair, straight nose, and long upper lip.

"Rev. Barker tells me that you lived for a time in London," he says to Sarah.

"Yes, I was in the service of the Rev. Mr. Waters of Kingsland Road in Islington."

"Ah. We were down in London's West End, on Brook Street in Holborn, so it's unlikely our paths would have crossed. You would see a change in England, I think. Things became increasingly difficult after the War. I, myself, was reduced under providence by misfortunes and losses, and I could no longer sustain my silversmith business."

"Do you plan to practice here?"

"It is my hope. I have also a very general knowledge of mechanics and some little of agriculture, so I hope by some manner or another to make my way."

He smiles towards little Sarah, Elizabeth, and Ann, who are clustered around their mother's chair. "Do you think your girls would like to see a piece of silverware?"

"Oh, indeed!" she says, gently pushing them forward. "And so should I." She hoists Ann onto her hip and walks over with the other two.

"I don't take snuff myself, but I carry this snuffbox as an example of my work."

The two girls stand at a respectful distance, craning forward as he produces the box from his waistcoat pocket.

"Look, Mama!" says Elizabeth. "There are flowers on the lid."

"Yes, it is beautiful," says Sarah.

She studies the delicate engraving, aware of how out of place it is in her simple home and bleak surroundings, hoping that this gentle, gifted man will, indeed, be able to make his way, as he had put it.

Not all the settlers are so amiable. When George returns from seeing the *Nautilus* transport, he tells Sarah that he found the party rough and vulgar. "I did not find one of whom I had the least hope of piety. I left them with the conviction that the fear of God was not among them."

By now, a steady stream of transport ships is sailing into the bay, and George continues to note each new arrival in his journal for the London Missionary Society. The H.M.S. *Menai* sloop of war that had escorted the settlers' ships arrives next, followed by the *Kennersly Castle*, the *Northampton*, the *John*, and the *Aurora*. On May 15, the *Brilliant* and the *Albury* arrive. George rides to the bay every few days and brings back such vivid impressions that Sarah almost feels as if she is witnessing this huge diaspora of British immigrants herself.

He returns one day after trying to retrieve letters and parcels from the *Aurora*—but could not, because the wind was too fierce—and he tells her, "I saw a woman today, a wife of one of the settlers, walking from the beach to the tents, who had not been confined a week. The poor creature was nearly fainting."

"Oh my goodness!" says Sarah, full of compassion and affinity. She is seven months pregnant with her fifth child.

Two months later, on a bitter midwinter night, she is woken at three A.M. on Saturday, June 3, by the first sharp contraction. The wind is howling around the house, but she is like a furnace at its epicenter. By daybreak, she is exhausted, and she can only turn her head from side to side against the pillows, no stamina left to push and hardly any to breathe.

The midwife wipes Sarah's face with a warm cloth—how she longs for Lena. "Rest for a moment," says the midwife, "then take a deep breath, and you will find the strength."

Sarah does as she is told, and the deep breath sends a jagged pain through her uterus. She feels as if the rest of her body no longer exists. There is just this pulsating, red heat in the deepest part of her. A clock chimes eight o'clock. It has been five hours.

"I cannot take much more," she murmurs.

Elizabeth and Ann's young voices sound in another room before their older sister quickly shushes them. Sarah opens her eyes. There is a streak of winter sunlight across the ceiling. She takes a deep breath, grips the bedclothes in her fists, and bears down with all her might. And then she knows there is another life in the room.

"Mrs. Barker, you have a fine son."

When George comes into the room he takes her hand, and rests his forehead against it. "Oh, my dear Sarah!" he says. "You had one of the sharpest births I ever knew you to have. I feared losing both you and the child." He grips her hand more tightly. "Merciful God, thank you for your help. O! That we felt more grateful for our mercies."

For two days, Sarah rests well, and her strength begins to seep back. But on the third day her abdomen is gripped by a very different kind of pain. Almost before she knows it, she is in the throes of violent dysentery. She is too weak to make frequent visits to the privy, and she has to try to deal with the fever, the extreme stomach cramps, and the profuse and bloody diarrhea in the confines of the bedroom.

Within a day, her infant takes the infection. Sarah knows that the greatest danger of dysentery is dehydration, and she urges her baby to drink her expressed milk, but everything passes straight through his little body. Even as Sarah slowly begins to rally, her son grows worse. By the eleventh day of his life, he can't drink or sleep, and all through the night they are fearful they will lose him. But he holds on. By the twelfth day, they have some hopes for him. The next day, a Saturday, the baby is able to rest, and they flatter themselves that he is better.

George preaches at the Sunday morning and afternoon services, and he sits up with his son until midnight so that Sarah can get some rest. He passes the infant to her then and goes to try and get some sleep in his office.

The moon is half full, and by its light, Sarah looks down at the pallid face of her son. Her mind keeps wearing away at the groove in her memory of the time she watched over her unnamed daughter, but she wrenches her mind away from the recollection, willing a different outcome. At daybreak, Sarah begins to drowse, but she is jolted awake when the child suddenly convulses and vomits all over her nightgown.

"George!"

He stirs instantly and is beside her. He stands looking down at the child. He says, "I fear he will not live long."

"I fear it also."

He rolls up his sleeves and pours water from the ewer into the basin on the washstand. He takes the infant and bathes and swaddles him while Sarah changes her night-gown. George lays his son down on the bed and they sit on either side of him. The small face is contorted and he exhales a whimper. His eyes and mouth are closed, and they wait for the next breath. It doesn't come. Then, the baby drags in a lungful of air. So it is through the day, as they expect every breath to be the last.

"Try to get some rest," says Sarah. "I will keep watch."

"I wouldn't be able to sleep. I will sit with you."

At four o'clock on Tuesday morning, the baby is seized by a strong convulsion. He twists and thrashes, his mouth stretched wide, groaning and whimpering. Sarah tries to soothe him, to hold him, to put cool compresses on him. Nothing helps.

"Oh dear God!" she says. "Let me take this on myself rather!" There can be nothing worse than this helplessness in watching her child in agony and not being able to do any-thing. Is this what it is like for George to stand by when she is in childbirth, unable to take away her pain?

At the last, the infant arches backwards in a convulsion, and then is still, and quiet, and slack. The first rush that Sarah feels is relief that it is over, before a stab of grief takes her breath away.

Somewhere, in another world, she hears George's prayer. "Lord, you do all things well," he says. "You gave and you have taken away."

The words lodge in her mind. "You give and you take away." But why? Why?

She fights against the knowledge that she has experience to draw from in how to deal with the death of a child. She knows that she will wash his body, wrap him in clean linens, feel the slight weight of him drop away as she places him in the small coffin, and follow that coffin when the people carry it on a ladder to the gravesite. But she can't begin the process. The cold winter day filters into the room, making gray silhouettes out of the tiny mound of the still baby, and of Sarah sitting motionless, her hand still resting on him.

CHAPTER TWENTY-TWO

A N ELDERLY MAN conjures the melody out of a curious, guitar-like instrument that is fashioned from an old tin can, a piece of wood, and strings. Others group around him, their fingers and palms pulsing over barrel-shaped drums. The dancers form a circle around the fire, the blur of their intricate, implausibly fast footwork stirring up clouds of dust. This is the celebratory *rieldans*, the Khoikhoi equivalent of a Celtic reel. A young dancer swings his hat in front of a lithe young woman and she laughs, offering him her hand. Another youth throws his shirt down on the ground; his dance partner shyly picks it up. Sarah recognizes these gestures as centuries-old, stylized courtship. The rhythm is mesmerizing, and she can't resist swaying her body instinctively to it.

Several families have come together to make this joint marriage feast in celebration of the couples George married last Sunday. Sarah and George always make a point of going to dine with newly married couples, and she is still replete with the excellent *potjiekos*—the melting pot of beef, *mealies*, potatoes, vegetables, and spices slow cooked over charcoal in a three-legged iron pot. As the early summer November day begins to turn toward dusk, Sarah leans lightly against George's shoulder and gives herself over to the rhythm of the boisterous *rieldans* and the jumping warmth of the fire. This could not be more different from their own quiet, restrained wedding at St. Mary's in London, and yet these Khoikhoi traditions no longer feel strange. They have been in Bethelsdorp for almost two years now, and she has grown more accustomed to its bleakness, almost finding a kind of beauty in it.

But it has been a difficult two years. Sarah is still haunted by the excruciating death of their son, and as George struggles on, overstretched, with the sole responsibility of the ministry and the increasingly onerous administration, it is difficult—close to impossible—for him to maintain discipline and order in this single-handed state. The attendance at church and school has dwindled. The buildings are run-down. There are pockets of drunkenness and immorality, and eruptions of unruly aggression amongst the people. He has begged the directors, repeatedly, for a mechanical missionary to help him to manage the temporal affairs at Bethelsdorp—even as he has bristled at their unsolicited interference and taken umbrage at their supercilious lack of understanding about the difficulties faced by missionaries struggling on their own out here in the field.

About a month after the marriage *rieldans*, Sarah goes into George's office to call him to tea and finds him at his desk, writing feverishly. Usually, Sarah loves to watch his hand flow evenly and smoothly over the page. Even when he pauses to dip the quill in ink and tap off the excess, there is an almost poetic reverence in the act. Now, he is scrawling, crossing out, inserting missed words.

"George?"

He throws the quill down and sits staring at the page in front of him.

"George, what is it?"

"John Campbell orders me to Theopolis."

"For how long?"

"To remove there permanently."

Sarah stares at his profile, taken aback, trying to make sense of this dislocating news. "But why?"

"Brother Ullbricht's health is failing, and he is thereby rendered unable to do his work. Since I was missionary there before, I am to resume my former field of labors."

Sarah can tell that there is more to it than this, and she waits, tense and quiet.

"Mr. Campbell writes that he and Dr. Philip are of the opinion that Bethelsdorp is in disorder, and they wish to send James Kitchingman in my stead. They imply that I am not able to perform the arduous task here." He stands up abruptly, his chair almost toppling, and turns away from her. "God knows their reasons for thus treating me! No one else, be it Mr. Kitchingman or Mr. Campbell himself, or any other, is able to perform the arduous task at Bethelsdorp with no help. I pity poor Mr. Kitchingman from my heart!"

"But did Mr. Campbell not tell you right here in this room that he would support you in any means or in any plans that could be adopted to better the state of the institution?"

"Is there any dependence to be placed on their word or their bond?" He covers his face with his hands and then, finally, he turns to look at her. The naked hurt on his face makes her heart clench. "Because I have been faithful, I am in disgrace!"

"Oh no! He should come and behold what you have done here and judge for himself," she says.

"Yes. He should come and reside here and let no one

deceive him about the real state of all things. I have made no false statements of any one particular. I have represented the station in its true colors, and woe be to him who comes after me. Their station is in disorder, and this is the way to lead to worse."

"Do they know the circumstances at Theopolis following the Makhanda uprising—how the state of the place is changed for the worse?"

"Indeed! Our place of shelter I built at Theopolis is now gone to ruins. Will they provide us with a residence at Theopolis before we remove thither?" He sits down again, hunching his shoulders forward as he grips his hands between his knees. "It is as impossible to conduct the affairs of Theopolis, alone and without rules, as it is in Bethelsdorp."

She goes to him then and runs her fingers through his disheveled hair, smoothing it, stroking it. "You have taken the disorderly state of things here too much to heart, and your constitution has been seriously injured thereby," she says. "You are not the person in strength of body that you were when you left England, nor even when we came to Bethelsdorp two years ago. They have sent no companion missionaries to you, and the very situation that has been detrimental to your health here is being assigned to you again in Theopolis."

"I am writing Mr. Campbell that I will proceed to Theopolis on no other conditions than the following," he says, counting them off on his fingers. "One: That I be stationed there as missionary, without interfering with temporal affairs. If they can't afford a person in that capacity, they must apply to the government for one. Two: That a residence be prepared for us in compensation for the one I have labored for here. Three: That the expenses of the journey be paid in full. Four: That a salary be allowed me there, as the neighborhood is become populous, and the station in every respect demands it."

"Take care not to write in anger," says Sarah.

"They have done me injury," he says, "and they deserve to know it."

After more than five years of sharing George's life, Sarah has learned that there is nothing to be done when a black mood takes hold of him but to be still and unobtrusive, and to wait it out. He will continue to go about his business quietly and methodically—too quietly, too methodically, like a blind man walking with exaggerated care. Over time—sometimes hours, sometimes days—the tightness around his mouth will begin to lose its edge, and she will know that the melancholy is loosening its hold.

The following day, without speaking, he shows her a letter. It is from the landdrost, Colonel Jacob Cuyler, and it is a glowing testimony of George's character.

She looks up into his face. His expression is self-effacing, almost shy. "Does he know of the directors' decision?" she asks.

"I don't know. But I take his testimony as a token of friendship."

She reaches out to touch his arm, then slides her hand around behind his neck to pull him close for a quick embrace.

"Now," said George, "will you ride with me up to Mr. Schoeman's farm? I feel it my duty to visit Brother Ullbricht in Theopolis, and I will need to buy a new horse for the journey."

They spend a quiet Christmas, and at first light the next day, George sets out for Theopolis. Sarah and the girls stand and watch as he walks his horse over the marshy flats towards the coast, a second horse in tow. He will travel east up the coast towards the Bushman's River. Even though the testimonial from Colonel Cuyler has helped to ameliorate his feelings of being ill-used by the directors, Sarah knows that his mind is still hurt by it. She loves him for his sense of duty in making this journey to Theopolis even in the face of his grievance, and she lets out her breath as she feels the uncomfortable, familiar displacement settle on her in the vacuum of his not being there.

As the old year turns to the new, Sarah is surprised to receive a letter from George much sooner than she had dared hope.

> *Theopolis, Dec. 30th 1820.*
> *My Dear Sarah,*
> *I am safely arrived at Theopolis. I found Bro U extremely ill, yet for the most part sensible. I conversed with him on Spiritual things & found his mind composed, resigned & comfortable.*
>
> *The journey was without incident, although the mare was very tender footed & the young horse ill, not being accustomed to travel. I spent the first night at the Bushman's River & at day light rode to Mr Sephton's party of Settlers at Salem. I slept at the house of the Revd. Wm Shaw who came with Mr Sephton's party on the Chapman. He was not at home being on his preaching tour. Mrs Ann Shaw made me welcome.*
>
> *I left Salem at daylight & arrived at Theopolis about 9 o'clock on Monday morning. On the peoples recognizing me, who were standing before the gate at Bro U's gate, they began to weep & thank God. I asked them if Bro U was living, they said yes & pointed to two men who were ready with their horses saddled to go to fetch me. I enquired whether Bro U had prepared a will & understood not. I wrote the Secy of Grahamstown to come &*

*do it without delay. Mr Onkruydt came in the evening
& by sitting & writing all night the will was completed.*

*Bro U took a sleeping draught that night, and yester-
day morning desired to be taken to chapel & could not be
made sensible it was not Sabbath until I came & spoke to
him on the subject. He was very weak & toward evening
delirious.*

*I rode to the mouth of the Kasouga River with Willem
Valentyn. You will be glad to know that he is well, but
the mission is in sad disrepair temporally and spiritu-
ally. Valentyn and Cobus Boezak observe that Bro U, for
nearly a year, has refused to administer the Lord's Supper
on account of the misconduct of some, thus depriving all
of the privilege.*

*Today Bro U has been much weaker & delirious
almost the whole day. He insisted on going to chapel "as
Bro. Barker would preach & he had not heard him so
long." This afternoon he is worse. He shall probably not
be alive when I come again.*

*I will send two men on horses back to Bethelsdorp and
they will bring this letter to you. I hope that you and our
Dear Daughters are well.*
Your affectionate husband,
Geo Barker

Sarah sits down to write a reply immediately so that
once the men and horses are rested, they can carry her news,
such as it is, back to Theopolis. She writes that little Sarah
is seated at the table alongside her, making scratchings with
a quill on an offcut of paper and believing herself to be writing to her father as well. She tells him that Elizabeth's new
pretend game is to be a teacher, "like Papa," and that Ann
dressed herself this morning, reasoning that it made sense
to put her dress on back to front because then she could

reach the fastenings. Also, that Ann's favorite new word is, unfortunately, "mine." She does not tell him that some of the people on the mission have been drunk, quarrelling, and fighting. She sees no point in burdening him with something he can do nothing about from so far away.

She also does not tell him that she suspects she might be pregnant again. This is something best spoken face-to-face, and she needs time to process the thought herself. She loves the private intimacy between them and the profound pleasure that George takes in her body. She adores her daughters. She wishes for a son. But the process of childbirth holds real terror for her now. She seems to suffer more than is natural. When she had helped Elizabeth in her confinement, her body was not as racked by childbirth as hers is.

"Oh my!" The exclamation brings her back to the present, and she sees that little Sarah has made a rather large ink blot.

"It doesn't matter," says her mother. "You can write around it."

She watches her child's intense concentration, knowing that she would do anything for her, that the agony of delivery is worth it for a moment like this. What makes the pain unbearable is to lose a child; the heartbreak compounding the physical pain. She is afraid that she does not have George's absolute faith in God's will. And she fears for her stamina.

As if aware of her mother's gaze on her, little Sarah looks up.

"Have you finished?" Sarah asks her.

"Yes, Mama."

Sarah takes the scrap of paper with her daughter's scratchings on it, encloses it with her letter to George, and lights a candle to melt the sealing wax. In George's absence, a letter has come for him from Brother Evan Evans in Paarl, and another from their friend Mr. Edward Thomas in London. She sends them along with hers, knowing how much George is comforted by correspondence from the outside world.

George is gone ten days. He arrives home just before sunset on the fifth day of the New Year. When news comes that he is on the road, Sarah readies the girls, washing their faces, changing their pinafores. She prepares high tea, putting out bread, cheese, a cut of cold meat, and, as a special treat, a chicken pot pie.

When the horses finally trot up to the house, the girls run out to meet their father. He reaches down and swings Ann up into the saddle before him to her squealing delight.

His eldest daughter reaches up to touch him. "You are wet, Papa!"

"Indeed. When I crossed the Swartkops River, the tide was high and I rode the lower drift. The horses swam and I got wet."

"How was the rest of your journey?" asks Sarah.

He hands Ann down to Sarah and dismounts, pulling the reins over the mare's head and thanking Pieter Platjes, who has come to take care of the horses. "Yesterday, I rode away from Salem after breakfast to the Bushman's River, and I had the most uncomfortable ride in all my life, on account of the wind and dust."

"Well, come and get comfortable now, and tell us all about it over tea!"

After George has blessed the food, Sarah asks, "How was Brother Ullbricht when you left him?"

"Extremely weak. He could not get up to ease nature—excuse my mentioning that at the high table. He did not know those around him."

"It will surely not be long now."

"He is prepared. The last time he could speak sensibly with me, I asked if he had a desire to come back again to life and health. He replied that he had no will or choice in the matter. He said that Christ is the ground of his hope, to whom he surrendered his whole self."

"Is he well cared for?"

"Oh yes. Mrs. Ullbricht is with him, and she has help." He takes a deep swallow of tea. "Ah! That is good. When I arrived at Salem, it was about six o'clock in the evening and I had been riding for four hours. Our Methodist brethren were holding their annual meeting, and I was requested to preach. I scarcely had time to take a cup of tea."

"Was the Rev. Shaw returned by this time?"

"He was, and I assisted him in administering the Lord's Supper. This was a very pleasant evening to me, the first scene of the kind I ever witnessed in Africa. Friends from other parts were present, and the congregation was considerable."

It is four days after George's return that a letter comes from Theopolis with the news that Johann Ullbricht had departed this life at six o'clock on the evening of January 4—one day after George left. And a letter also comes from Mr. Campbell in Cape Town. When George has finished reading it, he passes it to Sarah.

It is dated December 28, 1820, and signed, *With love to Mrs Barker, believe me to be, Your sincere well-wisher, John Campbell.*

"It ends better than it began," Sarah ventures.

"You were right; I should not have written in anger."

Sarah weighs her words, looking down at the letter in her hand. She notices how Mr. Campbell's script slants evermore downwards on the right so that, by the bottom of the page, the alignment is off by more than an inch. She thinks that he does not have so good a hand as her husband's.

She speaks carefully. "Well, although Mr. Campbell does request you to weigh calmly and deliberately the cause of your irritation before you write in future, he also states the case clearly: that the station in Theopolis is an important one and must not be allowed to go ruin, and that since you were a missionary there before, they wish you to resume your former field of labors at a time when there is most urgent need of them. This appears conciliatory to me."

George nods, but does not speak.

"Will you write your case to the society as he suggests?"

"No," he says. "I am resigned. I will write to tell him so—and to make amends."

Their removal to Theopolis is set for February. On Thursday the fifteenth, two of the ox wagons are loaded, and their sheep and cattle depart with the herders. The next day, the last two wagons are loaded, and in the afternoon, amidst the usual hullaballoo of calls and whip cracking, the family and the entourage of drivers and herders ride away from Bethelsdorp. Sarah looks back at the small group that has gathered to wave them off. Five years ago, when Sarah and George left Bethelsdorp for Theopolis the first time, Elizabeth had stood, with little Joseph on her hip, waving them off. Now Elizabeth is a member of the church headed by Dr. John Philip in Cape Town, and there is no intimate whom Sarah is leaving behind—just this bleak and barren place where she feels that neither she nor George has truly been able to leave their mark.

The first night, they get as far as the Swartkops River. "This is where your father got wet when the horses swam across at high tide," Sarah reminds the girls.

"Why is it called 'swart kops?'" asks Elizabeth. "The hills aren't black." The girls have picked up Cape Dutch from the people on the missions.

"Look at the shadows," says her father. "Don't you think they make the hills looks as if they have black tops?"

Elizabeth looks, then looks back at him and nods.

They spend the night with a settler couple, and, after breakfast, they ride as far as the Sundays River, about twenty-five miles east of Bethelsdorp. The river winds down to the sea on their right between magnificent sand dunes. "The people named this river 'Grassy Water' because the banks are always covered in green grass, no matter how hot and dry it is," George tells the girls. He calls up to Pieter Platjes, who is sitting alongside the driver of their wagon, "How do you say the name of this river in your language, Pieter?"

"It's *Nukakamma*, Brother Barker."

Ann tries it out—"*Nukakamma*"—and then repeats it several more times for good measure.

They spend most of the Sabbath at the Sundays River, and George holds an informal service, preaching from Psalm 99, "Exalt the Lord our God, and worship at His holy hill; for the Lord our God is holy." During the course of the day, it grows cloudier and starts to look like rain, so they decide to travel inland, up the Addo Hill. Away from the temperate effects of the ocean, up on the flat Quagga's Vlakte—named for the plentiful quagga that populate the wide-open plain—it grows unbearably hot. They cover some distance in the early morning on Monday, but the oxen—to say nothing of their herders—begin to flag in the scorching midday sun, and they are obliged to be still for the greater part of the day. Sarah, now three months pregnant, plucks her clammy undergarments away from her skin and waves a hand in front of her face, trying to cool her flushed cheeks.

"I have scarcely ever felt it hotter!" says George. This from a man who had sailed across the equator in his shirtsleeves.

In the late afternoon, when the worst of the heat begins to abate, the convoy shouts and grunts and creaks its way to life again, and plods as far as the Bushman's River to span out for the night. In their makeshift bed on the ox wagon, Sarah lies listening to the vast silence. The oxen shift in the distance. Ann briefly whimpers in a dream, then turns and settles. The black stillness pulses and breathes with hidden life.

When she wakes, George is already up. He never sleeps well on these journeys. She takes the girls to a sheltered place to relieve themselves, and by the time they return to their wagon, Pieter Platjes has brought a bucket of water up from the river and stoked the fire with kindling from the shrubs nearby. While water is warming for tea, they wash their faces, Ann squirming away from the chill, and they change their undergarments for fresh ones in the privacy of their ox wagon.

"There!" says Sarah. "All ready for the new day. Let's hope it isn't as excessively hot as yesterday."

George joins them for their Spartan breakfast of tea and corn bread. "We are going to take a new road today," he says. "Captain Cuyler told me that the Bathurst Road is better than the old one although it is longer."

Bathurst has been established as an administrative center for the British settlers, and Sarah's first impression is that she has been instantly transported back to an English village in Shropshire. But the indigenous giant wild fig trees and the coral trees with their scattering of bright red "lucky bean" seeds ground her in Africa again. They spend the night here, and the next day dawns surprisingly cooler, so they find they are able to cover more ground than expected. They press on, and reach Theopolis about six o'clock on the evening of Wednesday, February 21. As they plod slowly up the incline, with the Kasouga River winding to their right, Sarah feels a flicker of coming home. The curve of the landscape, the vast sky, the low scrubby bushes, the clean air, the haunting call of a flock of hadedas high overhead, all bring back to her, vividly, why she had first fallen in love with Africa.

Then the sharp jolting of the wagon brings her down to earth. The track leading to the settlement is rutted and unkempt. The vegetable gardens that George built are a straggle of plants gone to seed. Roofs are sagging, window shutters are missing or hanging from one hinge, all giving the impression of a decrepit, disheveled old man. The Theopolis Mission Station was right in the path of the Xhosa plunder in 1819. In the two years since, little has been done to restore the damage. To make this home, they will have to start all over again.

PART FOUR

Chapter Twenty-Three

O N A LEADEN FEBRUARY DAY, I drove east along Paddington Road through Homeland, one of the three historical districts in northern Baltimore, which I later discovered had been designed and laid out by the Olmsted brothers, whose father had designed places like New York's Central Park. The road wound through a mixture of Colonial, Georgian, Norman, Tudor, French Country, and Early American-styled architecture, and even in the dead of winter, the gardens looked promising.

I turned right at the picket fences and parked outside one of the brick-faced, semi-detached pairs of houses that circled the cul-de-sac.

"This looks too good to be true," I said to the real estate agent who was meeting me there.

"It may be," he said, grinning.

At this point, I had lived in twenty-five homes. The first leaving I remember is Namibia. On the night before our family left Windhoek for good, we had already moved out of the home that is still the template for every house I envision in any book I read. It was my brother's casement window in the front of the house that Heathcliff flung open when he called out to Catherine in *Wuthering Heights*. It was outside our dining-room window that Nabokov's well-dressed father appeared and disappeared when he was tossed into the air as part of a peasant ritual in *Speak, Memory*.

Our home all packed up, I stood at the darkened window of the Continental Hotel in Windhoek, looking out at the lights over the city. My brother, Peter, was in the room with me, and our parents were downstairs having dinner. Without warning, like a hiccup, or a sneeze, I erupted into tears. Peter, disconcerted, ran to fetch our parents. By the time they arrived, full of questions and concern, the crisis had passed, and my nine-year-old self couldn't find the words to describe the unfathomable sorrow at leaving this place. It was the only home I'd ever known, and I had loved the trace of Europe that still ran through it because it had been a German protectorate at one time.

The next leaving couldn't come quickly enough. Standing in front of the fireplace in the sunken lounge that had been the selling point of the ranch-styled house for my mother, I was again in tears, but this time it was because my urge to leave was like a flinch. I felt like an utter misfit in this South African goldfields town in the middle of South Africa where the bank had transferred my father after Windhoek. Since I had been uprooted from one place, I knew that leaving was an option, and I was desperate to go. I had already begun my love affair with Cape Town where both my siblings were living, and I became like Chekhov's Irena in *The Three Sisters* yearning for Moscow.

This is the pull and push, the loving and leaving, the belonging and not belonging, the yin and yang of migration. Nobody would choose to leave the place where she has roots, and memories, and a given sense of belonging, if there wasn't a compulsion, either pulling or pushing. It led me to nine homes in Cape Town and another seven in Johannesburg before I emigrated.

On that February morning in 2000, as I stood in front of the brick-faced double story in Homeland, I wondered how it might fit into my pattern of migration. Inside, there were three rooms downstairs and an equivalent three above. The rooms were beautifully proportioned, with high ceilings, and the floor plan was simple with an easy flow from one room to the next. Windows throughout the house let in the frail winter light onto oaken flooring. There was a basement with a utility half and a front half that cried out to be a cozy den. But *oh!* the place was a wreck.

There were festoons of cobwebs in the basement. The furnace looked like a relic from the *Titanic*. Some would-be carpenter had erected mismatched "beams" and a plastic faux-brick wall finish in an attempt to create a Tudor-look kitchen that was 100 percent out of place for a 1930s house. The avocado-green stove leached a stench of gas; the dust-caked hood over it looked held in place by a single screw. Layer upon layer of linoleum covered the wooden floors in the kitchen and entrance hall. Upstairs, the ceiling sagged in the second bedroom; the lavatory rocked on its pedestal; not a single window treatment matched another. But the bones of the house were good.

Douglas is someone who would buy a place based on the way it is furnished. His left-brain doesn't allow him much wiggle room to look beyond. After considerable placating preparation, I took him to see the house. He was horrified. I prevailed. When we took possession in May—the temperatures at 90 degrees with no air conditioning—and as we began the process of cleaning the caked egg and dog hair from the bottom of the fridge and scraping the grime off the paintwork, he became increasingly furious with me.

Now we have lived in the house for almost twenty years—longer than either of us has ever lived in any one place before. It is our nest, our lovingly restored and renovated home. It took coming halfway across the world for me to put a stop to my nomadic existence—for the moment.

Chapter Twenty-Four

WHEN SARAH, cumbersome with pregnancy, retires for the night on Saturday, August 18, 1821, a spring downpour is falling in such an unrelenting, perpendicular sheet that it is too much for the thatched roof of their dilapidated old house in Theopolis to withstand, and the rain is coming down in a steady series of drips onto the bed. George is still in his office working on his sermons for the next day, and she doesn't have the energy to go and call him. She blows out the candle and crawls onto the bed, trying to find a spot that isn't sodden where she can ease the weight of her belly.

She knows her time is near, and she longs for it to be over, dreading the ordeal, fearful of the pain, terrified of losing the baby. She tries to force herself to sleep, knowing she has to have it for the stamina, but the steady *drip-plop-drip* of the rain and her churning dread make it impossible. When George brings his guttering candle into the room, she is still wide-awake.

"My God!" he says. "The bed is drenched. You will be taken ill with the rain coming down upon you."

"There is nothing to be done."

"At least let me pull the bed away from under the worst of it. Come! Let me help you up, and you can sit in the chair while I move the bed."

She lets him do as he says.

"We will not be able to sleep in these wet bedclothes," he said, "And you are surely near your confinement—you cannot deliver in this state. Where will I find clean linens?"

She tells him, and she watches as he pulls the sheets off the bed, throws the sodden tangle into a corner, and spreads out fresh bedding, gladly obeying him when he admonishes her for trying to help. When he is done, he eases her onto the bed again, quickly takes off his trousers and boots, and slides in behind her, curving the front of his body along the length of her back. So held, she sleeps.

When she wakes, the rain has stopped, and there is a bright shaft of sunlight across the bed. She guesses it to be about six o'clock. There is no sign of George. It is still too early for church; he must have gone to inspect the effects of the rains.

He returns with the astonishing news that the Kasouga River has flooded its banks. "The river is more swollen that I have ever seen a river swollen in Africa. The water is half-way up the hill, and the ground is so saturated that there is nowhere for the flooding to go," he tells her. "I must go and inspect the rest of the village. You get some rest! I will take the girls with me, and thence to church."

Barely five minutes after they have left, the first contraction comes. It is mild, a slow start, and she breathes deeply, willing herself to relax. And this is how things are when George returns from preaching. Within half an hour, her labor begins in earnest, and it is time to send for Lena. When Lena had come to welcome them back to Theopolis, her broad, plain face was alight with joy, and the children had set up a chorus of delight. Now, with Lena here, Sarah's dread and fear subside, and she allows her consciousness to narrow down to the conduit deep inside her body where the baby has to pass through. Lena's low, soothing voice runs like a loop through her mind, and she loses all sense of time, even as time seems endless. The baby comes at five in the afternoon.

Once Sarah is cleaned up and the baby bathed, George sits on the edge of the bed, studying his son resting in the crook of Sarah's arm. "Seven hours," he says, looking up into Sarah's face. "You had a sharp time, but not so long as I have known you to be in labor." He bows his head. "The Lord is our helper and He alone is to be acknowledged. O, that we may be more grateful."

Tired and sore, Sarah wonders about *He alone is to be acknowledged*—but she, too, thanks God that her baby thrives. He is small but lusty, and he lets the whole household know volubly and in no uncertain terms when he is hungry, so the family has some late nights with him. Even when all is quiet and the house sleeps, Sarah, physically depleted, is watchful and wakeful. She keeps her baby close, his pulse and breath like her own. She is haunted, fearful that his quick heartbeat will falter, that his breathing will become jagged and uneven.

As the minutes and hours, and then the days and nights pass, Sarah slowly grows more trusting of this new little life. They settle on a name for him: Edward Thomas, for their London friend who had served as a witness at their marriage. After a week, Sarah ventures out from the sleeping room. Two days later, half wishing that she could keep Lena with them always, she sends her home to her own children.

As George also grows more trusting of Edward's strength, and of Sarah's returning stamina, he begins to return to the work of his ministry. He exchanges with the Rev. William Shaw and goes to preach at Salem. A shower of rain overtakes him on the ride back, and he arrives home fatigued and chilled, but buoyed by the experience. He comes into the bedroom where Sarah is breast-feeding Edward to change into dry clothes. He puts the backs of his fingers against her cheek to show her how cold and damp he is.

"I hope it was worth the drenching," she says.

"I enjoyed the day much," he says as he begins to strip off. "I had a very respectable congregation—such a one as six years ago I could not have had the most distant idea of ever witnessing in this part of Africa."

"There was a sizeable congregation for Mr. Shaw's service here too," says Sarah.

"How often have I wished the missionary brethren were near enough each other to exchange occasionally, but never expected to enjoy the pleasure of preaching to an English congregation by exchanging with their pastor. Mr. Shaw, by the bye, has a novel setup for preaching. He stands on an empty ammunition chest, with his Bible resting on his writing desk, mounted on a flour barrel. I followed that practice, too, when I preached in the morning and evening."

Sarah laughs at the image. "Is Salem much grown?"

"I estimate there are about seventy houses built there now. And here is something of interest to us. In the afternoon, I visited a very pleasing little Sunday school for the children of the Sephton party of settlers, and I addressed the school's teachers and children at the close. There being no school for white children in our country districts, the secretary of the Sunday school, who is a settler of that party by the name of William Henry Matthews, meets the children on Tuesday and Friday afternoons to teach writing and arithmetic. This will be something for us to bear in mind when it comes time to educate our children." He finishes tying his cravat and puts the tip of his forefinger, now warm and dry, on the round cheek of his son.

All through the spring, George preaches with fervency, and as the sight of a growing and attentive congregation puts life and energy into his soul, Sarah dares to hope that the blight of Bethelsdorp is beginning to recede. George is full of plans to build a new village at Theopolis and begins to search for the perfect site. By November, he is hard at work in his smithy, with the intermittent audience of various family members, building a truck to fetch and carry water. In April, before the winter cold had hardened the earth, he had begun to dig for water, first with the people and then by himself, at a little distance from the place where they lived. Theopolis is built at the meeting point of the deposits of the coastal belt and the harder inland soil made up of shale, mudstone, lime, and quartzite, and so they'd had to dig, by turns, through a stiff red loam and beds of stone. Until now, the only way to get the water from the wells had been to carry it, two pails at a time, attached to a yolk across straining shoulders. Now the whole family gathers to see George's water truck put to use for the first time.

He has fashioned a four-wheeled truck with a flat platform, and railings to keep the random collection of wooden and metal water pails from falling off. He guides the old horse of Elizabeth Williams between the shafts, lifts little Elizabeth and Ann into the back to find space as well as they can between the pails, helps young Sarah onto the seat in front, and climbs up beside her. He takes the reins, and with a "*Hah!*" they set off, with much clattering, to fetch the first load of water.

"This is the first horse I suppose that was ever put to such work at Theopolis!" George calls back to Sarah.

She stands with Edward on her hip, watching their careful progress down the hill toward the place near the Kasouga River where the well has been dug. Edward alternately lifts his wobbly head to look about him and then thumps it back onto Sarah's shoulder. When a flock of hadeda ibis sets up their racket overhead, Edward arches back in startled amazement, kicking at Sarah's stomach.

She takes in the picture of her African family—the loamy dust they are stirring up, the scrubby terrain of the *veld*, the vast, pale sky overhead, the quintessentially African birdcalls. It is a scene she could never have envisioned in Shropshire, much less London. Is she rearing African children, she wonders, despite their heritage? Certainly, little Sarah, just two weeks away from her seventh birthday, speaks more Dutch than English, even though they continue to speak their native tongue at home. Not too long ago, George had written a letter home to Wimbish, and when he asked their eldest child what she had to send to her grandmother there, the girl had answered, "*de groeten*," meaning "greetings."

Sarah turns back to the house to wait for the clanking and jostling of the various water pails to announce the family's return from the well. They are expecting the arrival of Dr. John Philip and his party to inspect the lands for the proposed new village, and there is meat to be cured, soap and candles to be made, and linens to be sorted for soaking and washing in boiling vats once the water arrives.

George and Sarah had first met Dr. Philip in Bethelsdorp, and he'd been none too gracious, using words like "deplorable" to describe the mission station. Since that time, it had become evident that Bethelsdorp was, indeed, as difficult a station to manage as George had complained it was, and James Kitchingman, for all his good sense, elevated piety, firmness of mind, and mild, conciliatory temper, had less success dealing with the landdrost, Colonel Jacob Cuyler, than George had during his tenure.

When Dr. Philip arrives at Theopolis in time for lunch on Monday, November 12, with his wife and a small entourage, he bows over Sarah's hand and looks at her from under his eyebrows. "Good day to you, Mrs. Barker," he says, "and thank you for your hospitality." His speech still has a trace of the town of Kirkcaldy, near Edinburgh, where he was born. He is a man in his mid-forties and has the slightly arrogant air of someone who is fully aware of his intellect. His thick hair is brushed back from his high forehead, and luxurious, bushy eyebrows dominate a face offset by a surprisingly curvaceous, full-lipped mouth.

Given their unsteady relationship in the past, George is as apprehensive about pointing out the site that he has chosen for the new village, as Dr. Philip is impatient to see it. They walk out immediately after lunch to take a look. The spot is further up the incline to the east, where Willem Valentyn had helped Sarah to become disentangled from the *wag-'n-bietjie* bush when she had explored Theopolis for the very first time. From here, they look down toward the trees that line the Kasouga River, to the peaceful plateau dotted with cows beyond, where Sarah had discovered the hidden glen. The air is clear and still.

"Hmm . . ." is the initial response from Dr. Philip. "This may do," he says, "but I wish to see more of the vicinity and the land before I make a firm decision." Sarah doesn't need to look at George to know how this lukewarm reaction will deflate his nervous anticipation.

On Tuesday, George rides with the visitors down to the mouth of the Kasouga River, where it ends in a blind lagoon just before it reaches the Indian Ocean. They ride east along the fine, amber sand of the seashore, then turn back north to ride over the greater part of the grounds of the mission station. The lands stretch further west to the Kariega River, creating both a border and good pasturage for the cattle, and down south to the coastline of the Indian Ocean, which has given the people a small industry burning lime from the seashells they collect along the beach.

The next day, George takes the party beyond the eastern property line, to ride along the coast as far as the mouth of the Kowie River where the settlers have just recently opened a small port. The day after that, the Rev. William Shaw rides down from Salem and takes the party in the other direction, west of the Kariega River. Finally, that afternoon Dr. Philip walks up to the site that George had initially chosen, decides on the spot for the church, and forms a plan of the village, pacing out the dimensions for the church, the schoolhouse, the missionary's house, and the schoolmaster's house, which will form the nucleus of the village.

Chapter Twenty-Five

M Y GENEALOGY FRIEND Kristine directed me to
the online site *FamilySearch*, and in no time, I got
lost in a web of crisscrossing possibilities as my
amateurish attempts to trace my family tree started to feel
like a ball of wool once a cat has been at it. Kristine, meanwhile, had tracked down the marriage license for Sarah and
George in record time, and she sent it to me as an email
attachment with no more fanfare than if she had found the
missing sock of a pair. It was more problematic for her to find
the provenance of Sarah Barker, née Williams. She combed
through the Shropshire Parish Records and British newspaper archives for marriage and birth notices that might give a
clue, but both Sarah and Williams are common names, and
it proved difficult to pin Sarah down definitively. Knowing
that her brother was named John was not helpful either,
given the regular occurance of that name. For both of us, it
became a jigsaw puzzle, a treasure hunt, finding one piece
that might lead to another and trying to follow the trail.

With a magnifying glass, I pored over a partial table of
Sarah and George's descendants in the master's thesis that

was based on his diaries . . . but it petered out before it got to my mother, or even my grandfather. So, I started at the other end, trying to work backwards, until my outline ended up looking like this:

Sarah and George
Their children
Blank
My grandfather: Reginald Barker
My mother: Joan née Barker
My siblings and me
My niece and nephew
My great nieces and nephew

But there was that murky no-man's-land near the top of the tree where I was confounded, and I couldn't break through to find the link that joined us. The time had come for me to do some on-the-ground searching.

In June 2017, I flew to the UK to visit the School of Oriental and African Studies at the University of London, where the archives for the London Missionary Society are housed. The university is at the northwest corner of Russell Square in Bloomsbury, within walking distance of the British Museum and RADA—the legendary Royal Academy of Dramatic Art that has been the training ground for the likes of John Gielgud, Vivien Leigh, Anthony Hopkins, Alan Rickman, Ralph Fiennes, Kenneth Branagh, et al. I took the London bus route 134 from Kentish Town in northwest London, where beloved friends had given me the use of their flat, down to Tottenham Court Station.

Whenever I go back to London, I fall in love all over again with the black-edged rectangular street signs attached to the buildings. This time, a particular one jumped out at me: Pratt Street in Camden Town. It triggered a connection to the street that runs along Baltimore's Inner Harbor, which was named for the first Earl Camden, Charles Pratt. If I hadn't lived in Baltimore, this sign name would simply have blurred into the countless others I passed on my southbound bus journey through London. We carry our stories and our histories with us. I looked down from the top of the double-decker bus on the throngs of people going about their business, each one of them carrying their own history with them.

I found my way down to the basement of the School of Oriental and African Studies, absurdly proud to be the possessor of an SOAS University of London Library Reference card, as if I were a *bona fide* researcher. I had expected the Special Collections Reading Room of SOAS to be dark and fusty with piles of teetering books. But as I took my place at one of the long research tables, the gentle light of the English summer morning came through the windows that ran along the length of one wall. There's something deeply convivial about sharing the muted studiousness of a library with others who are equally intent on their projects. Here, the discreet shutter of a camera punctuated the quiet now and then because, surprisingly but wonderfully, they allow you to photograph the materials, as long as you don't use a flash.

One of the first boxes that was brought up for me from the archive store contained two black-and-white portraits of Sarah and George. I recognized them from the copies that my mother had kept in a frame by her door—and which I now have on my desk in my writing studio in Baltimore. I turned over Sarah's photograph and read the dates: 1790 -1835. I studied it for a while, hesitating, but then I approached the librarian on duty at the desk.

"Sarah Barker is my great-great-grandmother," I said to her. "The date of her death is written here as 1835, but she actually died in 1836."

She took the photograph from me, considered for a moment, and then disappeared through a set of double doors into a room beyond. Some minutes later, she reemerged with the photograph and handed it back to me. I took it to my place at the long table and turned it over. The penciled date had been erased and corrected. It could hardly have been a smaller detail, but one tiny crease of history had been set straight.

The sheer volume of material in the SOAS archives is daunting. It would take months for me to go through each one of the seventy-five boxes that might include a letter from George or something pertaining to him, and I had to be ruthlessly selective in the two precious days I had. I chose to look at the earlier correspondence, thinking that, as he was learning about Africa and establishing the role he would play in his missionary calling, that material would be richest and give me the strongest insights. These are formal letters, being addressed to the directors, with phrases like "permit me to present you my sincere thanks" and "you will excuse my haste and brevity," but his earnest, deeply felt, easily hurt character breaks through, and they made me feel another degree closer to him, as I followed the formulation of his thoughts.

My heart jumped when I saw a letter from Sarah Barker listed in the catalogue, and I put in my slip for the box to be collected from the archive store. To my dismay, that partic-ular folder was missing from the box. But even as I searched for the missing folder, I inferred from the index that Sarah had not in fact written the letter after all. It was from her eldest daughter, her namesake, giving an account of the infant school she had established in Theopolis.

There was no letter from Sarah. As far as I could tell, none of her writing had survived apart from her two signatures on Elizabeth Williams's marriage certificate and her own. I couldn't hear her voice or follow her thought processes through her writing. It wasn't only that I had been unable to work out the direct line of descendants that connected us; I was still no closer to finding out exactly where, when, or into which family she had been born to begin with. I would have to keep relying on George's diaries—and my imagination— to try to fill in the gaps.

CHAPTER TWENTY-SIX

*N*O ONE KNOWS *how necessary it is for the African mis-sionary, when making an exertion like the present, to be himself present everywhere,* George writes in his diary on July 5, 1822.

At the start of this year, during the high heat of summer, wheelbarrows are made, timber is felled, the limekiln is prepared, the foundation for the new school is marked out, and digging begins for the new village at Theopolis.

On January 18, almost three hundred people from all over the mission, in groups of three and five and ten, come up the hill to the site of the new village to celebrate the laying of the foundation stone of the school. Sarah shepherds the children to the front so they can get a good view of what is going on.

First, the people sing, and the plaintive, interweaving close harmony of their ancient song sends a thrill of goose-flesh over Sarah's skin. George reads from Zechariah about Israel's past judgment and the promised future restoration—about how, in light of past captivity and promised future blessings, the nation was to repent and live righteously.

Willem Valentyn steps forward to help George pick up the foundation stone, and, sharing the weight of it, they make little, shuffling sideways steps to the marked place, where they carefully lay it down. The people erupt into song, the women ululating with their trilling call of joy, and George dusts off his hand, beaming. He bows his head to lead them in prayer, and when he dismisses them, they each go off, still sporadically singing, to their various activities.

Not all the events go quite so smoothly. A few days later, Sarah is pottering in the kitchen when she happens to glance out the window, and her attention is caught by the sight of George trying out the new cart he's been building and painting in his smithy. As it gathers momentum, it begins to weave about erratically, and then suddenly bursts into flames. Sarah sees George jump before she snatches open the kitchen door and goes running. The cart has come to a lopsided standstill against an outcrop of rocks and George is throwing handfuls of soil at it to put out the fire. By the time she gets to him, he is standing back, surveying the wreckage.

"What happened?" She stands aghast.

"It being without iron boxes in the wheels and without iron on the axel tree, I must suppose that is why it took fire," he says calmly, wiping his sandy hands off on the seat of his trousers. "I'll work in the smith's shop to set it going again, and it is likely to answer then."

Sarah looks at him and shakes her head.

"What?" he asks.

"I don't know what to make of you." She gives a half laugh. Sometimes the smallest thing can make him explode with anger, but now, in the face of something calamitous, he is acting as if it's nothing. "I expected you to be angry."

"Well," he says, "I understand this. And I know that it's within my power to fix it."

On June 10, George calls everyone together again to gather in front of Valentyn's house.

"Willem Valentyn," says George, "I present to you this stone, in the name of Dr. John Philip, as a reward for being the first with your house at the new village."

It had been Dr. Philip's express wish when he planned the village that the old, ramshackle Khoikhoi houses should be replaced with new homes built from brick or stone. "The traditional houses of the Hottentots are unfavorable to industry because they are too crowded for comfortable sleep," Dr. Philip had said. "There are no chests or closets or other places to keep things in them, so even if a woman is industrious enough to sew or knit, her work is spoiled by the filth of the place, and the children, and so forth. Delicacy is impossible in these houses because there are no divisions into rooms, so the sexual acts of married people are observed by all the other inhabitants—begging your pardon, Mrs. Barker." Dr. Philip had seemed, suddenly, to remember that he was in mixed company.

Dr. Philip was also adamant that the Khoikhoi at Theopolis should be recompensed for the thousand head of cattle they had lost when Xhosa besieged the mission station in the 1819 Frontier War. The tedious bureaucracy of constantly following up on this issue falls to George, and it constitutes a large part of the steady stream of correspondence that flows to and from his desk every week. It also necessitates his riding up to Grahamstown on occasion, and he returns from one such visit in April just in time for breakfast, having ridden the greater part of the night.

"I'm so fatigued," he says when he sits down at the table, "that I was wrong in the date in my diary. I was a date too late."

So fatigued is he that his mind is not properly on the job while he is making a batch of bricks, and he comes up to the kitchen cradling his right hand.

"What is it?" asks Sarah in alarm.

"I've damaged my hand. I could not get the right consistency of soil and water to pour the clay into the wooden molds. I drove the spade into the too stiff mixture with too much force, and injured myself."

"But that is a job you have done a hundred times!"

He sighs. "I know. I am simply too distracted."

Sarah takes his hand gently between her own and inspects it. It does not appear that there are any obviously broken bones, but it is already swollen and liverish with bruising, and the pain is bad enough at times that it makes George nauseous. It continues to plague him for months, sometimes flaring up so badly that it prevents him from doing anything.

By early June, as the cold of winter begins to bite, provisions run so low that George can't administer the Lord's Supper for want of wine.

"Even were it not for my hand," he says to Sarah, "I could not leave the mission station at this time. In the past three days, no less than twenty-four of our people have just wandered off the place without any permission. There was scarcely anyone to assist at the work today." Sarah is re-dressing the bandage on his hand, and he winces as she ties it. "I work and I work to try to give these people a life of dignity and purpose, but they simply come and go as they please, taking their children also from the work. I have no authority vested in me *by* the law, even though I am held responsible for control *to* the law. My heart is almost broken with grief."

By now, Sarah has come to understand that George's responses are not like those of other men. He takes things

to heart so personally, weighed down with such strong emotion, that sometimes he seems to her to be all feeling and no
thought. She tries to think of a practical solution. "Cannot
you seek the support of men like Willem Valentyn and
Cobus Boezak to compel the people to stay on the mission?"

"I have resolved to exclude everyone from the station
who refuses to come home within six days, and to remain at
home until the school shall be finished. I believe I could procure the approbation of our principle men to support such a
measure."

"In the meantime," says Sarah, "since you cannot leave
the station, I will ride to Grahamstown to obtain provisions
and money under the present exertions."

"I hate to be obliged to send you on such an errand."

"If you can spare Cobus, I shall ask him to accompany
me. He and I are old friends, and I'll be perfectly safe with
him at my side."

Sarah and Cobus are away just one night. On the way
home, they stop in Salem. Young Sarah and Elizabeth
have begun attending the girls' school there run by Mrs.
Matthews, and their mother hugs them close, inhales each
of their individual scents, hears about their latest lessons,
and counts with them the days until they will be home for
the holidays. Her heart aches for them, but George is adamant that they should receive a proper education at the small
academy that Mr. and Mrs. Matthews have established at
the Salem church.

When Cobus helps Sarah into the cart to sit beside him,
she turns and waves until her girls are out of sight around
a bend in the road. The two of them ride on in compan-
ionable silence as Sarah tries to calm the feelings that have
been stirred up in having to part from her girls. It is cold, but
the weather is fine as they pass by vibrant outcrops of aloes

along the track, the creaking of the cart and the footfalls of the horses making a cocoon of sound inside the vast silence around them.

"How long have your people lived here?" Sarah asks.

"Oh, hundreds of years, maybe even thousands. My *oupa* says his *oupa*'s clan lived around these parts since long ago."

"Is the clan made up of all your family members?"

"*Ja*. But also more than only family. Just people who have held together for a long, long time."

Sarah considers this for a while. Even though Scotland is far north of Shropshire, she knows something of the Scottish clan system. "Does your clan have a chieftain?"

"A *Kaptein*, yes."

"And who is your *Kaptein*?"

He hesitates, and ducks his head. Then he says, "I am the *Kaptein* now."

"Cobus!" She turns to him, and studies the strong outline of his profile under his hat. "You are so modest. I had no idea you held such an important position."

"It has not been for so long. Only when my father died last year."

It makes perfect sense. He is an instinctive leader. She thinks of the way he took control of the men who helped George to build their first house and how he is guiding the present exertions. She can't wait to tell George what she has learned when she gets home.

The next time Sarah goes to Salem, it is to bring the girls home for a few days' holiday. Young Sarah has slipped from childhood to girlhood in the six months she has been away from home. Her face is more slender, and she has acquired a quietly studious air of responsibility. Elizabeth has gained in confidence even as she has lost a tooth. They bring light and energy to the house, and when they bundle into bed with

Ann on their first night home, Sarah hears their whispers and stifled laughter for an hour before they fall asleep. So begins the cycle of joyous welcomes and aching goodbyes.

August, with the first hints of spring, brings a surge of building activity at the village as George's new ruling about the people remaining at the station on pain of expulsion begins to take effect. He finds men to prepare materials for their new mission house at four rix-dollars per day, and he helps them to fill the floor. He begins to ride brick to the house, and, once they have finished the foundation and leveled the floor, the brickwork can begin. One day, George forgets to roll down his shirtsleeves when he comes in for his tea, and Sarah notices that his fair skin is blend of tan and freckle, and that the dirt is ingrained in the cracks on his hands and under his fingernails.

Cobus Boezak and his men carry the beams and principal rafters to the school, and the blocks are fixed to carry the weight of the beams. On September 11, George assists in getting up one principal beam on the school. The next day, they manage to get up two. On the thirteenth, they finish setting the beams on the school, without anyone getting the least harm.

George works in the smith's shop, fashioning bolts for the school bell. The frame for the bell is fixed and hung in the center of the newly finished roof, and George hammers out a weather vane for the top of the school. The chimneys for the kitchen and parlor of the mission house and the schoolmaster's house are completed. George seeds cabbage, Indian corn, and vines. He employs a couple of the young men to help him plant seventy-six trees in the mission garden.

The more the new establishment burgeons, the more it starts to resemble a village such as Sarah might have recognized in Shropshire. Yet still, the scrubby vegetation, the smell of the earth, the feel of the subtropical air, the haunting bird cries—all of these place her firmly in Africa. And, as the village at Theopolis grows and spring arrives, Sarah finds that she is again with child.

CHAPTER TWENTY-SEVEN

ALL IS IN READINESS for Sarah and George to move with their young family into their new house on Tuesday, March 18, 1823. On the evening before, Sarah comes into George's study to keep him company while he completes his journal entry for the day. Instead of finding him at his desk, she is startled to see him seated on the floor, his knees drawn up with his back against the wall. His face is the color of dirty linen, he is covered in a sheen of sweat, and he is shuddering so violently that the ink well on his desk is tapping out a staccato rhythm. She knows this look from before; he is in the throes of a bilious fever. She snatches the throw from the chair and puts it around his shoulders, pulling his kerchief from his pocket to wipe his face.

"I must get to the privy," he says.

She is seven months pregnant and awkward with the weight of it, but she helps him to stand, pulls his arm across her shoulders, and walks with him out to the privy. She waits outside for him in the creaking silence of the night, which has now just the first suggestion of an autumn chill, trying to give him privacy while he heaves and strains inside. It is half-moon, and she can make out the silhouette of the new village up on the hill. She pulls the throw that she has taken from him more closely around her.

When he emerges eventually, she studies his face in the moonlight. He is still pallid and his eyes are like two dark caves under the cliff of his forehead, but he is not sweating and he manages a wan smile for her benefit.

"Let's hope that's that," he says. "I am resolved to get into our new house tomorrow if at all possible."

They rise early, and George leaves with the first load of furniture at about seven o'clock. Cobus Boezak comes with a cart an hour later for the second load, and when Sarah gets to the new house, George is setting up the beds. He is shaking, sweating, pushing himself to finish. When the sun goes down, that time when illness always seems to peak, he crawls into the bed that he has just set up in the front sleeping room. Sarah bathes his face, puts a bucket by the bed, and waits for the fever to break. Over the next days, they keep hoping he is getting better, but then the shuddering chills return.

For six weeks, George is so ill with the bilious fever that he cannot attend to anything.

On May 2, he finally writes in his journal in a shaky hand: *Have been severely afflicted & brought very low, but God has been my supporter. I never was more comfortable under affliction in my life.*

As he begins to recuperate, Sarah walks with him around their new home, from the parlor to the pantry, from the private sleeping rooms to the dining room, and back again, marveling at the space and comfort. And the glazed windows— what a difference those make! Not only in keeping out the drafts, but also in preventing the myriad *goggas*—Lena has taught them the Khoikhoi word—from crawling and flying into the house to take up residence.

Sarah is now so heavy with child that she knows her confinement could come at any moment. At around one o'clock on the morning of Saturday, May 5, she is woken by the all-too-familiar tug of a contraction. George is deep asleep—a rare thing for him—and she is loathe to disturb him, knowing he needs rest to regain his strength. All through the small hours of the morning, she breathes shallowly, trying to relax against the contractions. But a small sound escapes her just before dawn, and he wakes, instantly anxious for her. She has already been in labor for five hours.

"Shall I send for Lena?" George asks.

"I think it is too soon," she says. "I don't feel near my time."

George, weak as he is, walks with her through the rooms "to keep her blood pumping," as he puts it.

By one o'clock in the afternoon, she has been in labor for twelve hours, and no baby comes. At last, she allows George to send for Lena, who arrives with her calming vigor and her ancient Khoikhoi remedies. She smears Sarah's belly with oil from *buchu* leaves to ease the pain. She encourages her to squat, as her people have done in childbirth since time immemorial. Nothing helps. Sarah labors all through the afternoon and into the night until one o'clock the next morning, but still no baby comes. She has labored for twenty-four hours. Lena stays by her, with the timeless patience of her people, and in that supernatural hour just before night gives over to day, Sarah feels her waters break. At half past seven on the morning of Sunday, May 6, after more than thirty hours of labor, she gives birth to a baby boy.

Washed and cleaned, she rests in the bed, looking down at the child in her arms.

"Shall I bring the children in to greet him?" asks George.

"Not yet. I am afraid that all is not right with him."

As the day wears on, the baby cries almost incessantly, and by nightfall, it is as if Sarah is living a recurring nightmare. She watches, helpless, as he begins to convulse just as their poor, dead boy had done in Bethelsdorp. At half past eight the next morning, one day and one hour after his birth, he shudders and is still.

"No!" Sarah holds the small body against her chest, rocking back and forth.

"What shall we say?" says George. "God's judgment is still mingled with mercy. The dear infant died convulsed, and it were better for him to be bereft of life."

Sarah lifts her head to look at him. How can his faith be so unshakeable? Does he not share in her suffering? She feels only God's judgment, not His mercy. The gulf between her feelings and George's make him seem a stranger. She wants to rail against him. She manages to hold herself back, but she knows that she must do something, to act, to prevent herself from lashing out in hurt and pain. She draws in a shuddering breath, stands, lays her dead child on the bed, and carefully pulls the covers over him. Then she goes to the door of the sleeping room and calls for Lena.

"Please," she says to her. "Please, send for Cobus."

"What will you do?" asks George, when she turns back into the room.

"I will bury our child."

"Wait a day so that I can regain some strength."

"I will do it now."

"Sarah!"

"I will do it."

With the utmost gentleness, as if he were still sentient, she uncovers her baby, changes him into clean linens, and wraps him in a shawl, with just the little oval of his face showing.

By the evening all is ready. As Sarah releases the bundle of their child into the small box Cobus had made, George says, "Thus saith the Lord; refrain thy voice from weeping, and thine eyes from tears. And there is hope in thine end, saith the Lord, that thy children shall come again to their own border."

Cobus calls three other men into the house, and they take the box onto their shoulders. Sarah pulls a light shawl over her simple dress and falls into step behind them. They start the small procession down the hill. As they walk through the dusk, more people gather, the women keening in low voices. They walk past the place where the old settlement was, down across the *veld* towards the Kasouga River. They are headed for the sacred glen on the plateau beyond.

The men struggle as they slither down the side of the riverbed, step across the low stream, and climb up again on the other side, holding their small cargo aloft, taking care not to jostle it. Sarah guides them to the quiet glen, and they carefully lower the box beside the hole that Cobus has dug at the foot of a tree. Then, Sarah is momentarily at a loss. With no minister to conduct the burial, she is not sure how to proceed. She looks at Cobus for guidance, and he intuitively takes charge, indicating that they should lower the box into the ground. Sarah stoops to pick up a handful of soil, and throws it onto the box, so small and lost in the gaping hole. When the dull thump of the soil lands on the lid, Sarah understands with jarring clarity that it is the final physical gesture she will share with her child. She kneels and tries to touch the coffin one last time, but it is too low in the ground for her to reach.

"We commit his body to the ground," she says, still kneeling. "Earth to earth, ashes to ashes, dust to dust."

Cobus reaches down to guide her back onto her feet before he picks up the shovel and begins to fill the grave.

"Can we mark it?" says Sarah. She cannot bear the thought of an unmarked grave for her unnamed child.

Cobus finds a simple gray stone and places it at the head of the grave.

She stands unmoving for so long that at last Cobus touches her elbow said, "Come, Sister Sarah. Come. It will be getting dark soon."

She takes a few steps backwards with her eyes on the fresh mound of soil, then turns and walks away from the glen. She holds onto the roots of trees as she climbs down into the riverbed and up again the other side, the sand seeping into her boots and clinging to her dress. She trudges back across the *veld* towards the village with the men who served as pallbearers. When she stumbles on an uneven sod of grass, Cobus catches her even before she has broken stride, and it feels right that he should keep hold of her arm all the way up the hill until they come to the front of her house. He opens the door for her. She stops on the threshold. Inside are the intangible imprint of her dead child, and the unfathomable detachment of George. She turns and looks up into Cobus's face. His large black eyes are moist. She takes a deep breath, brushes the sleeve of his jacket with her hand, and goes inside.

CHAPTER TWENTY-EIGHT

A T ONE TIME, my brother, Peter, had considered the calling of priesthood. He settled for being a lay preacher, and, under the patronage of Archbishop Desmond Tutu, he founded a company called ACTS—African Community Theatre Service. One of its tenets was reconciliation through drama, and much of Peter's voluminous writing has a thread of Christianity running through it. Clearly, he inherited not only a physical resemblance to George.

Twice, Peter stayed with us in Baltimore, using our home as his base for a North American tour of *Bonhoeffer*, his one-man show about the anti-Nazi theologian and martyr. One Sunday morning, as I was watching *Meet the Press* I ran to call Peter. Barack Obama was a featured guest and I wanted Peter to see him, to share my enthusiasm about him. This was not long after then-state senator Barack Obama's electrifying speech at the 2004 Democratic Convention: *There is not a liberal America and a conservative America—there is the United States of America. There is not a black America and a white America and Latino America and Asian America—there's the United States of America.* And there was his message of hope: *It's the hope of slaves sitting around a fire singing freedom songs. The hope of immigrants setting out for distant shores. . . .* How could I not be captivated when he spoke so directly to me and my hope?

Peter had always been more actively involved in politics in South Africa than I was—to the extent that his mail was opened by the secret police during apartheid. Although I made a point of voting each election for the party that had evolved from the anti-apartheid Progressive Party founded in 1959, it was with such a feeling of what's-the-point futility against the monolithic and gerrymandered apartheid government that I was utterly disenchanted with the whole idea of politics. I didn't read newspapers other than for arts coverage; I didn't watch the news on television or pay attention to it on the radio, unless I had to read a newscast on air—it was simply too depressing. In America, though, I was surprised to find my interest in current affairs piqued.

Still, it was a good thing that I didn't have the privilege of voting until I was an American citizen because I simply didn't have enough of a grasp of the complexities to make any kind of informed decision. What made it intriguing was that I had no precedent to fall back on—no family tradition of voting Democrat or Republican, and Douglas was a registered Independent. I was a political virgin in America, so to speak. During my first presidential election cycle, when I still only had a green card and didn't have the right to vote, I watched the debates between a blustering Bush and a sighing Gore and found them both about as interesting as a pair of curtains. Then came my citizenship, 9/11, and the invasion of Iraq in quick succession—and things began to snap into focus.

Having grown up under apartheid, with responses that ranged from guilt to shame, it's no surprise that I would be drawn to the more liberal end of the political spectrum in America. Then, on a visit back to South Africa—still basking in a post-independence glow under President Nelson Mandela—sitting around a friend's dining room table in Johannesburg, the talk turned to President George W. Bush and his policies, and I had the disconcertingly familiar pang of feeling like a political pariah. Only this time, is wasn't for being a South African living under apartheid; it was for being an American living under an administration that was prosecuting a war with a cocky disregard for consequences, in the name of "weapons of mass destruction" that were not to be found. Had I simply exchanged one kind of shame and embarrassment for another?

By this time, I had formulated my political leanings in America, and I went into the 2002 midterm elections having done my homework and feeling relatively well prepared and confident. The big race in Maryland that year was for governor, and then-Lieutenant Governor Kathleen Kennedy Townsend, the daughter of Robert Kennedy, was a shoo-in. When she lost the election and Maryland elected a Republican governor for the first time in almost forty years, I started to feel as if I had a jinx. I had never been on the winning side of an election in my life.

When Barack Obama gave his galvanizing keynote address at the 2004 Democratic National Convention in Boston, I was already in the thrall of the party's nominee for presidential candidate. Four months earlier, I'd sent an email to Peter and our mother:

March 3rd 2004
I just wanted to write and tell you about a thrilling experience on Monday. Yesterday was Super Tuesday, when there were ten primary elections for the Democratic nomination of the presidential candidate, and I heard

that John Kerry would be attending a rally at Morgan State University in Baltimore at 8:30 A.M. on Monday the 1st. I got there early enough to be able to stand right up at the barrier in front of the podium where it was set up for him to speak.

There was much increasing activity, with media arriving, crowds of people, and special-agents, who were scanning the place for security. The special-agents then talked to us to say, "Don't keep your hands in your pockets; if you want to shake hands with him, keep your hands visible; don't give him a pen if you want him to sign anything because he will have a pen." It began to dawn on me that we were going to be able to get up close and personal with him! I had no paper with me other than a business card, which I thought would just have to do.

At about nine, some of the bigwigs from the Maryland legislature came in and made a few speeches, and introduced Senator Barbara Mikulski who is running for re-election. And then there he was. He is tall—probably about 6´4˝—and lean. He was wearing fawn slacks, a checked shirt, a sport coat, and burgundy loafers—casual but stylishly so. When it was his turn to speak, he shrugged off his jacket, took the hand held mic and launched into his stump speech—health care, economy, tax cuts, education, the war in Iraq, national and global security, and our place in the international community. He is ill, poor man, and his voice was hoarse, but he is so passionate and articulate—and presidential.

After his speech—about fifteen to twenty minutes— he came down to where we were all standing and began shaking hands and chatting with people who were close enough. There was a man who had edged in on my right and, as Kerry was still talking to him, he moved away from the man towards me and put out his hand ready to shake the next person's. I looked at his hand for a bit and eventually took the plunge and slipped my hand into his to shake it, upon which he looked at me, greeted me and was preparing to move on when I thought, "Oh no! this is too quick!" and I hastily asked him to sign the back of my business card, which he did, in a neat spidery script.

While he was signing it, I felt a spurt of courage from somewhere and asked him what his policy was on the arts. He couldn't hear me above the crowd noise and said, "What?" So I leaned up to repeat the question in his right ear. Then he said, "They'll be better than you've ever known." This struck me a bit glib so I pressed the point and said, "How do you plan to achieve that?" Again he didn't hear, and again I reached up and repeated the question in his ear. Then he stopped and looked directly at me, put his hand on my shoulder and said, "Through the schools, through the NEA" (the National Endowment of the Arts). He moved on to the next person, but he looked back at me and said, "My wife is very interested in the arts." And I said, "Yes, I know." She is Teresa Heinz Kerry, who married into the Heinz fortune in Pittsburg, and who is a great arts benefactor.

I stayed there just watching him work the crowd, and eventually off he went. It was so thrilling! Yesterday he went on to make pretty much a clean sweep on Super Tuesday, and there is no doubt that he will get the Democratic nomination and run against Bush. I felt as if I were a part of history. This is the man who could well be the next President of the United States, and he was so accessible—more accessible than he is even today, given that he will be the Democratic nominee—and I was there, and not only saw him but spoke to him and shook his hand, and I have his signature as a memento!

Yesterday I went to vote and it is such an extraordinary feeling for me to vote for a man whom I so admire, and whose ideologies I share and respect. Strange as it may seem as one of millions, I feel as if I can make a difference somehow. I can't really explain it.

When John Kerry lost the election and George W. Bush won a second term, I had to run away to my friends in England to lick my wounds. Kerry had represented the better part of America to me: humane, inclusive, cultured, thoughtful—without that tone-deaf, bring-it-on, we-are-bigger-and-better-than-everybody-else mindset that is the crass part of America.

The very first time in my life that I voted for a winning candidate was in 2006, when Martin O'Malley won the gubernatorial election that Kathleen Kennedy Townsend should have won four years before. No sooner were those midterm elections over than the wild and crazy presidential cycle began again. I was starting to learn that the country was always on some treadmill of an election cycle—House representatives every two years, presidents every four years, governors in the midterms, senators every six years—with barely a moment's respite once the election results were tallied. After Illinois Junior Senator Barack Obama announced his candidacy on February 10, 2007, and as the presidential race narrowed to Barack Obama and Hillary Clinton, and then Barack Obama and John McCain, Peter in Cape Town and I in Baltimore started to compare notes daily about our compulsive obsession with the *FiveThirtyEight* polling website.

On Saturday, January 17, 2009, no amount of Douglas railing against the idea of my standing around in subzero temperatures for four hours could dissuade me from going to Baltimore's War Memorial Plaza in front of the city hall.

Barack Obama, following the same route that Abraham Lincoln had ridden one hundred and fifty years before, was making a whistle stop tour en route to his inauguration. Wearing two pairs of socks, thick boots, long johns, corduroy pants, a camisole, a long sleeved tee shirt, a corduroy shirt, a woolen cardigan, a scarf, a long coat, a hat, fleece-lined gloves, and earmuffs, I stood in line at 12:30 with the thousands already gathered. A huge area around the War Memorial Plaza was blocked off, and the place was thick with police. At about one o'clock, the mass of people I was waiting with began slowly inching towards the metal detectors. The venue could take about thirty thousand people and they were expecting one hundred thousand, so there was every chance I wouldn't get in. But I did, and I ended up standing on a little patch of grass about a third of the way down from the temporary stage in front of the War Memorial.

The tall buildings around the space all had security guards with binoculars up on the roofs. There were police helicopters flying over from time to time. *It was 20 degrees Fahrenheit.* I stood on my little spot doing pliés and warming first one hand, then the other in my armpits. The Morgan State University Choir came out to sing. The Fort McHenry Guard presented the color guard. A glorious bass—they never said his name—sang the national anthem. There was an invocation by a bishop, whose credentials I couldn't catch. A woman from the Fort McHenry Guard led the Pledge of Allegiance.

Then I started to hear intermittent cheers in the distance outside the plaza, and I got a goose-bumpy sense that Obama was nearing. As with the John Kerry rally, there was a supporting cast of Democratic officials—Representative Elijah Cummings, Governor Martin O'Malley—until, finally, the loudspeakers announced, "Please welcome Dr. Jill Biden, Vice President Elect Joe Biden, Michelle Obama, and President Elect Barack Obama." It was 4:15 P.M., and I'd been out in the subzero temperatures for four hours. They appeared in the doorway between the hanging flags, the crowd erupted, and I became aware that my cheeks were bunched up in a wide grin as I stood in my little bubble of solitariness in the crowd.

"We began this train trip in Philadelphia earlier today," said the president elect. "It is fitting that we did so—because it was there that our American journey began. It was there that a group of farmers and lawyers, merchants and soldiers, gathered to declare their independence and lay claim to a destiny that they were being denied."

To witness his extraordinary eloquence in real time and to see how he connected with the crowd was mesmerizing. At the end of his fifteen-minute address, he said, "Join me in this effort. Join one another in this effort. And together, mindful of our proud history, hopeful for the future, let's seek a better world in our time. Thank you."

Out of the applause someone called out, "We love you!"

Quick as a flash, he responded, "I love you back." He came down from the stage, and, as John Kerry had done, mingled with the people at the front who had been queuing since six in the morning. As the crowd began to disperse, I walked up closer to the platform and over to the right. He climbed up the steps again to leave, waving and smiling, and as I watched his easy physical grace, I could hear the true baritone timbre of his voice—unfiltered by a microphone. My body was cramped from standing in one spot in freezing temperatures for five hours, and my hands, feet, and face ached with cold—but this ranked right up there with meeting Yo-Yo Ma backstage after a concert, or interviewing Plácido Domingo in his dressing room, or hearing the organ ring out at the exact moment when I turned and saw the rose window at Notre Dame Cathedral in Paris.

The Obama administration crystallized everything I had dreamed about America: the vision, the humor, the intellect, the sense of honor, the reserves of strength. Whatever happens, and however imperfect it might have been in certain ways, I will have basked for eight remarkable years under his presidency. Afterwards, I read that he wondered if he was too soon; if he was ahead of his time.

When I left work on Tuesday, November 8, 2016, having read the last Associated Press newscast for the day at 6:30 P.M., everything seemed to be on track. It had been a bizarre presidential campaign, to be sure, and how a bigoted, misogynistic, multiple-bankrupted, ridiculously coiffured individual who had a slip-sliding sense of truth and could only speak in Twitter sound bites had won the Republican nomination was beyond me, but that would all soon be a peculiar blip that might even seem amusing in hindsight. The nightmare that unfolded right before my eyes on my computer screen a few hours later made my insides drop away with shock.

The next day, a Persian friend of mine went home to Iran for a visit. She was born in Tehran and grew up in the midst of the Iran-Iraq war. It was fate, she believes, that brought her to America around the turn of this century—a combination of green card lottery . . . luck . . . work. Now, like many immigrants, she feels she has two counties but no home. There's this bond that we all share as immigrants, no matter where we're from; it's like coming across a compatriot in a foreign country. We don't have to explain the strange dislocation of displacement, the sense that, no matter how integrated we may become, we are always an *other*. My Persian friend and I built our friendship on this shared experience. She was more clear-sighted about it than I was—I was too idealistic—but it was our strongest initial connection.

Late that November, she sent me a message from Iran: *Just wanted to let you know that I may be back home with 20 months old twins!!! A boy and a girl! It hasn't been finalized but I just wanted to share this with you!!* I felt my body flush with gooseflesh. This was the happy outcome to years of heartache. She named the boy Alborz after the mountain range in northern Iran, and girl Dena for the range in the southwestern part of the country. *May they be as strong as mountains,* she said. The weeks turned into months as the new family became acquainted, the adoption paperwork made its way through the system, and the immigration process for the twins was set in motion.

The Executive Order 13769, signed on January 27, 2017, which limited travel to the U.S. from nine predominantly Muslim countries (including Iran) and by all refugees, didn't directly affect my Persian friend because she and her husband are U.S. citizens. But it did affect her sister and her sister's family, her cousins, her brother and sister-in-law, and her friends. And there was a stomach-clenching possibility that it could affect the immigration of her newly adopted twins.

The anti-immigrant xenophobia—*xeno*, from the Greek, meaning "foreigner," and *phobos*, meaning "fear"—was as jarring as a deeply personal affront. I knew it wasn't aimed directly at me—at least, not yet—but I took it personally, even as it zinged past me at some other intended target. Yes, I've had criticism leveled at me: *You are in America now; you should speak like an American.* I've been labeled a racist by someone who had never met me, for no other reason than that I grew up in South Africa. But those slings didn't threaten my immigrant status. I hadn't had to risk my life and my life's savings to wriggle under a fence, or cram onto an overloaded boat, or pack into a dark, airless van. That speaks to a kind of desperation and blind faith that I hadn't had to subject myself to. And I was exempt from a "fear" of "foreigners," not because of anything I had done or not done, but purely by the accident of having fair skin and hair; of not being a follower of Islam; of being South African rather than South American; of not being a native of a predominantly Muslim country. Douglas has argued for immigrants in court, and I asked him if I was at risk because of my dual citizenship, or because I was a naturalized citizen and not native born. It was a first-world problem—more of a luxury to worry about than a true threat.

But I *wanted* to worry about it. I didn't want to be exempt. I had been on the "right" side of discrimination before, and it was bruising. When I'd hunkered down in the abnormal vacuum of apartheid, I was guilty of Desmond Tutu's admonition that *if you are neutral in times of injustice, you have chosen the side of the oppressor.* And the very act of trying to work against the indoctrination of apartheid—*aparthood*—was so fraught with self-conscious effort that it, in itself, felt like an abnormality, and I despaired of ever being truly free of it.

Knowing that, living that, it broke my heart to see my adopted country being wounded by even more variations of divisive discrimination. It felt eerily, hauntingly, like living under apartheid again. But what could I do—one of over three hundred and twenty-five million people in the country—other than to align myself with my Persian friend and all immigrants in this country of immigrants; to speak; to write; to choose not to be neutral?

And when I met two small, shy, liquid-eyed immigrant twins who were named for mountains in Iran, I remembered how their mother had said, *May they be as strong as mountains.* I thought, *May our country be so too.*

Chapter Twenty-Nine

*R*AIN, George records in his diary on three successive days, from October 6 to 8, 1823. On Friday the tenth he writes, *Last night was a most awful night of heavy Rain & wind from the S.W. This was a tremendous day of driving Rain, not to be described. In the afternoon our privy fell & the window frames were falling from the houses not finished.*

At eight o'clock that evening, Sarah is hanging linens to dry in front of the kitchen stove when there is such an enormous crash that she feels it underfoot.

"What in the world was that?" calls George from the front room.

"Come and look in the pantry if anything has fallen, but I think it is thunder."

George comes into the kitchen. "I think it was David Jantjies's house. I'll have to try and brave the rain to see."

"No, I think it was on this side of the house."

"Then it must be the other part of the privy that has fallen."

He opens the kitchen door, braces himself, and goes out into the driving rain. He is soaked through in an instant.

Sarah stays by the open door, watching him go, the rain continuing to pour down in sheets, splashing over the threshold of the door onto her boots. George comes opposite the back door of the house of the temporal manager, Peter Wright, who stands silhouetted in his doorway with a candle. George looks up beyond Peter Wright's house and gives a great cry. He stands perfectly still in the rain for a moment, aghast it seems to Sarah, who strains her eyes to see what he has seen. He walks back to where Peter Wright stands and speaks urgently to him. Sarah catches the word "school," and then they both go off together. She waits for what seems like eons and is on the point of braving the rain herself to see what is going on when the two men return. George comes to the kitchen door and stands on the step, taking some shelter under the doorsill.

"The school has fallen, and we expect the houses to follow," he says. She stares at him, stunned. *All that work*, she thinks, *all that work* . . . As if intuiting the disaster, Edward cries inside.

"Go in!" says George. "Brother Peter and I are going over to the old place to see how all is there."

He doesn't return until after midnight. "We found most of the people drenched in their houses," he says. "One of the herders almost perished with wet and cold. He left the cattle and came home, but on his arrival at home, could not speak. Through mercy he recovered."

"There is nothing more to be done tonight," she says. "Try to get some rest, and we will see what can be done by the light of day."

It continues to rain the next morning, but she goes out with him to inspect the damage. One house, which was ready to thatch, is in almost total ruins. Three others, with the door and window frames in, are in heaps of wreckage. Then, they come to the school. One whole wall has collapsed, taking most of the roof with it.

"It was nearly finished . . ." says George. His voiced falters. "Our hopes, our expectations—destroyed with a stroke."

Even as they watch, another part of the school falls.

"Ah!" cries George. "Nothing compares to the loss of the school! The dear children deprived of the facilities of instruction, which this building would have afforded."

Another squall comes on, and they have to seek shelter inside.

In the afternoon, the weather turns a little fair, and the next day, Sunday, is clement, hot, and humid. The walls of the two main mission houses are wet through, and George and Sarah's has sunk considerably on the foundations. The gables and chimneys of both houses are soaked.

On Monday morning, it rains steadily, and it keeps increasing through the day. Peter Wright props up his house. Afterwards, he helps George to prop his, but by nightfall, they are extremely alarmed.

"The walls of the house are so very wet that we can expect nothing but the destruction of them," George says.

"I'm afraid for the children," says Sarah. "I expect every moment that the house will fall upon us. Can we at least put the children to sleep in your study out in the yard?"

After dark, once the children are safely settled in George's study, the rains begin to descend in torrents with thunder and lightening.

"This night is the most awful of all, the rain the heaviest," says George. "It's as if we are in the most distressing storm at sea."

George and Sarah can't think of sleep, and at about midnight, there is a knock at the door. George opens it to David Jantjies.

"Brother Barker!" He is wide-eyed and distraught. "One end of my house has fallen. Please—can my wife and family go be with your children in your study?"

When George comes back from settling the Jantjies family, he is wet through again. He changes into dry clothes, and he and Sarah sit down to wait out the night. When the thin line of dawn hints over the *koppie*, George says, "Never did I behold daylight with more pleasure than this morning." He ventures out into the showery, gray day to look at the damage.

"Our river is swollen over the whole plain," he reports back. "The people say they have never seen such a flood at Theopolis before—even the old folks. The flood washed away two kilns that were burnt. I estimate a hundred thousand bricks were spoiled."

"When we need them most to rebuild!"

"Even worse than that, it is a terrible blow to our trade in bricks."

The drenching, relentless rain is replaced by bursts of sudden showers throughout the day as George continues to prop up the house. The kitchen door is so swollen with the rain that they can't shut it, and George braces it closed with a stick.

In the evening, Sarah is in the kitchen busy with the relentless and seemingly futile effort of trying to dry clothes and linens in front of the stove when another sharp shower comes on. The new puppy, a gangly four-month-old, forces the door open to run inside. The stick that had been propping the door closed lands on the tabby cat, and she sets up a screeching cry while the stick clatters to the ground. In the split second that it takes for all this to happen, Sarah thinks the house is falling around her, and she screams. Even when she turns and sees what has caused all the commotion, she can't stop screaming. Her screams become tears of fright and anguish, and she gulps in big breaths, unable to stop her sobbing.

George, also fearing the worst, has come running. "What happened? What is it?"

She can only point. Ever practical, he goes quickly to the epicenter of the crisis and props the door closed again. Then he comes to put his arms around her. She is trembling, sobbing still, and inarticulate.

"There," he says, rocking her and running his hands up and down her back. "There. It's all right. You're safe. We're safe. It's all right."

Gradually, she quiets and rests against him in the circle of his arms. She pulls his handkerchief from his pocket, wipes her face, blows her nose. She takes a shaky breath.

"I'm sorry," she says.

"It is the shock," he says.

"I also think I am pregnant again, and you know how that affects my mood."

He holds her away from him to looks into her face. Then he kisses her forehead and her wet eyes, and pulls her close again.

The puppy is cowering in the corner. The tabby cat sits next to him, trying to look insouciant. Sarah goes and crouches before them, stroking them and speaking in a soothing voice. It isn't long before the puppy is wagging from his waist down and the tabby is purring and weaving around Sarah's skirts.

By December 20—just two months after the terrible flood, and so impossibly against all odds that it seems miraculous—the school is ready to be commenced. On this fiercely hot day, George calls the people together for the laying of the corner stone. Under the wide expanse of the

African sky, the people begin to sing and ululate in the way that never fails to make Sarah well up. George preaches from Ezra about the laying of the foundation of the great Temple in Jerusalem: "And all the people shouted with a great shout, when they praised the Lord, because the foundation of the house of the Lord was laid."

Cobus Boezak has been so invaluable in leading the team of builders and bringing timber that George has asked him to be the one to lay the stone, which he does with solemnity and reverence. To end, George leads the singing to the tune of "Rule Britannia." Even this incongruous tune the Khoikhoi people sing lustily, weaving their own intricate harmonies over and through a melody that is so completely unfamiliar to them.

PART FIVE

Chapter Thirty

On Monday, April 27, 2015, when I had been living in America for close to eighteen years, it was the twenty-first anniversary of South Africa's first post-apartheid democratic elections. That day, I sat in my home in northern Baltimore while, in West Baltimore, cars were set on fire, businesses were looted, and police officers were seriously injured in the city's worst race riots in a generation. It was the day of the funeral for the young black man named Freddie Gray, who had made eye contact with a police officer on a street corner in West Baltimore fifteen days before. When he fled, he'd been chased down, arrested, and put in the back of a police van. Half an hour later, he was taken to shock trauma in a coma. He died as a result of a spinal injury a week later.

On the day that the riots erupted in West Baltimore, emails and messages began to come in from friends and family all over the world asking if we were safe, and I had a chilling sensation of déjà vu. As people's lives were being turned upside down five miles away from me, as I agonized about coming halfway around the world just to witness more race riots, I was physically unscathed by it all—just as I had been, pretty much, by the Soweto Riots outside Johannesburg in June 1976, the police custody death of anti-apartheid activist Steve Biko in Pretoria in September 1977, and all the other ghastly milestones of apartheid.

Metaphysically, though, it was another matter. It was as if everyone I knew was turning to me and asking me what I thought, what I felt, how it compared. The questions unnerved me. I didn't want to be an "authority" on this; I didn't want to be the one to have an opinion. Part of my urgency to leave South Africa had been the hope that I could leave behind racism and its ugly implications. I didn't want to confront the notion that racism was still an abiding factor in my adopted country. But the comparisons were glaring—including the way I had an impulse to distance myself from the ugliness.

It was hard for me to believe that at this time and in this place, exactly forty-seven years after race riots erupted in Baltimore in the wake of the Rev. Dr. Martin Luther King Jr.'s assassination, there could still be such a *cri de coeur* of "them and us." I came to America naively thinking that they had taken care of all that with the Civil Rights movement. In the broad sweep of history, I calculated, the emancipation of slaves had come about in the 1830s in South Africa—three decades earlier than in America—while the laws governing segregation were abolished in the 1960s in America, three decades before they were in South Africa. Either way, America should have had its race relations sorted out by now. It didn't seem possible—I didn't want to believe—that America, a first-world superpower, a standard bearer for justice, and one of the strongest voices against apartheid, could still have its own wound of racism.

With disconcerting serendipity, the memoir *Between the World and Me*, by Baltimore native Ta-Nehisi Coates, was published three months after the rioting that followed Freddie Gray's death. As I drove to and from work each day, and Ta-Nehisi Coates's voice filled my car as he read his audiobook, he gave me the clearest sense I'd ever had of what it must be like for an American to inhabit a black person's body—*body*, in all senses of the word since he weaves it as a recurring theme throughout the book. I could sense the constant, lurking, over-the-shoulder fear on the Baltimore streets and in the schools, where making eye contact with a peer had the potential to turn fatal, just as making eye contact had turned fatal for Freddie Gray. I was deeply troubled by the racial polarization that Coates articulated—the them-and-us, his bitter expectation that the status quo of racial inequality was unassailable.

I needed another opinion. Tracy K. Smith became the next writer on my daily commute as I listened to her reading her memoir, *Ordinary Light*. Even though she took me with her through the process of her gradual awakening and identification of herself as a black woman, it struck me that she grew up in a family that could have been *any* American family. What brought it home to me even more intimately was that her father was stationed at Travis Air Force Base in California when she was a girl, as Douglas's father had been when Douglas was a boy. What made their lives—a young black girl and a young white boy—so very different? *Were* their young lives, in fact, so different?

D. Watkins, another Baltimore writer who became an insistent voice during the Freddie Gray tragedy, graduated from my MFA program the same year that I did, and in one of the most intense pieces he shared with us for a workshop, he described how, no matter what he drove, whether he was in a sleek Mercedes Benz or had crammed his six-foot frame into a small, beat-up car, he would invariably be profiled and pulled over by a traffic officer for no discernable reason. Once, as he sat in his car with the police lights flashing and the traffic officer laboriously went through the process of finding nothing whatsoever amiss with his papers, D. counted the number of illegal drug deals and drops going on around them.

It is as bizarre as it is illogical. I have a black cat. I could just as easily have a white cat, but I chose a black one. What difference does it make, really? When I get onto a bus, in a split second my mind subconsciously takes note of an elderly black man, a Latina woman with her daughter, a young Asian student, a middle-aged white housewife, and a young man who is so covered in tattoos that it's difficult to work out what ethnicity he is. I register the distinctions intuitively. How else would I know to give up my seat to someone who was elderly or had physical disability? But the truth is that every single person on that bus is just someone with an interior life, chugging away from point A to point B. Each one of us makes up the tapestry of this country. It's what the judge said at my citizenship ceremony—never to lose the unique qualities we brought from our native cultures as immigrants because they contribute to the rich fabric of America.

But still. How can I *not* be acutely conscious of racial distinctions when I have grown up under apartheid? How can I not be afraid of overcompensating to the point of coming across as patronizing, or of not being aware enough and being obliviously insensitive? I have to work every single day to bend my life away from a reflex born of years of subliminal indoctrination. Sometimes, too often, I still fail.

But when it dawned on me that I admired Barack Obama as simply a visionary President of the United States and not a *black* president; that I was awestruck by the grace and talent of Misty Copeland as simply an exquisite dancer, and not a *black* dancer; that I was thrilled by the success of Trevor Noah simply because he was a compatriot, it felt like a small victory over the apartheid DNA that was embedded for far too long. It's not that I was oblivious to their backstories—an amalgamation of Kenya, Kansas, Hawaii, Indonesia, German-American, African-American, Italian-American, Swiss-German, Xhosa—it is that I had instinctively responded to their exceptionality for what it *is*, not something that was parsed or seen through a scrim of preconception and prejudice.

And when I found myself at a writers' retreat in Vermont, and we sat around a dinner table—a white South African; a black MacArthur fellow and National Book Award recipient; a white Los Angeleno; a white attorney; a black debut memoirist; a white academic writing professor; and a woman whose public identity is ethnic black, but whose heritage is a mixture of two American Indian tribes, various European groups, and unknown African—and we could discuss the state of the nation and its problems, including race, with openness and frankness and lack of inhibition, I had a glimmer of what could be possible. Surely, it *must* be possible.

Chapter Thirty-One

"*To Whom it May Concern.*" George is doing a simultaneous translation from English to Cape Dutch as he reads aloud from a letter concerning a visit of His Majesty's Commissioners of Inquiry:

> "*Insofar as the Hottentot Proclamation of the year 1809 decreed that every Hottentot was to have a fixed place of abode and that if he wished to move he had to obtain a pass from his master or from a local official; and insofar as the Hottentot Proclamation made the registration of labour contracts compulsory if covering one month or more, and laid down conditions under which an employer could withhold wages for goods supplied by his servant; and insofar as the Hottentot Proclamation made the people subject to the ordinary Colonial taxes and to the public services exacted from Europeans, therefore His Majesty's Commission will examine the following:*
> "*The pass system for the Hottentot, and the risk of being flogged for offences against the labour laws;*
> "*The right to land ownership for the Hottentot;*

"The subjugation to compulsory service to which other of
His Majesty's Subjects are not liable;
"Children's apprenticeship without parental consent;
"Contracts of hire.
"The British authorities hope that these measures will
stimulate the Cape's economy by increasing productivity
of both the labouring classes (now given the incentive of
the profit motive) and the master class (now deprived of
indolence-inducing coerced labour).
"Signed, etc."

When George finishes reading, he folds up the letter, and there is a murmuring and a shuffling as the people meet each other's eyes with looks of unhoped-for expectancy, as if to say, *Is this too good to be true?*

"His Majesty's Commissioners have already visited Pacaltsdorp," says George. "In February, they will be in Grahamstown, and I will go and appear before them there to state our case."

"Perhaps Brother Barker can preach about angels on Sunday," laughs Cobus Boezak.

"Indeed I will!" George grins. "I will take the text from Psalm 103: 'Bless the Lord, ye His angels, that excel in strength, that do His commandments, hearkening unto the voice of His word.'"

The commissioners arrived in Grahamstown on Thursday, February 5, 1824, and they began to do business the following Wednesday. I imagine George in the painstaking process of collecting all the correspondence and cases to lay before the commissioners when his time comes. In the midst of it all, a parcel of mail comes from England, including newspaper articles and letters from their friends the Thomases in London.

"Listen to this!" says George, and Sarah rests Mrs. Thomas's letter in her lap. "*The Morning Chronicle* has a report about the proceedings in Parliament with regard to sending out the Commissioners of Inquiry to Africa." He reads aloud, "*The colonial government has appointed a commission of two members of the Court of Justice to visit the missionary stations within the Cape Colony. Judge John Thomas Bigge, assisted by Major William Colebrooke, will lead a Royal Commission of Inquiry at the Cape during the early part of 1824, with the aim of reporting on the rights and the status of the Hottentot people.*"

"Who would have thought that our business here should be attracting such notice in London?" says Sarah.

"I believe our situation has found support amongst those who are advocating the abolition of slavery in England," says George. "Oh, I wish that I may be able to conduct my part well enough!"

He leaves for Grahamstown on February 18, and, as always, he leaves behind a vacuum. At first, Sarah thinks that her debilitating fatigue and headache are just because she is missing him. But the next day, she develops a dry cough and a sharp, cramping stomachache that makes her double over with pain. She is by now six months pregnant, and she feels the adrenaline of panic, terrified that she will miscarry with George away and nobody to help her. The two older girls are at school, but Ann, being just five years old, is still at home, and Sarah does something she would never ordinarily have dreamed of doing. She walks to the children's sleeping rooms at the back of the house, keeping a steadying hand on the wall.

"Annie," she says, kneeling down on the floor where Ann has been making a cave under the bed with her little brother, "do you think you could go and fetch Lena for me?"

"Oh yes!" says Ann, and darts off without a backward glance.

It takes too much effort to stand again, and Sarah slides sideways, with her back against the wall. She stretches out her legs in front of her, resting her head backwards, and feels a prickle of sweat raising the hairs on her neck. Edward, with the instinct of an animal for a wounded creature, creeps onto her lap, negotiating her rounded belly, and rests against her.

When Lena comes, she crouches and looks into Sarah's face. "*Ai, ai, ai!*" Her broad, usually smiling face is pulled into tight lines of concern. "Come on, let's get you to bed." Once she has settled her, Lena brings Sarah a hot drink. Sarah takes a sip and almost gags.

"No, you must drink it, Sister Sarah! Your body needs the salt and the sugar." Sarah holds her breath and drinks down as much as she can stomach. "There! You rest now, see?" says Lena. "I'll go sit with the small ones. You just call if you need me!"

Lena stays in the house for the three days that George is away. He arrives home late and fatigued, and is taken aback to find Sarah in such a state. Lena gives him whispered instructions before she leaves, and he brings a basin of cool water into the room to bathe her sweaty face, keeping watch over her until his exhaustion gets the better of him. He shrugs off his jacket, tugs off his cravat, unlaces and toes off his boots, and falls asleep on top of the covers next to her.

At first, Sarah sleeps fitfully, her vivid dreams barely distinguishable from reality. As the gray light begins to change the outlines of the room, she drops into the deepest sleep, waking disorientated, hardly knowing where she is, even though she is in her own familiar bed with George, already washed and dressed, sitting watching her.

"What ails you?" he says.

"It is like nothing I have ever experienced before. My limbs are like lead, and there isn't a part of my body that doesn't ache."

"Shall I send for the doctor?"

"It is bound to pass," she says. "But now, tell me about your time in Grahamstown."

He studies her, as if trying to decide whether to push the point of the doctor. Then he says, "Well, I gave the documents to the commissioners as soon as I arrived at Grahamstown, but I spent the whole of the next day without being called before them. The following morning, I was sent for at nine o'clock. The commissioners began rather sharply with me, in loose conversation and loose interrogations not at all connected with the documents that I had put into their hands. It was not until the last that they alluded to them very slightly. But in the afternoon, I served as a translator for an old Hottentot woman from the district of Cradock, and then the commissioners were very kind and courteous. So, in the end, I was impressed with the reception I received by the commissioners on behalf of the station."

"And now?"

"Now we must wait for the commissioners' visit to the mission station," he says. "But put it out of your mind for now! You should concentrate instead on regaining your strength."

But by the next week, Sarah is running a high fever and is too listless to get up. Her stomach grows distended. "Just look at me!" she says, woefully. "I am like a beached whale with this bloating on top of the pregnancy." In the mornings, her fever abates, but then it rages again by nightfall, and when she starts to show signs of delirium during the third week, George sends urgent word to a medical man in Grahamstown to come. The doctor prescribes bed rest and hydration. With a blithe prediction that the fever will "run its course," he goes on his way. Sometimes, Sarah believes the doctor's prediction, and she feels better . . . but then the fever returns, along with the incapacitating lethargy and the bizarre dreams.

One day toward the end of March, George says to her, "The shopkeeper requires me to ride with him to the Kowie River. He wishes to inspect the lime industry from the sea-shells gathered there by the people. I would be gone only a few hours. You will be all right?"

Sarah assures him she will, and lies resting, watching the light play on the ceiling of the sleeping room. She hears George return much sooner than she had expected. He comes and stands in the doorway, his hair on end, a trickle of perspiration running down one temple, and his high collar looking wilted.

"As soon as we got over," he says, "I learned that His Majesty's Commissioners were on our side of the river, and returned instantly across the river to ride towards home with all speed. I had almost reached home when I was informed that the commissioners and the landdrost had lost their way just at hand. I must go and wait to see if they come."

He goes away again, sucking the life out of the room, and Sarah lies still, trying to make sense of all the comings and goings that George had described. She drifts in and out of sleep. He returns at dusk and sits down heavily on the straight-backed chair inside the door.

"They did not come," he says. "They were not three miles off Theopolis, but, as they rode, they could see nothing—not the residence of an individual. The reason for their passing us without calling is inexplicable. All that preparation—all for nothing."

Sarah pats the bed next to her, and he comes to sit down beside her. "Sometimes I feel like the long suffering Job," he says, "although, God knows, I do not have Job's patience."

She rests her hand on his, and they sit quietly in the quickening dusk, his disappointment and frustration almost palpable in the air around them.

At nightfall on Wednesday, April 28, Sarah is gripped by a tugging cramping in her abdomen, and she can hardly tell if it is her bowels or her womb. As the pain intensifies, she recognizes it for what it is, and asks George to send for Lena to come and help her with her labor.

"Oh, God. . ." she prays, but then a contraction comes, and she can't go any further. At the heart of her unspoken prayer is pure dread. She has been ill for more than three months, and she knows that she simply does not have the stamina to labor for more than thirty hours, as she did the last time when her boy died within a day. Lena comes, with her firm hands and her *buchu* unguents. She sooths and cajoles, and keeps up a steady flow of her easy chatter.

"My daughter, she is just as big as you—she's almost ready to pop. All these last months, I've been wondering, will I go here or there for a baby to come?"

The combination of Lena's pragmatic approach to the cycle of life, and the intimate circle of candlelight, beyond which the world doesn't seem to exist, conspires to give Sarah a sense of unexpected peace. After four hours in this insulation of the birth room, both women are almost caught off guard when, at about a quarter to one in the morning, Sarah is delivered of a son.

When George comes to her, he looks down at the way their newborn is robustly clutching a fold of Sarah's night-gown in his fist, his eyes still puffy from the birth. "You were much quicker delivered than ever before," he says. "Thus the Lord deals with us in mercy."

Within two days, Lena is called away to tend to her daughter's confinement, and George is turned nurse. As Sarah's health fluctuates, he takes over as much of the care of their son as he is able—everything, in effect, bar suckling the child.

"We are doing pretty well with it," he smiles, and Sarah tries to respond in kind. Now that she is no longer pregnant, she is rail thin. Her skin has taken on a translucence; her eyes and cheeks are sunken. The illness simply will not release its grip on her. The baby is strong and nurses well, but even that drains her own strength. As the autumn turns to winter, and as she watches her infant thrive, she despairs of ever being well again herself.

On August 12, with young Sarah and Elizabeth home from school, George takes the baby to church to baptize him. They have decided to name him John Williams, for Sarah's brother, and also in memory of Joseph. The whole family troops into her sleeping room before they set off for the church, and she looks at the scrubbed faces of her five children—Sarah almost nine; Elizabeth nearly eight; Ann, close to six; Edward just days away from turning three; and John not yet three months—young and vibrant and full of life, and she so depleted. They take their youthful vigor with them, and in the solitude of the empty house, Sarah allows the tears to come. She cries from utter exhaustion, from pain and discomfort, and even from a little edge of self-pity, which she quickly tries to push away.

She hears the overlapping of their excited voices returning long before they get back to the house. She sits up on the edge of the bed, stands shakily, walks over to the washstand to splash water on her face, and glances at her wan reflection in the speckled looking glass before she crawls back into the bed.

"Mama! I was allowed to hold the baby while Papa poured water over his forehead!" young Sarah tells her.

"Papa poured three times," says Elizabeth, "for the Father, and the Son, and the Holy Ghost."

George meets Sarah's eyes over their heads. "He was perfectly content," he tells her.

As John grows, and as Sarah's health continues to be poor, her milk is no longer sufficient for him, and he gets uncharacteristically fractious. A wet nurse has to be found, and losing the bonding intimacy of nursing John feels to Sarah like a reproach. By the end of September, she is still no better. George procures some port wine for her, and, come October, they try warm baths to ease her. On the seventh, the doctor is called again. He is called back the next day.

At last, on October 11, George writes in his journal that Sarah is *in a state of partial salvation from the medicine she had taken*. She has been ill for more than half the year.

Chapter Thirty-Two

"THERE IS A REMARKABLE EVENT taking place tomorrow morning," George tells the people after Sunday worship on December 19, 1824. "We will witness an annular solar eclipse."

This is just the sort of thing that fascinates George, and he has been avidly reading up about the difference between partial, total, and annular eclipses. "The word *annular* comes from the Latin word *annulus*, which means ring," he says, "and an annular eclipse is when the moon passes before the sun, making the sun look like a ring of fire. It will begin shortly after 10:30 tomorrow morning."

"How can you know the day and the time it will happen?" asks Willem Valentyn.

"I don't wonder at him knowing it," says Cobus Boezak. "A missionary is so knowing that there is no coming at the bottom of him."

George laughs his pleasure. "Astronomers are able to predict the cycle of the planets, and I read it in the papers," he says. "But now, it is very important that you should not look directly at the sun, for you will damage your eyes, and so today I will blacken pieces of glass so that you and your children may look through that to see the eclipse."

The next morning, the schoolmaster, Mr. Edwards, lets the children out of school at 10:30, and everyone gathers in clusters to watch through their pieces of blackened glass, while the moon's silhouette inches in front of the sun's disk as if a bite has been taken out of it. When the moon covers the center of the sun's disk and the ring of fire appears, a child laughs at the sheer magic of it. Another cries, and hides her face in her mother's skirts.

"Don't be frightened! It will pass," soothes Sarah, even as she wonders at the eerie, supernatural light. She holds up her piece of blackened glass to study again the unearthly outline of the sun in the peculiar dusk. She thinks, "And it was about the sixth hour, and there was a darkness over all the earth until the ninth hour. And the sun was darkened." But that event at the crucifixion, according to the Gospels, lasted for hours. Now, just as she has assured the frightened child that it will pass, the moon starts to inch away again within minutes, transferring the bite to the other side of the sun, until it has stopped overlapping the sun's disk altogether. As wondrous as it has been, when Sarah looks around her at the still upturned faces, she is glad to have things back to normal.

The eclipse coincides with the southern solstice, and that selfsame sun that was momentarily just a ring of fire around the moon bakes down its summer heat. For the remainder of the year of 1824, it is so excessively hot that whenever George has to ride out on business, he gets home drained and wet with perspiration. Even the fowls feel it, and all run into the church one day with much clucking and squawking. There is such a commotion of frantic creatures—fowls and people alike—running in all directions through the church, that Sarah eventually has to stop, pink cheeked and out of breath, and give herself over to laughter at the sheer ridiculousness of the scene.

Come the New Year, James Read arrives quite unexpectedly from Bethelsdorp to fetch the Barkers for a visit to mark the anniversary of the Sunday school there. Since the children are home from school, George and Sarah decide to enter into the holiday spirit and make a spur-of-the-moment excursion for a few days.

When they reach Algoa Bay, they find it much changed from when they had seen it four years ago. The town of Port Elizabeth now boasts three hundred people. George's old friend Mr. Frederick Korsten has been granted a piece of land on the adjoining beach to establish a whale fishery. The Red Lion Hotel houses a customhouse and public offices, and the town has named its first postmaster. In Bethelsdorp, the arch is finished on a bridge that Dr. Philip had encouraged as an undertaking for the strength of the people, and some other structures have gone up, too, although Sarah notices that there are not as many stone houses for the people as there are in Theopolis.

"I don't see any house here that is as fine as yours," she tells Willem Valentyn, as he guides the wagon through the mission station. He grins and nods.

Sara Read embraces Sarah with quiet pleasure. James Read Jr. is now fourteen years old, a slender young man with the high cheekbones, the softly curled black hair, and the olive complexion of his beautiful Khoikhoi mother. Little Ann takes a shine to this boy seven years her senior, and slips her hand into his when he allows it, becoming his little shadow.

It is a lively gathering for the anniversary, and Sarah is delighted to recognize the silversmith, Daniel Hockly, who has ridden down from Uitenhage.

"And how is Mrs. Hockly?" she asks.

"She is very well. She holds school in Uitenhage now. We have welcomed a son, Alfred, since we saw you last, and I am happy to say that my wife is with child again. We expect her to be delivered in the winter. And your family has grown, too, I see."

"Yes, indeed. Do you remember young Sarah and Elizabeth, who were so enthralled by the delicate engraving on the lid of the snuffbox you showed us?"

Daniel Hockly smiles, and assures her that he does.

"Ann was still a baby then. These are our two sons, Edward and John, who were both born after we left Bethelsdorp." Edward bends himself over into a formal little bow at the introduction. It looks comical, but he is so earnest that, although Sarah meets Daniel Hockly's laughing eyes, they both keep straight faces.

The pleasant company makes Sarah realize just how isolated they are up in beautiful Theopolis. She misses the proximity of the bay, and the flow of through traffic that brings lively society and conversation. There are visitors at Theopolis, to be sure, but as a destination, not as a thoroughfare, which encourages a different kind of interchange and conviviality.

When it is time to return home, there is a to-do because George's horse is missing and can't be found, and they have to go off without him. Little Edward is inconsolable. Sarah is at a loss to understand why this chance event has so distressed him until he says, "But he is our family, he belongs to us, we cannot leave him behind!"

She pulls him close and says, "He came into our lives for a while, and we may see him again, just as we will see Mr. and Mrs. Read and their children, or the Hocklys. But he is not truly family. Not like you. We would never, ever leave behind you or John or your sisters." At this, he quietens, and as they take the route by way of Uitenhage to the Koega River, Sarah thinks about the life of an immigrant's child. He has no extended family, no beloved grandparents or doting aunts and uncles to bolster him. There is no family tradition of place. Even when she was sent away from her home as a girl, she had gone to relatives in the same county. She understands now with a clarity that had not quite crystallized before that she will always have to be particularly vigilant to give her little brood a sense of belonging.

With Edward now contentedly playing with a pair of wooden oxen—*dolosse*—that Theopolis's carpenter carved for him, Sarah turns to George.

"We were not always so happy at Bethelsdorp," she says, "but a gathering like this made me realize that I quite miss the society that it afforded us."

"Yes, I felt it a privilege to be there and to take part in marking the anniversary in this way." The ox wagon creaks along at its plodding pace for a while, and then George says, "What would you think if I were to propose that we hold a missionary meeting at Theopolis for the first time?"

"Oh, I think that would be a fine idea!"

"I expect a visit from the governor, Lord Charles Somerset, next month, but perhaps after that," says George.

At intermittent stages through the rest of the journey, they return to the idea, planning who would come, how they could accommodate it, and Sarah conjures up images of a gathering of like-minded people populating their mission on a hill.

They have been home two weeks when George hears that the governor might be expected, by way of Salem from Grahamstown. It is almost ten years since the first time Lord Charles Somerset had visited Theopolis, when he'd superciliously regarded all from on high and left without even noticing all the hard work that had gone into the preparations in his honor.

The governor arrives about midday on the appointed day, with an entourage that includes his equally imperious eldest son, Colonel Henry Somerset, who is the commanding officer of the Cape Corps in Grahamstown, as well as a train of officers and soldiers. As intimidated as she had been when she had first met Lord Charles all those years ago, Sarah now considers herself a veteran, a mother of five, and quite up to the task of being mistress of her domain. She receives him civilly, and without trepidation. Even more satisfying is watching how George conducts himself. The entire party troops into the schoolroom, where his Lordship sits down, looking about him from under his hooded eyes.

"How long have you been holding school here?" he asks.

"Well, as your Lordship may be aware," says George, "we had devastating floods in the Albany region in October 1823, and we had to rebuild. Through the dedicated work of the people, the school was ready to be commenced just two months after that."

"How many pupils have you here?"

"We have about three hundred enrolled, but attendance varies. There are often demands on the children's time by their parents, and it is difficult to maintain strict attendance."

"Hmm. And the syllabus?"

"We use the monitor system, whereby older pupils take responsibility for the younger ones. Instruction is based on the catechism, and includes reading and writing from the Bible, as well as spelling and basic arithmetic."

"What is the medium of instruction?"

"Cape Dutch, your Lordship."

"I suppose that's all very well at the outset, but ultimately only English and Latin should be taught in the schools."

"With respect, Sir, I am of the opinion that for pupils to be obliged to learn in a language that is not their vernacular creates a barrier to their education."

"Well, I am a firm believer in the policy of Anglicization. This country is part of the British Empire, after all." He stands up before George can venture another opinion. "I'll take a look at some of the houses now."

He strolls out of the building, with his son, the officers, and the soldiers trailing behind him. After some perfunctory enquiries about which houses belong to which of the people, they are soon on their way, without saying what they think of the place. Sarah takes George's arm as they watch the carriage and horses bump their way down the track away from the station. She touches the side of her head to his shoulder briefly and gives his arm a squeeze. She is proud of the way he has stood up for his principles.

Plans go ahead for the first missionary meeting at Theopolis, and by the time it comes around, the seasons have changed. The early June nights are chilly, even though the sun warms through the days. And Sarah's season has come around again. She is more than three months pregnant, having conceived, she thinks, just after the governor's visit.

The missionary meeting is scheduled for Friday, June 10, and at teatime on the Tuesday of that week, the dog's urgent barking outside pulls Sarah to the window in time to see young James Read and Johannes Ullbricht dismounting. Calling to George, she runs out to greet these youngsters who are almost like an extension of her family.

"We all left Bethelsdorp on the Sabbath evening at eleven o'clock," says James, flushed and excited. "My father is just at hand to help with your meeting."

George instructs James and Johannes where to stable their horses, and Sarah pulls up two more chairs inside, so that they can all take tea together. In the evening, she pulls up two more chairs when Brother James comes. He is accompanied by Henry Helm, who is newly arrived at Bethelsdorp and the only stranger amongst them. He is a reserved man, and Sarah seats him next to her at the table, hoping to make him feel at ease. While the animated conversation goes on around them, she speaks quietly to him. She learns that he studied in Berlin and was ordained at the Lutheran Church in London, where he met and married an Englishwoman. She observes that his English is excellent.

When Brother Helm gives the sermon at the first service of the missionary meeting on Friday morning, he preaches fluently in Cape Dutch from the end of the parable of the Good Samaritan: "Then said Jesus unto him, Go, and do thou likewise." He takes the question "Who is my neighbor?" with which the lawyer had challenged Jesus in the Gospel account, and he likens it to the Europeans amongst the Khoikhoi.

"We are all neighbors in the eyes of God," says Brother Helm, speaking with quiet urgency in the hushed church. "We must all extend mercy to one another."

As she listens, Sarah questions whether she truly regards the people as neighbors in this sense, or if she can fault herself for thinking of the missionaries as "us" and the people whom they serve as "them." She loves Lena and often looks to her for help and guidance. She has long felt a bond with Cobus, and she depended on him utterly in her grief when she buried her child. But she wonders if, in some hidden way that she might not be fully aware of, she thinks of the European culture as being superior to the ancient traditions of the Khoikhoi. She suspects that George does. Does she? It is only when George closes the service with a prayer that her mind comes back to the reality of the church and the congregation around her. Henry Helm's words have hit a nerve.

Chapter Thirty-Three

ALL THIS WHILE, as I have been tracing Sarah's story, I've been going back home to South Africa every year or two—or, in the case of 2013, twice in three months for the funerals of my mother and my brother. But, really, am I going back home? Is *that* my home, where I am rooted with memories and friends and family, or is *this* my home, where I have planted myself with a house, a career, and an American husband who is homesick for South Africa?

My first time back was within six months, and it was as if I'd hardly left. It's true that I seemed to have a slight aura of exoticism because I now lived in a foreign country, but I picked up the threads as if I were simply visiting from Johannesburg. I stayed with my brother Peter in his flat, just as I had when I'd emigrated six months before; I caught up with friends; and I still felt in touch—part of the fabric.

Twenty years later, we were back at Millstream, the place where the mists roll in over the hills, where the air is unalloyed, where we'd been married, and where we return each time because of Douglas's longing for the place. I took a walk with two of the beloved and irreplaceable friends who invariably congregate with us there. They began to discuss the political situation in South Africa: the corruption, the dire consequences of then-President Zuma's ties to the wealthy Gupta brothers and their use of the London PR firm Bell Pottinger to exploit racial tensions for commercial gain. Although I knew the broad outlines of the plot, I felt completely out of touch as they talked. Many, if not most, of the names and details meant nothing to me; I was an outsider listening in on a conversation between two dear friends about something that was of vital, visceral importance to them—as viscerally important as the fallout from the 2016 American election was to me.

Between these two points, there is an evolving picture, an ebb and flow, of my connection to the country. There is the unique, red-earth smell of Africa when I first step off the plane. There's the instant when I hear the honking call of hadeda ibis and I know that I am truly back. It's trying to get used to drive on the left again and seeing Douglas in my rearview mirror frantically waving his arms when I forget. There's Julia flushed with pleasure when she picks me up at the airport, and there's Posy dropping her watering can with a cry to rush and embrace me when I appear at her garden gate. It's losing the instinctive sense of the value of the rand, and having to do a quick division by ten in my head to estimate the rough amount in dollars.

There's indicating to a young black woman that she should go ahead of me in the queue for no other reason than that she got there just before me, then registering her surprise because, in the old order, the assumption was that a white woman would go ahead. It's hoping that my small, instinctive gesture means that my logjam of subliminal apartheid conditioning is shifting. There's looking back up at my mother's face at the window of her corner apartment as I wave goodbye, wondering if this will be the last time I see her. It's Table Mountain lit up at night, looking like a giant, crouching elephant. There's my Cape Town home away from home in Ricky and Pete's house on the slopes of the mountain, with its vast expanse as their backyard. It's watching the unselfconscious ribbing and joshing from a neighboring table at a funky new restaurant near the SABC in Johannesburg, and seeing the encapsulation of Nelson Mandela's "rainbow nation" on wonderful display in the mixed races. So gradually that I was hardly aware of it, I was becoming the observer rather than the participant.

When I went back in 2017, it was to search for Sarah. My love affair with her had begun to crystallize about four years earlier when I was working towards my MFA thesis—a collection of essays about my immigrant experience called *Beyond the Baobab*. The final essay was, in effect, a love letter to Sarah, and it ends:

> *As I try to understand my own urgency to reach and stretch for something more, I wonder what made you leave your familiar, safe, predictable life in England for something that was so completely unknown and foreign. Perhaps I have inherited your wanderlust. Maybe it is you who has passed down to me that restless striving. And when I die, what country will I think of as my own?*

The more emotionally invested I became in Sarah and her story, the more I realized that I would have to go and pore over George's original journals, my closest link to her, and I eventually tracked the journals down at the Cory Library for Humanities Research at Rhodes University in Grahamstown. Since 2000, the Cory Library has been located on the ground floor of the Eden Grove Building, behind the Albany History Museum on Somerset Street, but it dates back to 1931 when the historian Sir George Cory, author of the six-volume publication *The Rise of South Africa*, bequeathed his research materials to the university and they became the nucleus of the library.

I flew into Port Elizabeth International Airport—near Bethelsdorp—and hired a car for the two-hour drive inland. My parents, and their parents before them, had been a part of Grahamstown for decades, and this was a journey I'd made countless times. But with a new awareness now, I noticed for the first time a sign for Colchester twenty minutes outside Port Elizabeth. It turned out that this little Eastern Cape town was, indeed, named after the historic town in the county of Essex, where my sister Anne first settled when she immigrated to England, and close to where George was born. I notched up another strand in the loops of serendipity.

As dusk started to close in and the road began to twist and climb higher towards Grahamstown, there was the first of a series of signs that said, "Welcome to Frontier Country," complete with the image of a cannon—an image that I thought was remarkably tactless. The Frontier Wars were Africa's equivalent of Europe's Hundred Years' War; from 1779 to 1879 Xhosa tribes and European settlers fought a series of nine battles and skirmishes in what became the longest-running military action in the history of African colonialism.

By the time I reached Grahamstown, it was dark, but the city plan that I'd carried somewhere in the recesses of my memory during the twenty years since I'd last visited offered itself up. I had to resort only once to asking directions to my Airbnb from an obliging, burly young rugby coach at St. Andrews College, where my father had once gone to school. Following the directions, I turned right onto African Street where Anne was born at No. 49, and I crossed Fitzroy Street, where my Grandfather Reginald and Grannie Jennie used to live when our family paid its annual visits.

Grahamstown is inextricably woven into our family lore. Reginald worked as a clerk in a solicitor's office there, his life a quiet struggle as he battled to make ends meet to support his five children and live up to the standards of his exacting Scottish wife, Jennie née McKenzie. Somehow, he managed to put all his children through Rhodes University.

My mother met my father at a dance in Grahamstown— he forever thought that the pale green dress she wore that night was white—and they were married in the Cathedral of St. Michael and St. George on High Street, where Anne was later christened. When my father died—too young, at the age of 63, from his third heart attack—his funeral was held at the cathedral.

My own involvement with Grahamstown was more tangential. We made those family trips once a year during the summer holidays; we visited Anne and Peter at their boarding schools there; when my parents took early retirement after my father's second heart attack, I spent my university vacations there; when my first love broke my heart, I retreated there to find comfort. It was the place I went to because it was historically bound up with my family's life. It was only when I went once a year each winter as a broadcaster to cover the National Arts Festival and watch it grow into Africa's largest arts festival that I began to experience the city in my own right. And now it had a vital pull in my search for Sarah.

On a wintry Wednesday morning in June 2017, I found my way to the Cory Library, which turned out to be within walking distance of my parents' old home on Huntley Street. The research library is maintained by Rhodes University primarily for its faculty and students, but it is also open to visiting researchers and the general public, who must be in possession of a reader's ticket. I presented myself at the front desk, duly bought my reader's ticket for two days' worth of research at R20.00 per day—roughly $2.00—and signed out George's journal in a huge, rather unwieldy ledger. The librarian settled me at an out-of-the-way desk in a side room and left me alone to get acquainted with this most tangible part of Sarah's history.

The library's records show that the diaries were bequeathed to the Cory Collection in the mid-1960s, around the time of the death of Harold Edward Hockly, one of Sarah's grandsons from a different line from ours. In 1948, this descendant had published *The Story of the British Settlers of 1820 in South Africa*, which became the standard history of the settlers, and I can only speculate that this was why George's diaries had been in his possession.

Somebody—Harold himself, perhaps—had bound the individual journals together into one volume, and I sat at my assigned desk in the Cory Library, turning it over in my hands. The tan vellum cover was worn, and the book boards showed through the marbled end pages at places on the inside cover. The diary is an inch thick and an unusual size, about seven inches wide by eleven inches long. George had made each of the sixteen individual signatures of the volume by folding six sheets of thick, creamy paper in half and nesting them together, one inside the other, before he stitched them together. I like to think that perhaps Sarah stitched them for him. His writing is close, edge to edge on each side.

Apart from its being precious, I found it beautiful. I smoothed my hand over it. I smelled it. I gingerly turned over each page as it crackled with age. I came across the blots, the watermarks, and the scratchings out. And as I read and deciphered and photographed, I took notes in my small black Moleskine notebook. Here was the lived account of

Sarah and George's "arduous undertaking," their journey by sea and land, their mission work amongst the indigenous Khoikhoi in South Africa's Eastern Cape, about thirty miles away from where I was now sitting.

Without any preamble or front matter, the diaries begin with: "*Journal*—," underlined, and then:

> *When we enter into important situations of life it becomes us to notice the judicial dealings of God in providence towards us. Thus, O God enable me to begin my Missionary voige (sic) and prosecute my labours among the Heathen, humbly relying upon thy faithfulness for the supply of all my wants, temporal and spiritual, and with gratitude acknowledging thy providential kindness in all that I receive.*

His writing, his thoughts, his aspirations, on these pages that he had touched, filling every space on each page with his handsome, slanting copperplate script . . . and as I read his account as he had originally written it two hundred years ago, no longer filtered through a typed transcription or on a computer screen, it shifted from being simply words and information into a conversation. I studied the elaborate "J" of Journal and the way his "d's" curled back over his words like a tail, in much the same way that I might listen for a sibilant "s" or a rolled "r."

In the day and a half I had available to me, I simply didn't have the time to read every word—and I struggled to make out some of them, partly due to George's old-fashioned handwriting, partly due to the wear and tear on the pages over the almost two hundred years. Still, as I paged through, the sense that I had of him—and, by association, Sarah—brought tears to my eyes with its immediacy. The physical, intimate contact with his actual writing was palpable; I internalized the words and the layers of meaning behind them differently. Phrases from their outward-bound journey jumped out at me: *I do not leave you* (meaning England) *with regret but with Joy . . . most of us are yet very ill owing to the swell in the morning . . . 15th (Saturday) crossed the line about 8 o clock A.M. & entered the southern hemisphere . . . The mountains of Africa were in sight by the light of the moon . . . came to an anchor about 20 minutes past 9 o clock A.M. to our no small joy, opposite Cape Town . . .*

There was a formality in the writing, which was not only a function of the audience—the stuffy old men back at the London Missionary Society—but also of the period. Still, what was coming through so strongly in his voice was his capacity to inhabit fully the instant of a momentous—and even a mundane—event. He was not simply recording a litany of "we did this, we did that." He painted the verbal pictures, and, in so doing, he placed me in the moment. It was thrilling to discover his innate gift for writing.

Returning from a lunch break, I stopped outside the Cory Library to take a photograph. A friendly, bearded man of around sixty, wearing a flat cap against the chill of the Grahamstown winter, asked, "How are you doing? Are you having a good time? Finding anything?" I assured him I was having a wonderful time. We walked into the building together, and he told me that he was the head of the library.

"Oh!" I said, touching the sleeve of his brown plaid shirt. "Are you Dr. Thomas? I have been emailing the library for years about access to the diaries of my great-great-grandfather, George Barker."

He laughed. "I get about eighty requests a day," he said.

He had a Cape accent and tawny skin, and as I walked back to my assigned desk, I wondered about his provenance.

I thought that perhaps it was not absolutely beyond the bounds of possibility that his forebears could have lived on one of the mission stations where Sarah and George worked amongst the people. I ran a check on my list of Khoikhoi people who were resident at Theopolis at some time between 1815-1834. There were four entries under "T," but they were all Trompetter—there was no Thomas. The serendipity didn't stretch that far.

Aware that my time was short, and trying to be strict with myself and pull myself away from becoming absorbed by every diary entry, I began to page through, looking for the overview. I took in the commencement at Theopolis; the commencement at Bethelsdorp; the blank page covering the period from February to September 1819, when George's feelings had been hurt by the directive from the directors of the Missionary Society and he had neglected to write anything down. I read the jottings in the margins about letters sent and received—the precious letters that were the lifeblood of their connection to England and the outside world.

At the bottom of one page, below the entry on June 2, 1820, where he wrote, *Worked in the garden. Sowed several sorts of small seeds, peas & planted potatoes*, there is a series of several, uncoordinated scribbles, as if a child might have got hold of her father's quill. Little Sarah would have been almost five by then, Elizabeth three, and Ann not yet two. Perhaps George wrote his diary entries with a child on his lap to free Sarah up for other duties.

All the while, I was searching for clues about her. He referred to her infrequently, and most often formally as "Mrs. B."—although sometimes he allowed his affection to show through, as in the entry on November 18, 1815: *This day the Lord gave me a daughter. My dear S. was taken ill about 4 o'clock in the morning & safely delivered about half past 1 at noon.* On

February 5, 1816, he mentioned that he could not attend a prayer meeting because "Mrs. B." was ill, but he made no mention of their first wedding anniversary the day before. On February 22 that year, while in Theopolis assisting the ailing Ullbricht, he wrote: *Received a letter from my dear S, which gave me great pleasure!*

And so I gleaned what I could at my assigned desk in the quiet of the Cory Library. But because this was George's account, my beloved Sarah remained oblique. As much as I had gained an essential insight, I knew that I would still have to rely on a combination of imagination and intuition to try to find my way to the heart of her, in this country that she had bequeathed to me.

CHAPTER THIRTY-FOUR

O N WEDNESDAY, NOVEMBER 9, 1825, Sarah feels
the first twinge low in her back, and although it is
enough to stop her in her tracks as she carries folded
laundry through to the linen box in the sleeping room, it is
not so piercing as some of the times before. She puts the linens down on a nearby table and rubs her lower back, encouraged, believing that it promises to be a good delivery. The
contractions come at irregular intervals throughout the day,
but they are not debilitating, and, in between, she can quietly go about the business of preparing meals, reading to the
boys, and changing the linens on the bed so that everything
will be clean and ready for her confinement.

A contraction wakes her in the small hours on Thursday,
and she twists, only half conscious, with a cry.

"Has it begun?" George, as always, is instantly awake and
alert.

She can only murmur her assent, "Mm."

"Shall I send for Lena?"

She waits for the spasm to pass before speaking. Then she
sits up and swings her legs over the side of the bed, panting

slightly. "It's been like this since yesterday. It's not so bad, but it's getting more frequent."

"I'll send for her. She could take care of the children, at least, and you can get some rest."

When Sarah sees Lena's square, smiling, and very welcome face, the first thing she says to her is, "How is your granddaughter?"

"Oh, she is fine, Sister Sarah. Yesterday, all she wanted was to play hide-and-seek. She put her head in my lap and pretended to sleep, and then jumped up, and I had to make as if I was frightened."

Sarah's laughter is cut short by a contraction.

"*Ai, ai, ai,*" says Lena. "Let us see where we are with this baby of yours now."

She puts her healing hands on Sarah's belly, staring off into the distance as she intuits what is going on inside. "Not there yet," is her prediction. "You just lie comfy here, and I'll get the little ones some breakfast. Then I'll bring you some rooibos, *nê?*"

Sarah is glad to give herself over to doing what she is told, and when Lena goes off to find the children, she hears their excited chorus of greeting. The contractions come and go, come and go, gripping her body and letting go in an inexorable rhythm throughout the day.

In the evening, Lena brings in a lamp. From the secluded space created by lamplight, Sarah looks through the window as the short, African dusk gives way to black night. It is a new moon, the stars especially vivid. Lena sits with the patience handed down through the millennia of her Khoikhoi people, talking sometimes, dozing now and then, but instantly awake almost before Sarah knows that another contraction is coming.

This clutch and release goes on throughout the night

and into the next day. Sarah marks the time from when the first spasm came the previous morning. The day and night have passed through a complete cycle, and she is no closer to delivering her child. Even though the pain is not unbearable—still not as fierce as times before—she is light-headed from wakefulness. No sooner does her exhaustion push her to the edge of sleep than another contraction comes and wrenches her back into consciousness.

George spends the night in the boys' room. When he comes to stand by the sleeping room door, she wants to cry. He looks as pale and drawn as she feels. The whole house is waiting for this baby to be born, and she cannot deliver it.

Lena comes and goes with cups of rooibos tea and bowls of porridge or thin soup. She soothes and she comforts. She runs her infinitely gentle and expert hands over Sarah's belly. At dusk, she brings in the evening lamp again, and Sarah watches the twilight and the night and the stars, while the contractions continue to rack her body in a constant rhythm.

With the first streaks of daybreak, George comes in and whispers to Lena. She quietly leaves the room, and George takes her place. Sarah, hands clenched, thinks with each contraction that she can't bear it any longer, and finds that, somehow, she can. And so a second morning passes. She has been in labor for forty-eight hours.

In the early afternoon, a spasm makes her cry out, and Lena comes running. The urge to bear down and push is almost a relief. She strains and pants and can't hold back a scream. But the baby does not come. Her waters have not even broken.

"Please . . . please . . ." She doesn't know to whom or what she is appealing, and hot tears run across her temples and into her hair.

George kneels by the bed and grips her hand. "Lord God, I ask in your name for relief for Sarah. I pray she no longer has to bear this pain. I pray that she turn to you during her time of struggling."

All Sarah can see is a white light of pain behind her eyelids, and then the light begins to splinter, and the pain subsides. She opens her eyes. Both George and Lena are at her bedside. "Who is with the children?" she asks.

"Little Sarah is taking care of them," says George, "but I will go to them." He stands, his own eyes wet. "Oh, Sarah," he says. He pulls her hand up to his mouth, and kisses it. Then he lays it gently at her side again, and walks from the room.

"Lena, what is happening?"

"I don't know, Sister Sarah. The baby is lying the right way. I don't know why it will not come."

For a third night, Lena brings a lamp into the room at dusk, but Sarah is unaware of the day changing to night. The contractions have begun to merge into a continuous stream of pain. Lena wants to change her out of her nightgown, which is rank with sweat, but Sarah can't summon up the energy to submit to it. She hears Lena's soothing voice although she can't distinguish the words any longer. She wishes that she would lose consciousness as she did when Ann was born, but she is so acutely aware of her body that she can feel her blood pulsing in her ears, the flush on her throat, the icy cold of her feet—all the disparate parts of her body pulling in different directions instead of converging on this one, crucial thing that has to be done. And then she feels the hot gush of her waters breaking.

At three o'clock on Sunday morning, the baby comes.

It is two full weeks after the ordeal of being in labor for almost three days before Sarah can venture out of her room for the first time. She is still frail, but their her newborn is a lively little thing who gives no indication of the struggle it was to give her life. By the time they baptise their fourth daughter Jane, Sarah is slowing growing stronger, but she is entering her thirty-seventh year now, and having given birth to nine children—and lost three of them—she finds that she can never quite regain her former strength after each confinement.

One Friday in late summer, news comes from the road that an ox wagon is approaching from Bethelsdorp. When Sarah hears the familiar hullabaloo of calls and stomping as the wagon comes to a creaking stop outside the house, she runs out to meet it with Jane on her hip. She sees the Rev. Adam Robson step down from the wagon and reach back up to assist his wife. Down climbs Sarah's lifelong friend, Elizabeth.

Although they have corresponded as regularly as the mail ship from Cape Town to Algoa Bay allowed, Sarah hasn't seen Elizabeth for seven years—not since she stayed with them here, in Theopolis, in 1818, after Joseph's death. When Elizabeth left Theopolis for Cape Town that year, her heart's urgent longing was still to return to Kat River to continue the work that she and Joseph had begun, but it was simply not practicable for a woman without the protection of a fellow missionary. She had settled in Cape Town, somewhat under the protection of Dr. Philip, to prepare herself for missionary service in whatever capacity it might present itself. And it had presented itself in the person of Adam Robson. He arrived at the Cape in 1823, and he and Elizabeth were married in 1824. He has newly taken up a position at Bethelsdorp.

As Elizabeth alights from the wagon, she looks about her, getting her bearings, in much the same way she'd done when

George had fetched her from Kat River in 1818. She catches Sarah's eye and her own light up, and then she turns towards her sons, who are clambering out of the wagon behind her. Young Joseph, born in Bethelsdorp, is now ten, and John, born at Kat River, a year younger. The two families converge, and in the bustle of greetings and introductions, Sarah and Elizabeth embrace, then draw back to appraise each other in a little space of quiet seclusion. Elizabeth looks both exactly the same and yet different. Her blue eyes are still clear and direct, her face unlined, but her brow is heavier, and her chin, with an extra little one appearing below her jawline, more set than ever. Sarah wonders what changes Elizabeth is seeing in her.

She pulls her in for another hug. "Oh, Beth," she says, reverting to her childhood nickname.

When George takes Adam Robson and all the children for a tour of the new village, Sarah stays behind with Elizabeth to help her settle into their rooms.

"Adam has a kind face," she says.

"Yes. He is younger than we, but he is man of infinite sense, ability, and deep faith."

"You've never told me how you first met."

"When he arrived at the Cape, he intended to work up north with the Bechuana, but the country was in a disturbed state and he was in ill health, so he was detained in Cape Town." Elizabeth pulls open a drawer and lays linens inside amongst the sprigs of rosemary Sarah has placed there. "We were in each other's company at Dr. Philip's church," Elizabeth goes on, "and since Adam had also studied at Gosport, we had much to talk about on that score at the beginning. Over time, it seemed destined that we should marry."

"Is his calling still with the Bechuana?"

"No, he will remain in Bethelsdorp. My hope had been for Kat River, but it is God's will that we should be in Bethelsdorp." She unpacks the last of the linens and firmly closes the drawer.

George invites Adam Robson to preach the sermon at the Sunday evening service, and Sarah and Elizabeth sit side by side in a back pew, flanked by their children, to listen to their two husbands, one as preacher and one as interpreter. Adam chooses a passage from Paul's letter to the Corinthians: "But we all, with open face beholding as in a glass the glory of the Lord, are changed into the same image from glory to glory, even as by the Spirit of the Lord." Adam speaks in English, as George translates for the people, of how each one of them gathered here together in the church is reflecting the glory of the Lord, and is transformed into the same image; of how each image is repeatedly reflected in the mirror of each other, again and again, *ad infinitum*, until they are all recurring images of the one Lord. Sarah is moved by the mystical possibilities of Adam's words, and puts her hand over her friend's. She is rewarded by a returning squeeze.

A party of singers from Grahamstown accompanies the next part of the worship, and they have with them two instruments of music.

"What on earth are those?" whispers Elizabeth close to Sarah's ear.

Sarah whispers back, "*Ramkiekie*. The people have played them for hundreds of years. The body is made from a hollowed-out gourd and it's strung with fishing wire." As an afterthought she adds, "I've seen them at wedding parties before, but never in a church."

They sit still then, listening to the haunting, interweaving singing, underscored by the repetitive chords of the two *ramkiekie*. Sarah takes in the flickering candle flames around the church, imagining in them the recurring images of a mirror in the mirror that Adam had preached about, thinking of the way that she has felt similarly reflected back in her friendship with Elizabeth since she was a girl.

When it is time for Elizabeth and her family to return to Bethelsdorp, she leans in close to Sarah to say in a low voice, "Don't have any more babies!" She pulls back and fixes her clear blue eyes on her. "Six is quite enough, and you're looking drawn and peaky."

"Oh, Elizabeth!" Sarah half smiles and shrugs as if to say, *What can I do?* She is jogging Jane on her hip because it is almost time for her feed, and she is showing signs of getting crotchety.

"I mean it," says Elizabeth. She puts both hands to Sarah's cheeks, and then turns to mount the wagon. So Sarah has the answer to her wondering about what changes Elizabeth was seeing in her when they met again after so many years. Evidently, she looks *drawn and peaky*. In truth, she feels it, too, sometimes. But she would not be without any single one of her precious children. She wishes she could have those she has lost too. And, as to the reason why she has this large brood in the first place, she loves George in every way. Not just as a companion and helpmeet, but in that deeply intimate, veiled, thrilling way too. When he turns to her and she feels her pulse matching his, she could no more imagine denying it than refusing sustenance to her children. Even if the consequences come at such a cost to her.

Halfway down the hill, Elizabeth looks back and waves. Sarah raises her hand in response, and Jane flails her plump arms in imitation. "Come on, little one," says Sarah, "let's get you fed."

They settle back into their quiet, steady routine. After tea one evening in mid-August, when the bite of winter is beginning to grow weaker, George says, "I am writing to my sister Sophia. I have told her that she stands high in your esteem, my dear, having gained your affection by her former letters, and that she cannot conceive how much a letter from her means to you."

"Certainly, I would always welcome a letter from Sophia," says Sarah.

"Is Aunt Sophia your oldest sister, Papa?" asks Elizabeth.

"Your Aunt Sarah is my oldest sister, then your Aunt Sophia."

"And Aunt Elizabeth is your youngest sister, is she not?" says her namesake.

"Yes, quite right. Can you remember your other aunt's name?"

"Aunt Lidia!" says young Sarah.

"Now, what about your uncles?"

"Uncle Thomas!" says Edward, looking up from the page where he is drawing a horse—or at least, that was what Sarah supposes it is; its legs are rather too short to be sure.

"Yes, Edward Thomas, you would be sure to remember that," says his father.

By pooling their resources, the children manage to name their other uncles: Nathaniel, named for their grandfather, Charles, Henry, and "Baby" Buttress, as they like to call him, even though he is, by now, twenty-four years old.

"Shall we ever meet them, Papa?" says Ann.

"Well, I don't know. England is a very far way off."

"Oh no!" Edward has broken the lead in his pencil.

"Take care, Edward!" George speaks sharply. "That is the only pencil you have."

Edward turns to look at Sarah, his gray eyes so like his father's. "Mama," he says, "will you write to your brother in England to send me out three pencils? Then I should be master of them, and my father could not scold me if I did break one."

Sarah meets George's eyes over their son's head, and she can't stop herself from smiling. George's face softens, and he reaches out to tousle Edward's hair.

When George gets up to stoke the fire, Sarah pulls towards her the letter he has been writing, skimming over the contents:

> *Our little Edward Thomas, who is five years old tomorrow, goes into the school. The girls are older and often mention your name, but alas the poor little things know nothing of Uncle or Aunt but mere name. Our last is a girl, now nine months old, called Jane, a lively, sweet little creature. We have six alive, four girls and two boys. Thank God they are well, have all the use of their limbs and their reason. This is often a source of great pleasure and always of gratitude. We sadly want a good school for them but I hope to have something done in this very soon, and indeed it is high time. The two older girls are able to read English but they want introduced to other society than we have here. The girls, young as they are, take care of the younger children and do most of the work in the house. They have little time to run about.*

Happily, the summer brings time for some running about. The Robsons and Elizabeth's two sons make a return visit for pure pleasure—no meetings or formal functions of any kind. On the second day, they take Adam's wagon and ride down to the sea. When George helps Sarah to step down, her boots sink into the soft sand, and she puts a hand up to her bonnet as she inhales a deep lungful of the heavy, salty air. The sky—just a slightly paler shade of blue than the sea—is almost cloudless, the temperatures already nearing 70 degrees, and the slight breeze seems to lift the air, to buoy it up.

In an instant, the children are off running, calling, laughing, dodging, like puppies let loose on a field. From the wagon, the two men unpack a pair of kitchen chairs for the women to sit on, and a hamper full of meats, cheeses, fruits, breads, and bottles of ginger beer. The women spread out two blankets, and Elizabeth calls to the three older boys to hunt for rocks to hold down the corners in case of sea breezes. In unison, Sarah and Elizabeth pop open their parasols and sit down on the chairs their husbands have set up for them. The calling voices of their children drift in and out on the buoyant air, Jane is deep into her morning nap on the blanket at Sarah's feet, and George has taken Adam to show him where the Kasouga River ends in a lagoon.

The warmth of the sun reflecting off the bright sand picks up the yellow-sprigged design at the hem of Elizabeth's dress. "What do you think about the new fashion of puffed sleeves?" asks Sarah.

"I like it not one bit. I not only think they look excessive, but they would never be practical for the kind of lives we lead."

Sarah laughs, happy that her friend's opinions on fashion continue to be the same as hers after all these years.

"I have started a sewing group at Bethelsdorp," says Elizabeth, "like the one I had at Kat River. The Hottentot women may not be quite as meticulous, but they still produce beautiful handiwork."

"I love to see the women so productive and proud of their work," says Sarah. "And, certainly, I would not have the time to keep myself and the girls properly clothed without the dresses that our sewing group produces. They have begun to sew men's shirts, too, and George is quite impressed."

"Mama!" Edward bounds up and comes to a sliding halt on his knees in the sand at her feet. "I am thirsty, Mama!" Fortunately, Jane is a deep sleeper and doesn't stir at her brother's boisterous arrival.

"Well, let's see what we can do about that." Sarah closes her parasol, digs its tip into the sand, and rummages in the hamper to pour her son a glass of ginger beer.

He trains his gray eyes on her over the rim of the glass as he gulps the drink down in one breath. "Thank you!" he gasps when he's drained the last drop. She takes the glass from him, and he scampers back to join the others. Sarah pours two glasses for herself and Elizabeth while she is at it, and settles down again under her parasol to watch the children and to savor the company of her friend.

"Did you hear about Robert Hamilton?" asks Elizabeth.

"What of him?" asks Sarah. It has been a long time since she had news of either of the other missionaries who made the journey to Africa with them.

"Well, as you know, Brother Robert married Sister Ann not long after we all arrived."

"Yes."

"Then, about six years after, while I was still living in Cape Town, she wrote to the directors deploring her state of mind, and saying that she was miserable and unhappy."

"Oh my!" says Sarah. "She did seem to be of a rather agitated disposition."

"Within months, she wrote again to say that she was unhappy with Brother Robert in New Lattakoo and wished to go to the Cape to earn her living—and indeed so she did. She left Brother Robert behind, and arrived in the year before we came to Bethelsdorp."

"Poor Brother Robert! He was always such an earnest man. This must have distressed him deeply. Does he remain with the Griqua up north?"

"Yes."

"And what have your heard of John and Mary Evans?

"They remain in Cradock. He ministers to the Independent congregation there."

The piercing voices of the children reach them, rising and falling with their game of chasing waves at the water's edge. One wave running at high speed up the beach nearly catches young Elizabeth. There's an impromptu conference as the children put their heads together. Elizabeth breaks away and starts bounding toward her mother. Sarah knows what the question is going to be, but she waits for her daughter to speak it.

"Please, Mama, may we take our shoes off?"

"Yes, you may."

Elizabeth spins around and streaks back to her comrades, calling, "She says yes!"

What a commotion, then, of dashing and shrieking and splashing and laughing. Sarah watches her namesake, who always keeps little John in her sights to be sure that he is safe. She stands with her baby brother now, holding his hand, right at the water's edge as the waves wash up to their ankles and recede, wash and recede.

"What an African scene," says Elizabeth, watching her children at play with Sarah's. "We never did anything like this when we were girls."

The men start to walk back from the direction of the lagoon, and George calls to the children to come for lunch.

As if on cue, Jane wakes, and everyone settles down for a picnic, not having to mind their manners too much, and scattering crumbs with abandon. Joseph and John Williams had started out the day shyly, but the boisterous play has relaxed them, and they seem a cheerful part of the family now. Sarah glances from young Joseph to her eldest daughter, born just a few months before him, and a thought suddenly flits across her mind that perhaps they could be life partners one day. But she looks quickly away, thinking it is much too soon to be trying to direct fate. Ann is luxuriously digging her bare toes into the sand, and Sarah thinks of what Elizabeth had said. This is not an English life, but it is a good life that they can offer their children in this beautiful country.

One night in early February when the summer begins to feel as if it will drag on forever, Sarah has washed her face, stripped down to her shift, and is plaiting her hair ready for bed. George comes in and stands behind her, watching her reflection in the looking glass.

"Do you know what day it is?" she says.

"The third? No, the fourth."

"It's the fourth of February."

He continues to study her face in the reflection.

"It is our wedding anniversary," she says.

She watches him calculate in his head. "Twelve years," he says. He steps in close behind her, and she can feel his fully clothed body through the thin fabric of her shift. He puts his warm hands on her shoulders, and drops his face into the hollow of her neck, inhaling her unique scent. She thinks of Elizabeth's admonition not to have any more babies, but she loves this man—this highly charged, emotional, deeply feeling, driven, and committed man—and she cannot parcel up that love into what is allowed and what isn't. She turns into him. Within two weeks, she is fairly sure that she has conceived.

In April, when she hasn't bled for two months and quite certain that she is carrying a child again, Sarah and George ride out as far as the Kariega River on the western boundary of the Theopolis property and down to the estuary where the river meanders into the ocean. The early autumn day is mild—temperatures in the 60s, George estimates—and the sun reflects off the pale, bleached sand along the beach, warming Sarah's face under her riding hat as they pause, their horses shifting under them, to look out at the Indian Ocean.

"You're particularly radiant today," says George, glancing sideways at her.

She loves to choose her moments to tell him they are expecting a child, and always remembers the first time, in the cramped and dingy cabin on the *Alfred*, when a tear had slid over the bridge of his nose.

"It is because I am carrying your child," she says now.

He turns his head quickly, and he stares her full in the face. Then he maneuvers his horse around so that he can be close to her, their knees touching where hers are suspended from her sidesaddle, and he reaches to take her gloved hand.

"I pray it will not be so long a birth this time," he says.

She leans toward him, and, negotiating their hats as best she can, she puts her cheek against his.

"You are well enough to ride?" he says.

"I am perfectly well."

"Then, let us mark this beautiful day by riding along the beach to the mouth of the Kasouga River."

CHAPTER THIRTY-FIVE

GEORGE, SARAH, and the younger children are coming out of church one Sunday in mid-August of that year, 1827, when a constable arrives with a letter for George. This is such an unusual occurrence that George breaks the seal and reads the letter at once.

"It's from the landdrost, Major Dundas," he says. He runs his eyes quickly over the letter. "He states that, in consequence of a threatened invasion of the colony by a large body of Xhosa on the frontier, he has to request that all the able-bodied men we can muster may be held in readiness if required to assist in opposing them." He looks up at the constable, who is still astride his horse. "Tell the landdrost that I shall make a list tomorrow, and we await further instructions. Will you take some refreshment?"

"No thank you, sir. I must ride to deliver messages to the settlers," he says. He touches his cap, turns his horse, and spurs it into a canter down the hill.

Sarah looks at George's set face. "You hate this," she says, "enlisting our men to fight."

"It is not what we are here to do," he says.

But the Xhosa raids were a fact of life. After the Fifth Frontier War in 1819—when the Xhosa prophet-chief Makhanda promised his people that he would "turn the British bullets into water"; when a thousand Xhosa lives were lost in Grahamstown; and when a besieged Theopolis was all but decimated—the British pushed the Xhosa further east. But the Xhosa, who had occupied this land for millennia and were being encroached upon from the east by the expanding Zulu kingdom, continued their forays into the Albany district.

Within a day, George has drawn up a list of able-bodied men, and they are in readiness, waiting for orders. No orders come. Nobody can settle to anything, as if lives are being put on hold on an off chance, and the mission station continues on edge from day to day, waiting for a directive. It comes on Saturday. George sends out word to the seventeen men, and they come with their families to meet at the school. He reads aloud from the order, "*The enlisted men are requested to be at the East Barracks in Grahamstown at eight o'clock on Monday morning next. The settlers are likewise ordered out, to be at the same place at the same time.*" He folds up the document. "You will need to travel tomorrow night to be in Grahamstown at the appointed time. We will hold a prayer meeting for you tomorrow afternoon before you go."

Sunday dawns muggy and hazy. When the enlisted men gather with their families at the church in the afternoon, George calls on each of them to stand as he reads their names.

"Almighty God, we commend to your gracious care and keeping these men: Corporal Matroos Boardman . . . Corporal Stoffel Boezak . . . Sergeant Plaatje Boezak . . . Sergeant Alcaster Coenradt . . . Sergeant Gideon Jack . . . Corporal Jan Jacobs . . . Corporal Piet Jager . . . Sergeant Klaas Klaas . . . Corporal Stuurman Kleinbooy . . . Sergeant

Cupido Kobus . . . Sergeant Daniel Links . . . Corporal William Norris . . . Sergeant Stuurman Plaatje . . . Sergeant Hendrik Scheepers . . . Sergeant David Schnapps . . . Sergeant Jan Soldaat . . . and Corporal Piet Spandeel. Defend them day by day with your heavenly grace; give them courage to face the perils which beset them; and grant them a sense of your abiding presence wherever they may be."

The sun has never quite come out during the day, and the interior of the church is dim in the late afternoon. Sarah looks at the straight backs of the men as they stand, silhouetted like stone sculptures. Each one of them is a superb horseman and an excellent shot, like their fathers, and their fathers before them. But how can this be right? How can they be sent to fight for the British when the British authorities don't regard them as fully-fledged citizens? And how can they not be fully-fledged citizens in a land where their ancestors have lived for thousands and thousands of years? She feels washed over with sadness, and when she turns over in bed later that night, sleepless in her seventh month of pregnancy, and hears the soft jingle of bridles, the scrape of hooves, the low voices of the departing men, she feels a sting of tears, as if she were the one sending a husband or a son or a father off into a conflict. It has just passed new moon. The men will have little light to guide them on their night ride.

They are just seventeen men out of the hundreds who live at Theopolis, but they have taken the life of the place with them. It is a subdued, almost listless, settlement going forward, and George has to work that much harder to try to inject a spirit of hope and faith.

September brings news of a pending visit from Sir Richard Bourke, the lieutenant governor of the eastern district of the Cape. He has been recently appointed acting governor of the entire Cape Colony while Lord Charles takes a leave of absence, and, George guesses, Sir Richard has the expectation of superseding Somerset in due course. The acting governor—like his cousin, the writer and thinker Edmund Burke—was born in Dublin, Ireland, and appeared to support the liberal Whig party in Great Britain in its recognition of public opinion and the political participation of the English middle classes.

The packhorse and servants of the lieutenant governor arrive on the morning of Monday, September 17, and he and his retinue follow during the early afternoon. He is a tall, imposing man, who still carries himself like the major general he was during the Napoleonic Wars. Sarah takes in his hooded eyes, straight nose, cleft chin, and wiry curls receding over a high forehead, before they all set off to tour the school.

The schoolmaster is midway through the fourth multiplication table when the party troops into the schoolroom to be greeted by a chorus of scraping chairs and one or two stray pieces of dropped chalk.

"Good afternoon, class," says the lieutenant governor.

"Good afternoon, Sir Richard," they chime back in English, which suggests some diligent rehearsal.

Sir Richard turns to the class monitor. "And what have you been learning today?"

George steps in to be a quiet and deft interpreter.

"We read about the parable of the unforgiving servant, and how Jesus says we must forgive other people just as God forgives us, and then we wrote that down, and now we are learning the times-four table."

"Very good." Sir Richard turns to the schoolmaster to nod his approbation and says, "Do carry on."

The pupils sit down and they pick up where they had left off with their multiplication tables, while Sir Richard strolls through the school twice.

George has told several of the people in the village that he plans to bring the lieutenant governor to visit their houses, and, once the tour of the school is over, their first stop is Willem Valentyn's home. George points out the stone on the front of the house with the name and date, marking that his had been the first house to be completed at the new village. The window frames are painted yellow, the dung floors are polished to a mahogany shine, and there is not a single thing out of place inside. Willem and his wife, Elizabeth, are shy but gracious hosts.

When they emerge from the Valentyns' house, George turns to the lieutenant governor. "Sir, one of the houses we will visit belongs to a man named Cobus Boezak, who is a *Kaptein*—a chieftain—of his clan. In the past, it has been the tradition for a *Kaptein* to be recognized by the government through the presentation of a copper-headed staff of office. Would you consider making such a presentation?"

"On your recommendation, I would gladly do so."

"May I fetch the staff now?"

"Please do!"

While George runs back to his study to fetch the staff, Sarah slips into the role of guide and interpreter for the next house they visit. When they come to Cobus Boezak's house, his bulk momentarily blocks the doorway before he steps aside and invites them inside. His wife, Marta, keeps her new house immaculate, and it smells of coriander. Its front room is dwarfed by the influx of people in the lieutenant governor's party, and George comes in through the doorway as Sarah is making the introductions.

Sir Richard raises his voice above the hubbub. "Cobus Boezak," he says, and a sudden hush falls over the crowded room. "By the power invested in me by the British government, I confer upon you this captain's staff." As Sarah translates, George steps forward and places the staff in Sir Richard's outstretched hand. Sir Richard continues, "I present it in honor of your leadership amongst the people, and the contribution you make to our colony thereby."

Cobus's face is a study of surprise, joy, and disbelief. For someone usually easy with words, he is dumbstruck, and he stumbles out a thanks as he accepts the staff. He turns to show it to Marta, and then he looks up directly at Sarah. As their eyes meet, and he silently acknowledges her part in this, she feels as big a rush of pride as if she had been honored herself.

The lieutenant governor dines with George and Sarah that evening.

"It is quite a village you preside over up here, Mr. Barker," Sir Richard says. "I must say that I was surprised by the number and quality of the houses."

"We have a core of hardworking people who take pride in the place and in what they have achieved here. I do not believe it is simply my bias that makes me think our houses are superior to those at other missions stations I have visited."

"I would agree with you. And it is exactly this kind of initiative that we must reward. As you may know, I am in the process of drafting an ordinance that would allow the Hottentots to move freely without carrying passes. They should have equal status with the Europeans, and should also be able to acquire ownership of land. It is time that we restore the proper degree of dignity to these people."

George breaks into one of his rare smiles. It lights up his face.

With Sir Richard's visit successfully accomplished, Sarah begins to feel the familiar turning inwards, as the time of her confinement comes near. Her labor begins in the small hours of Saturday morning, on November 3. Sarah calls for George at two o'clock, and he sends for Lena within the hour. The moon is almost full, and, once again, it serves as Sarah's marker—almost her talisman by now—as her contractions wax and wane. The larger Sarah's family grows, the more the older children are able to take care of the younger ones and to help around the house, and so the less they see of Lena. The pleasure and relief, now, of seeing her broad, comforting face is the one saving grace of having to go through this ordeal again. The aromas of *buchu* and rooibos waft around her in the candlelit room, and she feels the clench of her tension release under the warm, firm pressure of Lena's hands on her belly.

"*Ai!*" Sarah tenses again at Lena's sharp exclamation.

"What?" she can hear the edge of panic in her own voice.

"I am feeling the baby's head up by your ribs, instead of down by your hips. *Sjoe*! This is not going to be so easy. But you just push like normal, Sister Sarah. I will take care of you."

Sarah has no option but to push. By daybreak, the contractions are already coming closer and closer together, and the baby is moving through the birth canal much more quickly than Jane had done. That much is a relief. But even in the constriction of pain and pushing, Sarah knows that all is not right. As much as she is able to blot out the pain of childbirth each time once it is over, the primal instinct of it returns when it comes again, and this is not like other times. She can feel pressures and strains and protuberances where they should not be. Lena, usually so centered on Sarah and her well-being, is absent from her this time, her focus entirely on the unborn child, and Lena's concentrated tension transforms into fright and panic in Sarah.

Then Lena speaks. "It is coming now . . . and it is her buttocks first, thank you, God. I was scared a foot or a knee would come first. Now push for me. That's good. One hip is out . . . and now the other. *Ai!* Her leg is squashed. Push for me again. Good. I have one shoulder now . . . and the other. Now wait, don't push! I'm going to turn her so her face is down. Good. Now push again. And here comes the back of her head . . . and I've got her. She is a fine, big girl." Sarah manages an unsteady laugh that is half a cry.

When Lena brings the child to her, Sarah sees that her legs are still held tightly against her abdomen. Sarah tries, gently, to straighten them, but they remain folded in, and the right hip and leg have dark red smudges of early bruising. Still, as strangely frog-like as she looks, she is a hearty little creature, and she latches onto Sarah's breast quickly.

By the end of the second week of her life, the baby has straightened her legs. The damage to her right leg from her breech delivery is severe, though, and the swelling has turned stiff and hard. She is miserable. Sarah, still unwell herself, asks George to help her grind together *buchu*, ginger, and dandelion with a pestle and mortar, as Lena has instructed her to do. They mix the herbs into a thick paste with charcoal and hot water, spread the mixture onto cheesecloth, and apply the poultice to the baby's swollen leg. They repeat the poulticing all day, and the next. Any improvement to the leg is infinitesimal—it remains swollen and hard—but its little owner appears less wretched, and Sarah takes that as an encouraging sign. Still, from a fear based almost in superstition, she is afraid to name the child, in case she loses her.

Bit by bit, George picks up the threads of running the mission station—receiving callers, preaching, baptizing, writing, riding to the Kowie River mouth to attend the opening of a new Methodist chapel, extinguishing the shopkeeper's chimney after it catches fire, trying to adjust differences between some of the church members, and excluding Ditz

Trompetter from the church for having used most disgusting and obscene language when quarreling with another woman. And, also bit by bit, Sarah and her newborn gain in strength.

On December 17, at first light, George has the wagon ready to go to Salem to fetch the older children home for the summer holidays. Sarah stands on the doorstep, watching the wagon sway and lurch its way down the hill. Three-year-old John, wearing new breeches for the first time, is making the journey with his father, and she listens to the running commentary of his piping voice as it fades into the distance: "I can see so far from up here.... Look at the cows up on the *koppie*, Papa.... I can see everything.... Is that an eagle?"

"No, I think it's a . . ." But by now they are too far away to hear. Sarah looks up and thinks she can spot a hawk. She holds her baby in her arms, while Jane waves with an up-and-down flap of her wrist for as long as that particular novelty lasts. Sarah thinks, *I shall see them by the end of day. . . . I shall see them by the end of day*, over and over, like a glad mantra.

When she watches her eldest daughter climb down from the wagon with lithe grace in the late afternoon, Sarah's postpartum emotions teeter. Five years ago, she had taken a girl-child to school, and now here is a girl-woman. The months-long stretches of time between the holidays are too much for a mother to keep track, as she ought.

"Oh, my dear girl!" Sarah says, hugging her namesake close with one arm as she cradles the baby in the other. She sniffs audibly but laughs to cover her tears. "How lovely you look!" She releases her to examine the bright eyes and the clear, pale skin, while she smoothes her hand over the dark hair highlighted with George's auburn.

Young Sarah giggles, and reaches to cup her baby sister's cheek. The other three come flocking around to see their youngest sibling.

"She's a rather large baby," says Edward, who is still small for his age.

"Oh, I love her," says Elizabeth, slipping a finger into her little sister's fist and smiling at the instinctive grip.

Ann stands on tiptoe for a closer look. Sarah shifts to give her a clearer vantage point.

On the Sunday before Christmas, the whole family of nine Barkers troops into the church. George preaches from the fourth Commandment about remembering to keep the Sabbath day holy, and then the congregation turns towards the back of the church as the family gathers around the font. Once again, Sarah's eyes are drawn to her eldest daughter, who is cradling their newest family member with the utmost care. Sarah remembers how George held their first child in the church at Bethelsdorp, as the dust motes hung suspended in a shaft of sunlight, when she was baptized. Almost twelve years later, she is holding her baby sister, who is wearing the same christening gown that their mother spent hours embroidering with a honeycomb smocking stitch.

"Dearly beloved," says George, "you have brought this child here to be baptized, you have prayed that our Lord Jesus Christ would vouchsafe to receive her, to cleanse her, and to sanctify her." He stoops to take the small bundle from young Sarah's arms, and says, "Name this child."

"Mary Ann," say her siblings in unison.

CHAPTER THIRTY-SIX

Bethelsdorp, February 14th, 1828

Dearest Sarah,

My first news is that on the morning I arrived, February 12th, Sister Elizabeth was delivered of a son—half-brother to Joseph and John, and younger brother to Alfred Robson, now but one year old. Mother and child are both well. Brother Robson informs me that they intend to name the child Cornelius, in honor of the older son of Dr. Johannes van der Kemp, who works now as an assistant at the mission station founded here by his father.

After my late start from Theopolis, I arrived at Bethelsdorp only at about two o'clock in the morning, much fatigued after the ride. Yesterday, I gathered with our friends for the Sunday School Anniversary, and I preached from Revelation: "Blessed is he that readeth, and they that hear the words of this prophecy, and keep those things which are written therein: for the time is at hand." I selected this passage since the Bible class was to read the 22nd chapter of Numbers, after which I catechized them. The report for the Sunday School was very pleasing & the meeting interesting. The resolutions were moved by

*Brother Robson, myself, Brother Read, Cornelius van der
Kemp, and others whom you do not know, and all were
seconded by the like number of Hottentots.*

*It is very hot here. This evening, I shall ride to
Cradock's town, and return here to take the services on
the Sabbath, both morning and evening. I plan to leave
Bethelsdorp between 2 & 3 o'clock next Monday morning
to return home, by way of Salem to visit the children.
Sister Elizabeth sends you her love, as do I.*

GB

O N MONDAY, Sarah can't settle to anything, knowing
George is on the road. She finds herself half-hoping
that he might surprise her and arrive early, as he has
done before. When he does get home, at about eight o'clock
on Wednesday morning, he brings with him news not only
about Bethelsdorp but also about the meetings of the anti-
slavery movement in England.

"It was much talked about amongst the Brethren at
Bethelsdorp," he says. "Dr. Philip has just published *Researches
in South Africa* in England, and the publicity surrounding his
book, combined with the high regard that the abolitionist
movement has in the public opinion, makes the issue of the
legal status of our people potentially embarrassing for the
government, so the timing is opportune for the cause."

"If they prevail, how soon do you think it would be before
we saw anything being put into practice here?" Sarah asks.

"There was much discussion about that. It appears that
Sir Charles Somerset has been permanently removed from
the position of governor, and we were in general agreement
that this bodes well for events to move forward in favor of
the Hottentots. I have greater faith and belief in Sir Richard
Bourke, and I believe he has done excellent work for the

cause in the two years he has been acting governor. However, rumor has it that Sir Richard will not be given the position permanently. There is talk of Sir Lowry Cole being transferred from his present governorship at Mauritius to come and govern at the Cape, and we should then have to wait to learn his views on the issues."

"And meanwhile?"

"Meanwhile, we continue to do the best work we can."

In the recurring cycle of comings and goings from the school at Salem, the children return home for the winter holidays, and the whole family gathers around the fire in the parlor after tea in the evening. Young James Read, now almost seventeen, is serving as a junior assistant at the mission station, and he comes to welcome the children home. Ann's eyes light up when she sees him.

George is working at his writing table assembling three small wooden picture frames that he has cut, mitered, and sanded for a series of watercolor portraits the three older girls have painted at the school. He seems to Sarah even more withdrawn than usual, and she tries to guess at a possible reason for his melancholy.

"Is this the portrait you painted?" James asks Ann.

"Yes."

"You've captured Elizabeth's likeness well."

Ann beams at him.

George taps a pin into the corner of a frame to secure it. "James, do you remember Brother Evan Evans, who presided over my ordination in Bethelsdorp?"

"I do indeed. I was only seven or eight at the time, but it made a deep impression on me."

"I received the sad news today that he died in Wales on January 29. I plan to give a kind of funeral sermon for him in the church tomorrow."

Now Sarah understands the reason for George's sadness. "How long had he been ill?" she asks.

"He began to suffer from ill-health in the early part of last year, I believe, and returned home last August," says George. He takes a soft cloth and rubs his fingerprints from the glass of the frame before placing the portrait facedown onto it. "Although I did not see him much over the years, we had corresponded regularly. He was a fine man, of good convictions, and I shall miss our exchanges."

Sarah thinks about Evan Evans going home to Wales to die. She wonders if she would want to go back to Shropshire if she knew that she was dying. Is that still her home, where she was born and had her formative years? Or is this her home now, here, where she and George have made a life, and where she has given birth to all her children? She doesn't know.

It is six weeks later, on August 1, that George receives the report of Ordinance Fifty from Acting Governor Richard Bourke, and he sends word to James to come and sit down for tea with the family. Watching George pour glasses of port for the three older members of the gathering around the high table, Sarah muses that it is almost worth it to live through his lows in order to witness his joys; the one extreme is as profound as the other. He has seldom been more buoyant than he is made now by this ordinance, so hard fought for, by so many people, and so conclusively won. For as long as George and Sarah have been engaged in their mission work in Africa, the Khoikhoi—those who didn't come under the protection of the mission stations—have suffered under an indentured labor so stringent as to be close to slavery. At long last, this ordinance from the acting governor will begin to redress that.

With grace said, tea poured, and plates filled, George reads aloud the salient points of the ordinance. "It states that henceforward, *Hottentots and other free persons of color are to be subject to no laws to which Europeans are not also subject.* I believe that this would include the pass requirements and the so-called 'vagrancy' practices. Freedom to move and freedom to own land are also explicitly decreed, as are all contracts of service."

"Does this mean any law that makes a distinction between Europeans and persons of color will be forbidden?" asks Sarah.

"It does not, as yet, address the Xhosa people, but as it relates to other free non-European inhabitants of the Colony, yes."

"And so the equality of our people at Theopolis and Bethelsdorp and beyond would be decreed by law?"

"Yes."

There is a silence at the table as this sinks in.

"When will this ordinance be the law of the land?" James asks.

"The British Parliament must still ratify it," says George. "Even then, it will remain to be seen if the laws that are written on paper will be executed in life."

"But it is a start," says Sarah.

"It is a start," agrees George.

One of the first indications of the new order comes in September. George is away at Bethelsdorp for the opening of the new chapel at Port Elizabeth when Sarah is drawn outside by a clamor of men calling, horses whinnying, women ululating. She stands at her doorway shading her eyes, watching as women and children streak down the slope towards a group of men on horseback. The small valley echoes with shouting, cheering, singing, even a rifle shot fired into the air by a rider at the back. The commando that was called up in readiness against the threatened invasion of the Xhosa has come home. The closer they get to the village, the more people join, until there is a seething mass of pure jubilation. Sarah goes to greet them.

When he sees her, Sergeant Klaas Klaas jumps down from his horse, pulls off his hat, and holds it over his chest, beaming at her. "We got the order this morning, Sister Sarah. We were free to go."

When George reaches home late that night, finding all well and the people all returned from the commando, he says, "This is thanks to the ordinance from the acting governor. It abolishes all forms of compulsory service for our mission residents."

Next morning, he comes to the breakfast table with a copy of London's *Morning Chronicle*. "The paper gives an account of a resolution passed in Parliament on the motion of Sir Thomas Fowell Buxton, who is the leader of the abolition movement in the British House of Commons. He is the one who assisted Dr. John Philip in drawing up the motion respecting the Hottentots—and now the Duke of Wellington's cabinet has supported the motion."

"It's official, then?" says Sarah.

"It is. May the people appreciate the advantage they have received."

PART SIX

Chapter Thirty-Seven

AS THE MOMENTOUS YEAR OF 1828 winds down and the days grow hot, the family—all of them, the older children being home again for the holidays—ride down to the sea to spend a few days there. Edward is still a little fellow for seven years old, but he is bright and gregarious, and much revered by John, two-and-a-half years his junior. The three older girls are lissome and slender, with a blend of pale skin and auburn hair that clearly marks them as sisters, though each has her distinct personality—Sarah responsible and demure, Elizabeth with a tendency to take charge, and Ann spilling over with love. Mary Ann has passed her first birthday, and even though the unevenness of the dry, silky sea sand flummoxes her, she can get up quite a head of walking speed along the firm sand near the waves. In the normal routine of their lives, Jane is a happy minder of her baby sister, but now she is much too entranced with her older siblings and trails around in their wake. George in his shirtsleeves and Sarah under her parasol sit on the blanket with their shoulders touching, watching their seven offspring cavorting at the water's edge.

"With God's will, there will be an eighth come June," Sarah says.

George sits perfectly still for a few moments. Then he shifts to put his arm around her and pull her against his body. He says, his mouth against her ear, "I pray you will not suffer."

Full of sun and languor, their skin prickly with sea salt, the family rides back to the mission station on the extremely hot morning of the last day of the year. As the day begins to cool toward evening, they all gather together with the people of Theopolis for a prayer meeting to close out the year of 1828.

And here, George's diaries abruptly end. After the last entry on December 31, 1828, he wrote:

> *This ends the Fourteenth Year since I left my Father's house to sojourn in a strange Land. Mercy & goodness have followed me all the way. Here I erect an Ebenezer & say, Thus far the Lord hath helped me.*

Then, there's nothing more.

When I first made this discovery, on a Monday in August 2012, I was in the Special Collections Reading Room at the National Library of South Africa in Cape Town. At first, I thought there'd been some mistake; that not all the photocopied diaries had been brought over for me from the off-site vault. But no. There is no trace of any further diary at the National Library of South Africa, or at the Cory Library in Grahamstown, or in the London Missionary Society's archives at the School of Oriental and African Studies in London.

As all my searches for more dairies turned up fruitless, my disappointment felt as if it would tip over into despair. I had lost my only conduit to Sarah—as tenuous as it was. How could I possibly find her to try to fill in the rest of her life? What about the child she was carrying at the end of

1828? How would I be able to trace the slim genealogical thread that links me directly to her? I felt the loss of her as sharply as if she had died in my lifetime.

My mourning for her spanned a time of very present grieving. On the eve of America's Independence Day in 2013, my brother Peter called me from Cape Town to tell me that our mother had died. The distance stretched between us over the Atlantic as I listened to the silence, unable to speak, trying to make sense of this news. It was only because of my mother that I had the link to Sarah at all, and the threads of loss twisted and meshed together.

Three months later, my brother's fight with cancer took a sudden, fatal turn, and he died two hours before I was about to leave for the airport to go to him. My grieving became unmanageable. When I spoke, the words came out in uncoordinated lurches, and the weight of sorrow was so overwhelming that, months later, I had to get out of bed in the small hours of the night and crouch down, sobbing in raw cries that sounded inhuman even in my own ears.

My mother lived to the wonderful age of 97, and so although the actuality of her loss was worse than I could have imagined, we knew that she was living on borrowed time for years, and every day was like a gift. Peter, though, was too young to die, and the fact that I didn't get to him in time made his death unbearable. It was these feelings that I drew on when I tried to imagine Sarah's unfathomable sorrow at losing a child.

But as she learned, and as I did, too, time does heal—to a certain extent—as they say it does, and when I turned to Sarah again, I discovered that I could find other ways back to her.

I made a follow-up visit to the National Library of South Africa in Cape Town in June 2017. The Special Collections Reading Room there has that contemplative, almost church-like air that is a hallmark of all the archives and libraries where I have gone searching for Sarah. It is a gentle room with natural light filtering through five tall, arched, wooden sash windows that face onto the avenue leading to the Company's Garden, where Sarah had surely once walked.

Again, the box marked MSB57 BARKER, GEORGE, had been pre-ordered on my behalf from the off-site manuscript collections, and it waited for me on one of the long, gleaming tables. The box contains folders with photocopies of George's diaries from 1815 up to—and stopping abruptly at—1828. Most precious of all, the box also contains a file of some of George's original letters, written on thick, creamy paper with sepia ink in his handsome copperplate.

Although you are allowed to photograph the materials in the Cory Library in Grahamstown and the School of Oriental and African Studies in London, you may not at the National Library of South Africa—at least, not in the Special Collections Reading Room. So, I took out my black Moleskine notebook, pressed out the crease to start a new page, and began to transcribe the letters.

Chapter Thirty-Eight

IMAGINE AN AIR of quiet industry in the parlor in Theopolis. Every now and then a candle fizzes or a log collapses and sends out sparks in the grate. A moth knocks intermittently against the latticed windowpane as if it wants to become part of the cozy glow inside and escape the cool September evening that hasn't yet quite turned to spring.

George's pen scratches on the page, punctuated by pauses when he dips it in the inkpot, taps off excess ink, and then resumes the scratching. Sarah is hemming a calico-print dress that one of the women finished at the sewing class earlier in the day. Young Sarah, now nearing eighteen, is preparing lessons for the mission's infant school, where she teaches upwards of a hundred children ranging in age from eighteen months to seven years old. Her pupils include her four youngest siblings—Jane aged seven; Mary Ann, five; young George Nathaniel, four; and Harriet, aged three, the youngest of the Barker brood that now numbers nine.

Jane has at last recovered from her long, mysterious illness, and she looks sleek and plump as she sits at young Sarah's feet teaching Mary Ann how to plait her hair. They are doing it with a kind of dumb show because they know better than to make a noise when their father is writing at his desk. Little George and Harriet are absorbed in paging through a precious picture book newly published by Dean & Munday on Threadneedle Street in London, and mailed by their Uncle John Williams.

George lays down his pen. When he speaks, Sarah gives a little start since it had been so long since anyone has said a word. "I'm replying to my sister Betsy's letter," he says. "I believe the simple fact of Walden having become an electioneering town, as she informs us, will make the people of Wimbish politicians. I am glad Betsy gave us this information—little pieces of news like this are cheering." He picks up his sister's letter and scans it again. "I should really like to hear what my father and Thomas say of the man for whom they voted. If Betsy had told us, I should then have known whether they are Whig or Tory."

"Do you suppose that news has reached them about Parliament's resolution on the emancipation of slaves?" Sarah asks.

"Surely. This is what I have written Betsy about it." He hands his unfinished letter to Sarah, and she holds it up to the candlelight to read.

Thank God this will be an honour to Britain. I am not in the way of slavery, there are none in this part, the Settlers were prohibited from having any at the first, but there are about Thirty Thousand slaves in this Colony, and at Cape Town men are sold every week like cattle, every week slaves advertised for sale in the news papers. Many people at Cape Town live like gentlemen by letting out their slaves, slaves constitute their riches. O! What a blessing it will be when slavery is no more. I sent the Government Ordinance to Thomas, which made the

*Hottentots free, for they were formerly as bad as slaves but
thank God they are free. Slavery destroys all the feelings
of humanity. It makes the masters tyrants and the slaves
brutes, but many in this colony are sadly annoyed at the
prospect of losing their property in men.*

Sarah hands the letter back to George. "Let us hope it
will soon come to pass," she says. "The emancipation will
bring about great change, I think, considering the changes
we have seen here amongst our people."

"Yes, the civil freedom of the people is working wonders
every day. In fact, their state is so much improved that they
no longer need the protection of the mission and many are
now impatient of the restraints necessitated by institutional
life." He stares into the fire for a moment. "I cannot help but
wish that so many of our best people—people like Cobus
Boezak—had not departed for Kat River."

A hundred families with eighteen ploughs, twenty wagons, and nine hundred head of cattle have left Theopolis
for the settlement that James Read Senior has set up at Kat
River so that the people can own the land they work. When
it had come time for Sarah to say goodbye to Cobus, she'd
felt a sense of deep sorrow and loss. He was an integral part
of Theopolis for her, and she feels the place diminished
without his energetic presence. "I must suppose that this is
how we serve them, though," she says, "to help them become
free and independent again."

George studies her. Then he nods. "And despite the
loss, the Sunday morning congregation is still four hundred
strong. There also seems to be an increased interest in agriculture at the institution."

"And the sewing school continues to encourage habits of
purpose and industry," says Sarah.

"I daresay we still continue to fulfill our mission," says
George.

Sarah looks over at her namesake, who has been following the conversation with interest. Both her older daughters are living examples of what Sarah means: she has loved them, nurtured, supported, and encouraged them, and they are now ready to make their own way in the world—Sarah running the infant school at Theopolis and Elizabeth at Salem assisting Mrs. Matthews in the duties of her boarding school. Ann, about to turn fifteen, will be home from school next year, and then it will be time for her to begin finding her own path too.

Young Sarah smiles at her mother, and then stands up. "Come along, children," she says. "It is time for bed."

As the four young children trail after their eldest sister, George comes and sits by the fire. "It has been in my mind also to write a letter to the directors in London. At the end of next year, if spared, I shall have completed a period of twenty years service, and I feel a great desire once more to visit our native land."

Sarah is too taken aback to formulate a response.

"Since the last letter which I received from my parents in June informed me that they were then both living," says George, "I have been often ruminating whether my father and mother may not have been spared to see me yet again, and I should like to see them once more in the flesh."

"Are you weary of the missionary work?" Sarah asks.

"Far from it. Should my request be complied with, I have no desire to remain in England, or to leave Africa to see it no more. Yet I do feel a strong desire to refresh my spirits among those whom I esteem. Another reason is that Edward would be fourteen years of age by then, and, really, the prospect of apprenticing him to advantage in this colony is so dreary that I wish I could get him home for that purpose." He is starting to speak more quickly now, as if trying to fill her silence. "I should prefer printing and bookbinding for him, as he might then be of essential service to the missions, a printer being much wanted in connection with our work here in Africa."

"So you would take him with you?"

"Oh, indeed! If I went, I should not leave any part of my family behind. But our family is so large, and the expense would be so great, that I fear my request shall miscarry. Were it otherwise, I might stand a chance of going. A passage may be taken at Algoa Bay so as to save the cost of going to Cape Town to embark, and the elder children accompanying me may be of service to the course. Our Sarah is now as efficient for the work in our infant school as any one in this part of the colony, yet a visit to England would tend still more greatly to her improvement. In any event, I shall make the request and, if refused, shall not be disappointed."

"Do you still consider England home?"

He is quiet for a moment, considering her question. A log subsides in the grate. "I should like to see my family once again," he says, "but have no desire to remain among them. Their winters are too cold. Our children do not know what ice is. And I am not so anxious about leaving our family behind us in the colony now. Its aspect is so much improved, and is improving, so there is a prospect of a comfortable living for industrious people. We have been able to procure a fair education for the elder children and can leave them to the providence of God." He shifts the log with his boot, and a flame flares. "And you?"

"This is my home now," she says.

CHAPTER THIRTY-NINE

O! What a blessing it will be when slavery is no more.

I WAS IN THE NATIONAL LIBRARY of South Africa when
I first read these words that George wrote in a letter to
his youngest sister Elizabeth, on September 16, 1833, and
I felt a flush of relief run over my whole body.

During my years-long search for Sarah, the more urgently
I dug into her story to find her, the more afraid I became
of what I might uncover—like someone on one of those
television shows, *Finding Your Roots* or *Who Do You Think
You Are?*, finding out that their ancestors were slave owners.
I was already so invested in her that I didn't know what I
would do if I unearthed information that showed George
or Sarah, or both, as colonizing racists. I couldn't gloss over
the way that George referred to the traditional healing and
beliefs of the Khoikhoi as "witchcraft" in his journal. He was
there to evangelize about Christianity, and evangelize he did.

In another letter to his sister, George wrote, *From our
schools we hope to see a new and improved race of natives spring
up, whose knowledge will be much more extensive and their
habits and manners every way superior to the present race.* The

Khoikhoi—the "present race" he refers to—were certainly different from the English, but by what standards would their habits and manners be made "superior" through the mission schools? And when he wrote, *The Hottentots have improved in industrious and provident habits during the twenty years I have known them, far beyond your conception, still they are below the English standard*, it is all too clear that he held the English standard to be superior. But who is to say?

The Age of Discovery that saw Francis Drake, Christopher Columbus, Vasco da Gama, and others fanning out across the earth during the fifteenth and sixteenth centuries must have been as thrilling as the Space Age during the twentieth century. My mother and I huddled over our transistor radio on July 20, 1969, to listen to the crackle of history when Neil Armstrong took his "one small step for man, one giant leap for mankind" on the surface of the moon. The apartheid government regarded television as the "devil's own box, for disseminating communism and immorality," so we couldn't join the rest of the world in watching the historic step on the screen, although I've watched it many times since. Perhaps when Sir Francis sailed into Plymouth on September 26, 1580, after circumnavigating the earth, there was an epoch equivalent of Walter Cronkite announcing, "Man on the moon!" followed by, "Whew! Boy!" and a laugh as he took off his glasses and rubbed his hands together in pure glee.

But when those early forays of discovery around the world began to catch and snag on the Americas and South Africa and India, when trading posts became possessions and turned into the fodder of empire building, it was like lava inexorably shifting a landscape. It's not enough to say that all societies have been colonized to some extent—whether it might have been the migration of black Africans into the

KhoiSan regions of southern Africa in the fourth century, or the Norman conquests in Britain during the eleventh century. Even though our global history is shot through with pockets of colonialism, too much of it had devastating consequences—to the extent that the term "colonist" is now as pejorative as the word "Hottentot" became.

Growing up in an unbalanced, dysfunctional society is what I imagine it must be like to grow up in an abusive family. It is all you know, your family dynamic, and you accept it as such. As you begin to disengage, though, and air and light from the outside world begin to stir the sediment, you start to recognize it objectively for what it is. In the broad sweep of colonialism, then, and in the particular case of black Africa, I had to wonder if I could dare to hope to have a story that wasn't tainted by colonialism, or one that had any legitimate relevance at all. If Sarah, as a white missionary settler, had planted me in Africa, did her story matter?

Well, it did to me. Even if it didn't fall into the narrative of black Africa, it was the only story I had. And it mattered to me not only because Sarah was my bloodline—if *her* story was irrelevant, then so was mine—but because, with the exception of aborigine groups like the southern African San from the Stone Age, we've *all* come from somewhere else. South Africa, like America, is a hodgepodge with its multilayering of San, Khoikhoi, black African, Portuguese, Dutch, Malay, French, German, English, Jewish.

But still, I was haunted. Migration is one thing, but forcing your ideas down someone else's throat is quite another—and colonialism, imperialism, call it what you will, exaggerates that a thousandfold. What if I was wrong about Sarah and George?

Then I read those letters in the National Library in Cape Town, and I hovered over phrases like, *It is really astonishing how soon men become imbued with prejudice against those who happen to differ from them in colour,* and, *You perceive how the welfare of the native rests solely on the missionaries.* At a time when Britain was still in the process of abolishing slavery throughout its empire; in a society that considered Britain to be the superior nation; during an age when women were still barred from owning property or voting, George, it seemed to me, had been on the right side of history.

Ultimately, it made no difference. Apartheid, with all its ugly ramifications, still became entrenched in law a hundred years later. But I was flooded with relief to know that Sarah and George had stood against its fledgling form. Very few have the power to bring about change in history. But in the minute, all-but-forgotten microcosm of their particular place and time, they tried to make a difference. And that made all the difference to me.

Chapter Forty

"I hear that I am threatened with a prosecution," George says.

Sarah is setting the table for tea, but she stops and stares at him, horrified, with a plate suspended in her hand.

"My letter was published in the *Grahamstown Journal* about that disgusting and uncalled-for outrage that I witnessed toward the Xhosa Chief." He pulls out his chair at the head of the table and flops down. "The letter has been applauded by all well-meaning people, but gave umbrage to the parties concerned."

"But I thought you simply signed your letters '*Philanthropist.*'"

"It appears I have been discovered. My efforts have been attacked, but in a very feeble manner. I doubt that it will come to anything." George seems sanguine enough, so Sarah carries on about her business of preparing the tea. "I believe the time is gone past when oppression can be practiced with impunity," he says. "Our press is the balance of power, and I hope to see the Xhosa treated as men and not as brutes."

"Does the press take up your point of view?"

"It depends. From the very beginning, there has been

an outcry from certain quarters against the ordinance that put the Hottentots on an equal footing with the Europeans, and now there is a measure on foot that will tend to nullify that law should the act pass. The editor of one of the Cape Town papers advocates the cause of the natives, the other paper the contrary." Sarah lays cutlery in front of him and he absentmindedly straightens it, though it's quite straight already. "Dr. John Philip has written against it in the Cape Town papers and addressed a petition against the measure to the Legislative Council. I have written three letters to the *Grahamstown Journal* against the introduction of the proposed law—and I am now expecting abuse."

"Did you observe when we were last in Grahamstown how even some of the settlers lately from England treat the non-Europeans poorly?" asks Sarah.

"Yes, and I perceive how the welfare of the natives rests solely on us missionaries. Here is an ordinance proposed aiming at the people's liberty, and not an individual to defend their right but the missionaries."

The tea is ready, and Sarah calls the family to the table. With all the children home for the winter vacation, there is a boisterous commotion of footsteps, scraped chairs, and voices pitched from shrill to mellow. After he has said grace and shaken out his napkin, George picks up the conversation again, in the way that he likes to do to encourage discussion about the topics of the day around the table.

"It is a universal fact," he says, "that when civilized men come in contact with uncivilized, they always encroach on the rights of their neighbors. The strong oppress. It is really astonishing how soon men become imbued with prejudice against those who happen to differ from them in color."

Edward says, "Mr. Matthews has informed us of the manner in which the African slaves have been treated in the American colonies."

"Precisely," says his father, "and I doubt but that the English folks who are emigrating to America feel indignant at the manner in which the blacks have been treated there. But I can tell them, from effects which we have witnessed among our settlers, that it will be a miracle if they keep above the prejudices for any length of time. I wish I could give them a lecture before they embark."

"But our people at Theopolis don't look so different, Father," says Ann, referring back to his earlier comment. "Why would they be treated differently?"

"To use their own expression," says George, "*A Hottentot is a Hottentot*, and by that I mean that some people continue to view them and treat them as degraded beings under all circumstances, and in all places, and with all they come in contact with. If he seeks employment, his wages are beat down. If he takes an article to the market, he is generally taken advantage of. If he enters a shop with money in his hand, he is looked upon with disdain. And the only reason is—or, if I may so express it, his unpardonable *sin* is—he is a Hottentot. If he is travelling with the wagon, those who have one, he must not unyoke his oxen here, nor there, because he is a Hottentot. It is unimaginable the effect which such prejudices produce on the aborigine mind!"

George's voice has become tight with anger. He takes a deep breath. There is absolute silence at the table. When George speaks again, his voice is calmer. "But why fear? Our work must prosper, the cause of God will triumph. Justice, humanity, and right shall prevail against oppression, and English liberty shall be established because it is based on the Word of God."

With Ann and her two brothers home from school, George wishes them to write to his parents. The two older girls clear away the tea things, and take Jane, Mary Ann, young George, and Harriet to get them ready for bed. The cold July night is beginning to close in, so Sarah brings candles, and the letter writers settle down with pen, ink, and paper at the table. Sarah is in the process of sewing a jacket for John, and she joins the children at the table to pull taut the gathering for the tops of the sleeves and set them into the armholes. From time to time, she glances over at her scribblers to watch their progress.

Ann's script is beautiful, and her face is a study of concentration as she makes careful sweeps of the pen to create elegant copperplate loops. Her penmanship is so much more graceful, Sarah thinks, than the elementary lettering she had learned herself as a girl. With the conversation around the tea table evidently still on her mind, Ann writes, *Most of the Hottentots begin to assume the appearance of Europeans as most of them wear shirts, very few of the Sheepskin cloaks are to be seen now, only one or two of the very old people. Their manner of living is very simple. They have a bucket with a pot or two and almost all of them with a teakettle for they are very fond of tea. Some of them have a table and a form*—Sarah interprets this as a long seat—*or two or three three-footed stools with a chest in which they keep all their riches, clothing, money, basins, spoons, and plates if they have any.*

"When you have finished," says George, "leave room at the bottom of the page for me to add a post script."

"Yes, Father," says Ann.

"I intended that the two elder girls should have written," their father says, "but the postage of so many letters all at once would have come heavy."

"They have written before," says Sarah, "and they can write again another time."

When it is Edward's turn, he writes, *As we are all at home for the midsummer holidays (or rather midwinter there) Father wishes us all to write to you.* Sarah thinks how like him it is to take that leap of understanding into someone else's season. Edward writes about his siblings, and the infant school, and ends with an account of a journey he took with George: *Last April I rode to Algoa Bay with my Father on horseback a distance of about one hundred and twenty miles, in two days, to attend an auxiliary missionary meeting, and as we were coming home we had to wade a very deep river, which rather frightened me. At School I learn History, Grammar, and Geography, and am as far as Vulgar Fractions, in Arithmetic. Give my love to all my friends.*

John is rather more formal. He begins, *It is with much pleasure I now take up my pen to write a few lines to you. I am a little boy, my name is John Williams Barker. I am ten years old and live in Theopolis where there are all Hottentots. Some Hottentots have very curious names. Our chief Magistrates are Class Hunter, Piet Hunter, Willem Sailor, Valentine Jacobs.* John's letter is the shortest, and Sarah is touched that he devotes a fair portion of it to her: *Mother is quite well and busy making a jacket. Mother makes all my clothes except one jacket I have made by a Tailor.*

John is proudly sporting his new jacket when winter starts to turn to spring, and the cycle of leaving comes around again. It is time for him to return to the school at Salem with Elizabeth and Edward.

CHAPTER FORTY-ONE

GEORGE IS BECOMING agitated by the surges of cattle raids being carried out by the Xhosa people in the Albany region. In the summer, broiling tensions spill over sporadically into the buffer zone between the Fish and the Keiskamma Rivers, and herds of settler cattle are brought to Theopolis for safekeeping. On December 11, 1834, a newspaper headline blares, CAPE GOVERNMENT COMMANDO PARTY KILLS CHIEF OF HIGH RANK.

On Christmas Eve, a Wednesday, Sarah is on her knees in front of the washtub in the kitchen, bathing Harriet. Little George has finished his bath and is dressing himself in the fire's glow, his damp hair spiking up at the crown of his head. So gradually that Sarah can't be sure when she first became aware of it, she hears a strange, throbbing sound that seems to echo through the valley from the far distance. She can't place it. It is unlike anything she's ever heard before. She lifts her head to listen and imagines that she can hear isolated shouts rising above the curious hum. She sits back on her heels, her motions arrested, trying to make out what the sound could be.

The back door of the kitchen bursts open with such sudden force that it crashes against the wall, making Harriet cry out with fright. Willem Valentyn stands silhouetted in the doorway.

"Sister Sarah! The Xhosa are coming! Thousands of them. Where is Brother Barker?"

"I don't know—the smithy, I think."

"I will look for him. Come! We must all go to the schoolhouse. We will be safer all together there. You go! I will go find the others."

Willem runs out, leaving the outside door ajar, and Sarah pulls Harriet out of the tub, enveloping her in a towel. "Get dressed quickly," she says, speaking in a low voice so as not to alarm the child still further. "I will go and fetch your sisters. George," she looks over at her youngest son, "stay here with Harriet. Don't either of you move until I come back!"

She runs through the house, calling for young Sarah, Ann, Jane, and Mary Ann. "Bring your mantles, and come through the kitchen! We will take as much food as we can carry."

As Sarah and her six children make their way over to the schoolhouse, they join a throng of people from all over the village already streaming in that direction. Willem Valentyn has done his job well. There is a bottleneck of people at the door of the schoolhouse, and people start to shove and shout in their panic.

"Stay calm!" George raises a clear voice over the uproar, catching back the panic just as it is about to peak. "There is room for everyone. Form two queues, and we will all get inside more quickly that way."

The noise that had so puzzled Sarah is now a rumble, and as the last stragglers from the village are urged inside the schoolroom and the door is closed and bolted, the first wave of Xhosa warriors swarms over the hills. There, they stop, still some distance from Theopolis, and their seething presence hangs in the air.

Willem is talking to George in a low, urgent voice, and Sarah moves closer to hear.

"Already, Chief Maqoma has gathered an army of ten thousand men," Willem is saying, "and they have swarmed over the frontier, killing, looting, burning . . ."

"I knew there would be terrible repercussions after that Xhosa chief was killed," says George.

"Our friends at Kat River have been hard hit."

"They are coming!" shouts Klaas Klaas.

Willem whips around, takes up his rifle propped against the wall, and runs to a window next to the door. From where she stands, Sarah can see a phalanx of Xhosa pounding down the hill toward the village. Willem props open the window, lifts his rifle, and Sarah watches as the tension drops away from his body. He squeezes one eye shut, pulls almost gently against the trigger, and the report echoes round the schoolroom. There is a spurt of disruption in the Xhosa mass. At the other window, Klaas echoes Willem's shot and also hits his mark, making the phalanx scatter into more disarray. Willem calmly reloads, fires again, and brings down another warrior. By now, other men have joined Klaas and Willem at the windows and add to their fire. The Xhosa try to regroup, scatter again under fire, and then finally retreat, carrying their dead with them.

Sarah has often heard of the deadly accurate shooting of the Khoikhoi. She never imagined she would have to witness it. The stench of gun smoke hangs in the room. A child whimpers.

Willem calls over to Klaas, "How many guns have we got?"

"Twenty-five. Some unserviceable."

Like Klaas, some of the others from the commando called up that November in 1827 are still settled at Theopolis, and now they organize a watch at the windows as dusk comes in. Sarah takes stock of her children. Little George, at five and a half years old, is on the brink between frightened and fascinated. Harriet is wide-eyed and has wedged herself securely between young Sarah and Ann, becoming a little tremulous if either of them moves. Seeing that they are safe enough, Sarah sets off around the room, stopping at a family group here and there, to offer what help and comfort she can.

There is no further movement from the Xhosa, but the threat isn't gone. As the shadows get longer, there is a pinprick of fire on the slope of the hill overlooking Theopolis—then another, and another. By nightfall, the refugees in the schoolhouse are completely surrounded by the jumping fires of the invaders on the hills. As the flickering lights hover, seemingly suspended, they look to Sarah like some looming, malevolent creature. Surely, it will be impossible to sleep with this threat hanging over them.

Daybreak has only just warmed the eastern *koppie* when the watchman calls out, "Three of them are coming."

George scrambles up from where he had fallen into an exhausted sleep just an hour ago, wrapped together with Sarah in her mantle. "I'll need a translator, please," he calls.

Sarah rises, too, and pulls the mantle around her. She is stiff and chilled, despite the summer warmth. *This is Christmas Day*, she thinks. George and the translator walk to the door of the schoolroom, and he pulls back the bolts. Willem, unbidden, pushes a pistol into the back of his waistband where it is hidden by his jacket, and he walks outside with George and the translator. Sarah edges to the window so that she can see her husband. As the two parties walk toward each other, George raises his hands in a show of peace. He comes to a standstill in front of a powerfully built man with a balding head, high cheekbones, and a broad nose. His prominent collarbones are etched under his dark, gleaming skin in the morning light. George is a tall man, but he looks utterly vulnerable as he stands, bareheaded, turning from the translator to the Xhosa warrior and back again, to conduct this peculiar exchange. After what feels like an age to Sarah but is probably no more than five minutes, George and his two companions turn away and walk back towards the schoolhouse, while the three Xhosa men walk back up the hill. Sarah realizes that her fingernails are biting into her palms, and she unclenches her fists.

"That was Chief Maqoma himself," says George, raising his voice so that everyone in the schoolhouse can hear him. "He says that Salem and Grahamstown have been overwhelmed." Sarah is winded with shock—*Elizabeth, Edward, John, overwhelmed in Salem!* "He told me that we are completely surrounded, and we are threatened with death if we do not submit at once." A murmur stirs the attentive silence. "Now, I must tell you," says George, "that I shall not submit. It is my duty to protect our village and the institution to the utmost of my ability. But it is a choice that I cannot make for you. If you wish to submit, then you must do so. I would caution, however, that there is no way of knowing what would become of you if you did. Chief Maqoma will return tomorrow for my answer."

Salem and Grahamstown have been overwhelmed.... Salem and Grahamstown have been overwhelmed.... George's words run in a loop through Sarah's mind. Had the children found shelter in the church at Salem? Were soldiers from Lombards Post stationed there, as they have been during other threats? Throughout the day, as she tries to find enough food to go around for the refugees, as she smilingly speaks words of comfort to the families taking shelter in the schoolhouse, her mind is at Salem. *Salem and Grahamstown have been overwhelmed.* Over and over again, she drags her mind back from the verge of her worst fears, and refuses to think them.

When she comes to Lena, sitting with her daughter and granddaughter, Sarah's brave façade cracks. "Elizabeth and Edward and John are at Salem," she says, her low voice shaking as she speaks out loud for the first time the terrible fact that is crowding her mind.

"*Ai!*" says Lena. "Why aren't they home for Christmas?"

"Elizabeth had to stay behind with some of the children from Mrs. Matthews' school, and her brothers were going to come home with her in the New Year."

Lena takes Sarah's hands in her hard, capable ones, and Sarah sees her own worry reflected back in the beloved face of this woman who has helped her give birth to the three children who are now so vulnerable in Salem. "If we are still safe, then they are surely also safe," says Lena. Sarah tries to believe her.

Men from the old commando covertly escort families, one by one, to and from their homes to fetch food or clothes or medicines, but the schoolhouse is their refuge, as hot and crowded and airless as it is. In this close proximity, it takes just one baby crying to start up a cycle of screaming children and shushing adults and frayed nerves. Faces gleam with perspiration. There is an acrid smell of fear.

George prays with the people. "O God, you have bound us together in a common life. Help us, in the midst of our struggles for justice and truth, to confront one another without hatred or bitterness, and to work together with mutual forbearance and respect; through Jesus Christ our Lord."

"Amen," comes the uneven rumble of voices from around the room.

Sarah watches George stepping carefully through the refugees, talking to them, trying to get a sense of whether they will go or stay. In the evening, he holds a Christmas service, and the nativity story of the young family taking refuge in a stable has never seemed more apt. Sleep, such as it is, is fitful and intermittent, and, at daybreak once again, the call comes that Chief Maqoma is approaching the village. When George goes out to meet him this time, the exchange is shorter.

When George returns with Willem and the interpreter, and the schoolroom door is bolted again, he says, "I told Chief Maqoma that I would not submit, and that the people of Theopolis have informed me they will not submit either. He is displeased. He reiterated that we are completely surrounded, and again threatened death if we do not surrender. He says that he will give us one more day to think about it."

George holds prayers for the people. They eat, wash, and relieve themselves as best they can, and they hope for sleep at night. Sarah tries to be a comfort to the people, and she takes some consolation from that herself. But when she stops, even for a moment, thoughts of Salem squeeze into her mind, adrenaline races through her, and she has to turn away to hide her welling tears. She *has* to appear strong for the people and her family, and the pretense holds her terrified imaginings at bay.

The next day, Chief Maqoma doesn't make his dawn appearance, and Sarah can guess from the strained faces around her that the people feel as apprehensive and unsettled as she does, not knowing what to expect, to fear, to hope. When the chief and his entourage come down the hill around midmorning, his exchange with George is more vehement, and Sarah can hear his raised voice through the open window. George's face is drawn and pale when he comes back to the schoolhouse. He is clearly shaken by the chief's outburst.

"The chief's patience is wearing thin," he tells the crowded schoolroom. "He says that the longer we delay, the worse it will be for us. Again, I must say to you that you are free to make your own decision about whether to stay or to surrender."

There is silence. No one moves, or even shifts.

George nods. "Then, let us pray." He bows his head and leads them in prayer. In a far corner of the room, a woman starts a low, keening song. Other women join, and then the men. Soon the whole room is awash with the interweaving harmonies of this ancient music of the Khoikhoi. Sarah looks across at George, her eyes brimming over. George comes to join his family and they all sit, surrounded—embraced, almost—by the voices of their people.

It is a turning point. The chief does not come the next day, or the next, and the suspense of waiting drags from minute to minute. As unsettling as these meetings have been, they've become familiar, and the absence feels ominous. Food and water are getting low, and the air is fetid with unwashed bodies. And yet the people are taking endurance from one another. What could so easily have been a melee of panicky self-serving has instead become formidable resolution. For the next two days, Chief Maqoma sends his deputies to talk to George, and George continues to relay the steadfast message that Theopolis will not surrender. And, all the while, the thoughts haunt Sarah: *Salem and Grahamstown have been overwhelmed. . . . Salem and Grahamstown have been overwhelmed. . . .*

On New Year's Day, there is no morning visitation from either Chief Maqoma or his deputies. George decides to lead the morning prayers early, preaching from Psalm Eight about how the simple, unquestioning faith "out of the mouth of babes and sucklings" could give them strength to silence the enemies who were seeking to overcome them. But as he preaches, Sarah hears the same strange, throbbing sound that she heard in the kitchen on Christmas Eve. One by one, the people catch the sound, and George breaks off. Added to the sound now are calling and stampeding.

"The cattle!" shouts Willem Valentyn.

By the time they reach the windows and the pull back the bolts of the doors, the Xhosa are driving a herd of cattle up into the hills. The people stand, helpless, as the cattle disappear over the ridge, with the dust left hanging where their hooves have stirred it up. The tension of the week and the outrage over the loss spill over into fury and confusion, and George has to shout to be heard above the din.

"Brothers and sisters! Brothers and sisters! We must remain calm. It is the only way. We will put all our lives in danger if we pit our paltry selves against the Xhosa masses." Gradually, the uproar begins to subside, and George can speak more quietly. "We will set up guards to try to stop further incursions, but the most important thing is that we protect our community and keep ourselves safe."

"But if they can steal our cattle from under our noses, it will make them more bold," says Willem. "What if they rush us?"

"It is in God's hands. We must stand firm, but without provocation."

Klaas Klaas organizes the men to guard the cattle in twos, and the refugees in the schoolhouse fidget and fret, all semblance of their routine during the previous week evaporated. An old woman drops a bowl by mistake and the clatter makes the whole mass rise as one in fright. Sarah keeps careful watch over her two youngest children in particular, their eyes overlarge in their pale faces. And the undercurrent of agitation about the three at Salem remains a constant, strident pedal note.

As night closes in and people try to settle down to sleep, the restless turning and whispering throughout the schoolhouse sounds to Sarah like the disturbed flurry of bird wings. George comes over to be with his family, and he has hardly sat down before his body slides prone, and he falls into such a dead sleep of pure exhaustion that Sarah puts her ear to his chest to be sure that his heart is still beating, like that time seventeen years ago when she nearly lost him to the bilious fever. She pulls her mantle over him and settles down to keep watch as he and the children sleep, with young Sarah as companion.

She is still awake and the inky blackness of the sky through the window is starting to lose its density when the two guards outside give a sharp call that galvanizes the room. Within minutes, all the able-bodied Khoikhoi men are gone from the schoolhouse into the predawn. George stands, his hands clenched at his side, a muscle jumping in his jaw. Sarah can only guess at what was going through his mind: he will not fight, but neither can he stop the men from fighting.

Outside it is pandemonium—men shouting, cattle bellowing, feet drumming. High above the mayhem comes a high, piercing scream, trailing off into a dull thud in the sudden silence that follows. Then, the commotion redoubles, with guns firing and horses neighing. The noise stays at this pitch, and Sarah stands, unseeing, envisioning in her mind's eye the fracas outside. Imperceptibly at first, but then with gathering speed, the noise begins to inch away until it is almost like an echo. Sarah finds that she is clutching George's hand.

Klaas Klaas and Willem Valentyn stagger into the room, covered in blood, carrying the body of a Khoikhoi man whom Sarah knows by sight. A woman screams and forces her way through the crowded refugees towards the men. As

Klaas and Willem carefully lower the man's body to the floor, the woman breaks into a keening and plaintive ululating that is picked up by the other Khoikhoi women in the room. A group of children, their faces blank with shock, edge closer to the man and the sobbing woman kneeling next to him. Sarah counts seven children, ranged in age from about twelve to three years old. When the woman sees them, she smears the tears away from her cheeks and takes deep, shuddering breaths, trying to calm herself as she pulls her children into a collective embrace.

George goes to the group and stands with his head bowed. He speaks in a low voice, and Sarah can only just make out his words.

"Trusting in God, we pray together for our brother as we come to the last farewell. Lord Jesus Christ, grant that our brother may sleep in peace until you awaken him to glory. There is sadness in parting, but we take comfort in the hope that one day we shall see him again and enjoy his friendship. Let us console one another in the faith of Jesus Christ."

A ragged murmur of "amen" goes through the schoolroom.

The man will be buried within hours, as is the Khoikhoi custom, and the focus now is centered on these preparations. In the midst, Sarah sees Willem take off his hat and show it to his wife, Elizabeth. It has holes on either side. A Xhosa spear had shot clean through it. As Elizabeth Valentyn understands the implication, she grips the lapels of Willem's jacket, looking up into his face, close to tears. He pulls her against him, resting his cheek on the top of her head.

It is too dangerous to go far afield to bury the man, so the men dig a grave nearby. When it is ready, six Khoikhoi place the man's body on a board from one of the trestle tables in the schoolroom, hoist their burden onto their shoulders, and make a solemn procession outside, followed by the woman, her seven children, and George.

When they return within half an hour, a phalanx of support gathers around the woman and her children. Fear and depression hang over the room like an insidious fog. How long before the Xhosa return to carry out their thwarted raid on the cattle? How long before they rush the schoolhouse, killing all inside it? The shadows grow longer, and the dangerous nighttime closes in.

A shot ricochets through the valley. In the split second that it takes for the realization to dawn that the Xhosa do not possess guns, the people look at each with shock and wonder. Sarah hears that same strange, throbbing sound echoing through the valley, interspersed now with shouts, screams, and more gunshot. A crowding rush to the windows shows the scarlet uniforms of a British regiment on horseback. In the melee, the scarlet clashes with the throngs of Xhosa on the hillside, inching them backwards, until they seem to pour over the ridge of the *koppie* and disappear from sight. An infantryman breaks away and canters down the slope.

"Is the Reverend Barker here?" he calls in English. Sarah has never been gladder to hear her native tongue.

George unbolts the door, and goes out to meet the soldier. Through the open door, the conversation filters into the schoolroom.

"It is a miracle that you are alive," says the English voice.

"Is Salem safe?" asks George.

"Both Grahamstown and Salem are safe."

The flood of relief turns Sarah's legs weak, and she sits down abruptly on the hard floor of the schoolhouse.

CHAPTER FORTY-TWO

S ARAH WAKES to the quiet click of the bedroom door.
George had risen and dressed without waking her, but
the mechanical hinge betrayed him. She lies facing
the window with her eyes closed, the early morning winter
light filtering through her eyelids. She takes stock: today is
Tuesday, July 26, 1836. She had come to bed early last night
and slept well, but she still feels heavy with fatigue.

She rolls over onto her back, and the rising nausea is so
sudden that she just barely throws herself out of the bed and
makes it over to the washbasin in time before she vomits
violently. When it is over, she kneels down and leans against
the leg of the washstand, trying to remember what she ate
last night. Fresh poached fish, green beans, and boiled potatoes. That wasn't it. She brings her hands up to her breasts,
and feels them through the thin fabric of her shift. They are
swollen. She is pregnant. How can this be? Her monthly
bleeding has become so erratic that she thought it had come
to an end for her time of life. She is forty-six years old.
Harriet, the youngest child, is six.

In the coming weeks, there is no doubt that Sarah is
carrying a child. It is her sixteenth pregnancy. But there is
something peculiar this time. She feels sharp cramping in

her womb. She finds blood spots on her undergarments. George fears a premature birth, or even a miscarriage. She fears it, too, but she tries to keep his spirits up and maintain a quiet composure the better to protect the child.

When spring comes, George has to think about his duty to visit the congregation at Kat River 120 miles away. The settlement, devastated by the Sixth Frontier War, has been further left destitute by the temporary absence of James Read Sr. He has travelled to England with Dr. John Philip—along with a delegation that also includes James Read Jr. and a deacon of the church at Theopolis named Andries Stoffels—to give evidence before a parliamentary committee about the interests of the indigenous people in South Africa.

Sarah had traveled to Kat River with George in March, and was profoundly distressed to learn that Cobus Boezak had died shortly after he had moved there. What a sadness, she thought, for him not to have had more time to enjoy his new freedoms. She visited the place where he died, and tried to envision his energy filling up the place in the short time he had there.

Ever since that stay in Kat River, Sarah has taken a deep interest in the settlement, encouraging George in what he is able to do for the people there. At her urging now, he begins to make plans for a return journey in early November, and he works many late nights preparing for it, while also keeping up with the business of running his own mission at Theopolis.

One night, towards the end of October, Sarah retires early and lies drowsing in the sleeping room while George sits up late at his desk. He comes through around midnight, moving quietly so as not to disturb her. A hard knock comes suddenly at the door, and Sarah flies up in the bed, startled.

"It is just a knock on the front door," says George. "I

must see what it is at this late hour. Lie down again, and I will return quickly."

Sarah tries to do as he says, but she feels her womb contracting with deep pain. She is only five months pregnant. It is much too soon to give birth; the baby would never survive. She sits up, cradling her rounded belly, and rocks back and forth, as if to lull the child. This is how George finds her.

"What is it?" The alarm is sharp in his voice.

"I am having contractions."

"What can I do?"

She breathes hard in and out through her nose. "Please, help me to empty my bladder."

He holds her and supports her as she crouches over the chamber pot and then guides her back onto the bed. She slides down onto her left side, leaving a smear of blood on the sheet. She lies still, breathing shallowly, her eyes closed. The clutching contractions ease a little, and that helps to ease her panic.

"Who was at the door?" she asks after a while, without opening her eyes.

"It was Hendrik Buys. His wife, Hannah, is confined. I sent for Lena."

She nods. "Good." She lies perfectly quiet then, drawing in slow breaths, willing her baby to be still.

George watches over her for half an hour, then he strips down to his shirt and slides in behind her, laying his arm along her outer thigh. And so they sleep.

When George disengages himself from Sarah in the early morning, she wakes to the realization that she has passed the night without mishap. *Thank God*, she thinks. *Thank God.*

"Rest today," says George. "Stay in bed and rest."

And so she does. Young Sarah brings her tea when she returns from teaching her infant school, and she has beads of moisture in her auburn hair.

"It has begun to rain," she says. "The clouds are almost black in the west. We will have a thunderstorm, I think."

As if on cue, there is a low rumble, and Sarah listens to the accelerating rhythm of huge drops of rain outside the window. She pulls herself up in the bed and picks up the cup and saucer from her night table. Directly overhead comes a sudden thunderclap. Sarah jerks with the shock of it and gives a cry; the cup falls from her hand, shattering and spilling on the floor. Young Sarah is instantly at her side, and her mother looks up into her face, clinging to her upper arms.

"It is starting again," she says.

"Shall I call Father?"

"Help me first." She fears she will not be able to stop it a second time, but she asks young Sarah to help her as George did last night, going through the motions exactly—almost like a ritual—of emptying her bladder, climbing back into the bed, lying on her left side, breathing deeply, willing her baby to be still inside her. Again, she falls asleep, again George watches over her, and again she manages to pass the night without mishap. She looks at a patch of clear October sky that she can see through the window. It will be a beautiful spring day.

Come November, Sarah starts to feel the familiar discomforts of a pregnancy that is now into its sixth month. Her feet and ankles are plump with swelling; she is hungry all the time but gets indigestion when she eats; she struggles to get comfortable enough to sleep well, and, when she does, George—ever the silent sleeper—tells her that she snores. Still, although she suffers from low back pain, she has had no more alarms about early onset labor, and she is able to be up and about.

"My duty to the congregation at Kat River is on my conscience," George says. "I had thought of being with them for the first Sabbath in December, but I am uneasy about leaving you."

"I hate to be the cause that keeps you from them," she says, "but could you think of delaying to the end of the month, then we shall see how it is with me—"

"Certainly," he jumps in, even before she has finished speaking.

He continues to watch her every move, coming to help her if she so much as lifts a teapot or stretches her back to ease the low ache. With the visit to Kat River postponed, George is preparing for a quick, two-day trip to Algoa Bay. Their daughter Elizabeth, now a young woman of twenty, and Edward, aged fifteen, are to set sail for Cape Town. There, Elizabeth will learn the system of running a school, and Edward will learn the printing trade. The directors of the London Mission Society never granted George's request to visit England after twenty years of service, and Cape Town is the next best option as a place for Edward to be apprenticed.

Sarah would have given anything to be physically present to see her children off on this new chapter in their lives, but her condition is too precarious. As with the momentous event of George's ordination, she has to give the charge over to her lifelong friend. Elizabeth and Adam Robson had moved with the four boys from Bethelsdorp to minister in Port Elizabeth four years earlier, and they will take George and the children into their home before seeing the young people off to Cape Town on December 10. Sarah will have to put her trust in Elizabeth to be her eyes and ears and heart once again.

She remembers how she had once told George, *This is how we serve them; we make them free and independent*, with reference to both the Khoikhoi at the mission and their own children. She understands, intellectually, that this is how it should be, but her emotions don't follow the logic. She feels hollowed out inside as she envisions the time stretching into months, and maybe years, before she sees these two dear young people again. Might young Elizabeth settle in Cape Town? Will Edward's new trade ground him there? With little George Nathaniel off to school at Salem alongside his brother John, there are now only five girls at home, ranging in age from six to twenty-one. She wonders how all nine of her children—soon to be ten—will choose to make their way in the world; what professions they will follow; whom they might marry; where they will live. Will they think of themselves as Briton or African?

When George returns from Port Elizabeth, he brings a letter from her old friend that undergirds his own account of the children's departure for Cape Town so vividly that she can clearly see in her mind's eye the snap of sails as they take the wind and the ship starts its westward voyage, and she can feel in her heart the mixture of anticipation and anxiety in her two children. And now, the pending trip to Kat River begins to loom over Sarah and George like a gathering storm.

At last he says, "I am duty bound to visit the settlement at Kat River, and my fear is that if I delay it too long, I shall not be home in time for your confinement in February."

"I share your feelings," she says. "Your whole soul is bound up with the destitute congregation at Kat River, and I cannot, in all conscience, keep you from them any longer. You must go as planned. Indeed, the weather being warm, you should leave on Monday rather than Tuesday, so as to have a day in Grahamstown to rest yourself and the horses."

"I will consult a medical man at Grahamstown and send out medicine for you," he says. He hesitates, as if to say more, but he checks himself, and she doesn't press it.

So, on the morning of Monday, December 19, George leaves home at eleven o'clock to ride to Grahamstown. He pulls her carefully against his body and speaks close to her ear. "Unless the rivers prevent me I shall be back in the third week."

"Do not allow my situation to make you uneasy," she says. "God will take care of me."

He mounts, and she stands in the doorway, leaning a shoulder against the jamb, one hand resting lightly on the swell of her stomach, raising the other to wave each of the many times that George turns in the saddle to look back. She stays standing, watching, long after he is completely out of sight. Even after sharing her life with this man for almost twenty-two years, her melancholy at being parted from him is as acute as ever. A sharp twinge in her womb brings her back to the present moment. She pushes her shoulder away from the doorjamb, steadies herself with her hands on her belly, and turns into the house to go and help young Sarah prepare for her own forthcoming visit to Grahamstown while her infant school is on its summer vacation.

Sarah puts on a smiling face for the children. Her longing for George, Elizabeth, and Edward makes her mood subdued, like walking from sunlight into shade, but her other seven children are all home for the holidays, so the house is full of cheer and she basks in it. She spends the day contentedly enough, sorting and packing with young Sarah, and, with the summer light still slanting into the dining room in the late afternoon, the family enjoys a lively, hearty supper.

Not too long after young Sarah and Ann return from putting the younger children to bed, their mother rises and says, "I think I must retire too."

"How are you?" asks Ann, with some concern.

"I feel myself painful, but it is nowise alarming."

She strips down to her shift, pours water from the ewer into the basin to wash her face, and plaits her hair—moving cumbersomely with the weight of her pregnancy. She climbs into the bed, and, just as she is about to blow out the candle, young Sarah knocks and comes in to make sure that she is comfortable.

She bends and kisses her mother's forehead. "Sleep well, dear. Be sure to call if you need anything." She blows out the candle and quietly pulls the door ajar behind her.

Sarah doesn't expect to sleep; she is too uncomfortable, and the bed feels desolate without George. But, as it happens, she falls into a deep sleep—only to be woken at midnight by wrenching pain. At first, she can't move because of the intensity of the pain, but she knows that she must call for help. She turns to the edge of the bed, rolls out of it and, by holding on to the bedpost, a chair, the corner of the washstand, she makes it as far as the half-open door. There, she is incapacitated by another excruciating spasm.

"Sarah!" she calls.

Like her father, Sarah is a light sleeper, and she immediately calls a response. "Yes, Mother, I am coming!" She runs, her bare feet padding on the floor.

"I am ill."

"I will bring a light."

"Oh God!" cries her mother. She feels the hot gush of blood down the insides of her legs, and she watches it pool at her feet, the spreading stain visible even in the darkened room. She is suddenly faint, swaying. Young Sarah catches her, half guiding, half carrying her back to her bed, calling to her sister, "Ann! Go and call Lena!"

Young Sarah lights a candle and looks down at her mother's face. "Oh!" It comes out on a sob. "I shall send for Father."

"No!" says Sarah. "Don't call your father back. He is gone on a good work. God will take care of me. We ought to consider the hundreds at the Kat River who are destitute of a minister." She has already delayed his journey too long. Now that he is gone, she can't call him back again so soon. If she has to give birth to their child without him—for the first time in all her life—so be it. It will be a wonderful event for him to come home to in the New Year. And if, God forbid, the baby were lost, he would be spared that at least.

When Lena comes, Sarah knows all will be well. Her bed is stripped, her nightshift changed, the blood cleaned away, and the room is soon redolent of rooibos and *buchu*.

"*Ai*, Sister Sarah," she says. "Your baby is eager, isn't it? Two months too soon! Can't wait to come into the world."

Sarah manages a wan smile.

Lena bathes Sarah's face, runs her healing hands over her body, and Sarah is so comforted that tears of relief ooze from under her eyelids. The excruciating pain has subsided and the spasms that come are the all too familiar contractions she has experienced over the past twenty-one years—since she first gave birth to this beautiful young woman standing at her bedside.

Daylight creeps into the room. Young Sarah blows out the candle, and the lingering scent makes Sarah think of the sanctuary of a church. Lena guides her with calming directives of when to push and when to rest. *I can do this*, thinks Sarah, *the pain is not so bad*. The pain is truly less than she has ever known before in childbirth.

The morning sunlight is bright in the room when Lena says, "Almost there. Now a big push for me!"

Sarah feels the urgent release of delivery, and waits for the baby's cry. It does not come. The silence in the room stretches.

Lena comes to stand over her, and strokes her hair back from her forehead. "Sarah, my darling,"—it is the first time she has ever called her anything but 'Sister Sarah'—"your little girl is stillborn. She was too small and weak."

Sarah closes her eyes. The insides of her eyelids are red. Her nostrils are filled with the metallic smell of blood. She can't sort exhaustion from grief, sorrow from dull acceptance. This pregnancy has been precarious from the start.

Lena leaves her side to take care of the afterbirth, and young Sarah comes to sit by the bedside. She takes her mother's hand, gripping it tightly. Sarah turns her head and looks into her daughter's eyes. She can see her own sorrow there.

"What time is it?" she asks.

"After nine o'clock."

A tremor runs through her body. Then another. She begins to shiver. Her heart is beating in her ears, her breathing ragged.

Lena puts an extra cover over her and reaches beneath it to massage her stomach. "The bleeding will not stop," she says, and Sarah senses an alarm she has never heard from her before.

Sarah's shivering is making the bed frame knock, and a cold sweat starts to trickle over her scalp. She clenches her teeth and tries to still her shuddering body, but she cannot. This is different. She has never experienced this before.

"Has your father been sent for?" she asks.

"Yes. I dispatched a messenger to him about two o'clock this morning."

"That's right." It is difficult to speak for the shivering. "I know he will be here as soon as possible."

The clock in the parlor chimes ten.

"*Ai, ai, ai*—nothing will stop this bleeding!" Lena is frantic.

Sarah looks up at daughter standing over her, and sees her face askew with tears. Behind her is Ann. Sarah doesn't know how she came to be there. With supreme effort, she turns her head. John and young George stand at the foot of the bed. In a cluster next to them are Jane, Mary Ann, and little Harriet. On each one of their faces she recognizes the blank shock that she had seen on the faces of the seven children in the schoolhouse when the Xhosa killed their father. And she understands. And grief pushes up through her throat.

"What, shall I never see him again?"

"He will be here as soon as he can," says young Sarah.

She closes her eyes, the warmth seeping from her body, her breath coming in a shallow pulse, jarred by her shivering. She is with George, riding hard from Grahamstown. Vivid fragments of memory move in and out of focus. . . . Looking down at his vulnerable face when he said, "Sarah, will you do me the honor of accompanying me to Africa as my wife?". . . . The tug of sexuality when he slipped a hand under her cloak to take hers on the coach ride from London to Plymouth. . . . Drawing back slightly to look at him in the dim light of the cabin on the *Alfred* and watching a tear make its way over the bridge of his nose to plop onto the makeshift pillow when she first told him she was carrying their child. . . . His cold skin as he slid into the cot aboard the *Alfred* and whispered, "The mountains of Africa were in sight. By the light of the moon I could see this land I have long wished to see.". . . The letter where he described this as "the beautifullest country". . . . How he had pulled her carefully against his body and spoken close to her ear, "Unless the rivers prevent me I shall be back in the third week." With the pulse of her shallow breathing, she thinks, *I must wait for him. . . . If I can only wait. . . . Will I be able to wait?*

The clock strikes quarter past ten. Using all her strength, she reaches her hands out toward her children, and feels them gripped. Five minutes tick by. Her hands grow warm from her children's touch. Her shuddering quietens. She feels a deep flush of comfort as if she is sinking, moist and womblike, in the cocoon of the bed.

Into the stillness of the room, she says, "Amen. Even so, come, Lord Jesus."

CHAPTER FORTY-THREE

GEORGE ARRIVED at twenty minutes past noon. He had covered the thirty-five miles in a desperate four-and-a-half-hour ride, but he reached home two hours too late.

His plan had been to consult a medical man in Grahamstown, not only to send out medicine for Sarah as he had told her, but also with the intention of describing the real state of the case to the doctor, and of taking his advice about whether or not to proceed farther to Kat River. He had not dared to mention this to Sarah before he left.

At seven o'clock on the morning of December 20, 1836, he'd been sitting at breakfast in the house of a friend in Grahamstown when the messenger from Theopolis arrived. George immediately became alarmed, rose from the table, mounted his horse as soon as he could, and rode as fast as possible. About halfway to Theopolis, he met another messenger with a note saying that Sarah was now dangerously ill and advising a medical man to be sent for. George sent the messenger on to town and quickened his pace towards home.

What must that ride have been like for him, fearing the worst, wondering if he would make it home in time? As he starts up the hill at Theopolis towards the village, he sees the schoolmaster, Thomas Edwards, evidently on the lookout for him. One look at the schoolmaster's face is all he needs to confirm his worst fears. He dismounts, removes his hat, rubs his hand over his face. Barely conscious of what he is doing, he hands the reins of his horse to Thomas Edwards, and plods the rest of the way up the hill on foot. When he arrives at the door of the house, he finds the children half frantic. Young Sarah puts her arms around his neck, part comforting, part seeking comfort.

"Oh Father!" she says. "Mother is happy—I am sure she is in heaven, she died so comfortable."

The house is filled with the keening and weeping of the mission people. Lena, usually so sanguine about the cycles of life, sobs without restraint. George walks to the sleeping room, pauses on the threshold, then closes the door behind him so gently that it doesn't make a sound.

The curtains are drawn against the heat of the day. The room is dim and has a strange, dusky smell, quite unlike the scent he has always associated with Sarah's warm, sleeping aura. Someone—Lena, perhaps—has washed Sarah's body, clothed her in her church dress, and folded her arms across her breast. She looks, as young Sarah had described her, comfortable. The small bundle of her stillborn child lies at her side.

He wants to reach out and take Sarah's hand, but something holds him back; something almost akin to fear. This is the beloved, intimately known form of Sarah, but not the essence of her. He looks at the curve of her mouth and her full lower lip, at the shape of her ear where the lobe meets the soft line of her jaw. There isn't a part of her that isn't exquisitely familiar. But where is her essence?

"Dear God," he begins. But the prayer will not come. He

feels himself sway, and he buckles to his knees. As he kneels there at her side, he loses all sense of time and place.

✲

When Thomas Edwards sent a third messenger to Grahamstown to carry the news of what had happened to the Monros and the Macdonalds, the messenger met the doctor on the road, and turned him back. Messrs. Monro and Macdonald arrive on horseback at three o'clock the following afternoon.

George has hardly slept. He is dark-eyed and disheveled, even as he tries to appear strong for the children. John Monro grips him by the shoulders and looks deep into his face, murmuring a prayer. When he sees George's self-control begin to collapse, he guides him into the parlor and puts the door ajar. George stands facing away, staring out of the window with vacant eyes.

"My feelings are not to be described," he says, his voice husky and unsteady. "I apprehended the worst and thought myself half prepared for the event, but when the stroke came, I found my strength perfect weakness."

John Monro looks around the parlor, sees a decanter of brandy with glasses on a small table, and pours a shot to bring to George.

George takes a sip and inhales deeply. "Thank you," he says. "I have been rather poorly, not so much from the sickness as from the shock my nervous system has received." He takes another sip. "I know—I feel—I ought to submit. I have been preaching resignation to the will of God for more than twenty years, but I find the precept hard to practice now. I have but one helpmeet for me." He sits down, cradling the glass in his hands, staring into it. "Yet I dare not murmur. I rather desire to be grateful. I can look back on near twenty-two years of uninterrupted happiness in the society of her whom God gave, and whom God has taken away. I have lost my friend and councilor, the guide of my youth and the solace of my riper years. . . ." His voice breaks, and he is quiet.

John Monro puts a hand on George's shoulder. After some minutes have passed, Brother John speaks carefully, "I have been wondering what your wishes are about the internment. My wife and Mrs. Macdonald are following by wagon, and I doubt they will arrive until after dark."

George wipes his face and clears his throat. "It is so hot," he says, "and there has been so much blood spilled, I don't believe we can keep her body above ground until tomorrow."

"Yes, I think it will be best to proceed before sundown."

Willem Valentyn has already built a coffin, and, when the time comes, he and Klaas Klaas carry it into the sleeping room, where Lena and young Sarah are waiting. The four of them, with a grace that seems unworldly given the awkwardness of their task, silently wrap Sarah and her child together in a mat and reverently lift their burden into the box. Lena scatters a handful of dried cypress leaves into the coffin before Willem nails the lid closed.

"With faith in Jesus Christ, we receive the body of our sister, Sarah, for burial," says John Monro.

"Deliver your servant," murmurs George, "and set her free from every bond."

Willem calls four other men from the mission, and they lift the coffin onto their shoulders to carry it from the house and out into the throng of people waiting outside. The crowd makes a pathway to allow them through and falls in behind George and the children, all quickly washed and changed into their church clothes. George holds Mary Ann and Harriet by their hands; Ann walks with John and Jane; and young George keeps close to his eldest sister and Lena.

In the oppressive late-afternoon heat, sweat streams

from the faces of the pallbearers, but they walk on steadily. Within the tight-knit group of the family comes the steady tramp, tramp of their footsteps over the *veld*, and all around the wailing and low ululating of the people. They walk down the hill, heading for the trees that line the Kasouga River. The river is flowing, fed by the summer rains, and the men, with their precious burden, have to cross by the stones, balancing carefully, precariously. On the far side, they haul the coffin, hand over hand, feet slipping, muscles straining, up the steep bank to reach the plateau beyond. Where they go, the family and the people follow, the singing and keening never faltering.

They come to the sacred glen where, thirteen years ago, Cobus helped Sarah to bury her unnamed son. The air is redolent of red clay from the newly dug grave. They set the coffin down, and the low ululating trails off as the people shuffle quietly into the glen. There is, then, absolute silence.

Before he begins the burial rite, John Monro turns and addresses the people of Theopolis. "You have lost a mother," he says.

CHAPTER FORTY-FOUR

I WAS, BY THIS TIME, so steeped in Sarah's story that I felt as if I had been living her life—to the extent that even the circumstances of her death, which I had barely been able to imagine at the outset, were clear to me now through the mosaic of letters that George wrote to his brother and the directors of the London Missionary Society, and a loving obituary that was printed in the *Grahamstown Journal*. I had become so immersed in the process that when one of Sarah's descendants contacted me by email one day, I was momentarily disorientated. In my focus on Sarah and my connection to her, I had lost sight of the diaspora of descendants she must have through her nine children. My mother had four siblings and I am one of ten cousins in our generation—I can't even begin to do the arithmetic of how this must multiply exponentially.

Jane, who was just eleven years old when Sarah died, went on to marry Daniel Hockly, the son of the silversmith whom George first met off the *Chapman* at Algoa Bay in 1820. Jane lived to the wonderful age of ninety-seven, and the descendant who contacted me out of the blue was from that line. It was her great-grandfather, one of Jane's sons, who had bequeathed George's diaries to the Cory Library at Rhodes University in the 1960s, and she had tracked down my address through the library to see if I could fill her in on some of the details about our mutual ancestor, Sarah.

Truthfully, I felt a little twinge of envy that this very distant relative had mapped out so clearly her ancestral link to Sarah. All this time, I had been trying to wrestle with the genealogy that would show me how her bloodline made its way down to me.

As I continued in my amateurish, more-by-good-luck-than-good-management way to sift though the notes and files and pieces of memorabilia that I had accumulated in my search for Sarah, I came across an envelope that my mother had labeled *Old Family Photos*. When my mother died in 2013, it fell to me to bring her precious things back with me to America, and this was amongst several envelopes of snapshots. This particular envelope includes a 4 x 3 inch black-and-white group photograph, dating from the 1890s to judge by the style of the clothing. On the back, again in my mother's handwriting, is this schema:

ARTHUR

GEORGE		SYDNEY
EDITH	MINNIE	JESSIE
HESTER (OSCHSE)	WILLIAM	GEORGE (SENIOR)
		NORAH
KATIE		LILLA

REGINALD (b. 1881)

Amongst the many stories of her ancestors that my mother used to tell me were the ones about her large family of aunts and uncles, and some of the names—Arthur, Sydney,

Jesse—echoed back at me from her telling. As I studied the schema, I realized that the George (Senior) in this instance was not Sarah's husband, but her son, who looked in this photograph for all the world like Johannes Brahms in his later years. Reginald, who was born to George (Senior) and Hester (Osche) in 1881, was my mother's father.

And so—in a sudden instant—there it was. Somehow, I had imagined that there was an extra generation in there somewhere, as there was for Jane's descendant, but it turned out to be simpler than I had been making it. I could—finally—trace the trajectory backwards from me . . . through my mother . . . through my grandfather Reginald . . . through my great-grandfather George Nathaniel . . . to Sarah and George. The deeply satisfying click of homecoming this gave me at last was like a key turning smoothly in a lock.

Young George fought in the Eighth Frontier War before he settled in Tarkastad further north from Theopolis across the Winterberg range. There, he became the proprietor of *The Tarka Herald* and the mayor of the town. Now I remembered my mother mentioning that her father was born in Tarkastad.

The whole diaspora of nine children did Sarah proud, each in their way. Young Sarah married George Monro, the son of the minister who conducted Sarah's funeral. Elizabeth, who never married, put her teacher training to practice in Paarl, forty miles from Cape Town, where she kept a school. Ann married her beloved James Read Jr. shortly after Sarah's death, and supported him throughout his ministry, much as Sarah had supported George. Edward married a young woman named Maria Anathasia in Cape Town. He—the one who had been able to envision the opposing northern-southern seasons when he wrote to his grandparents from Theopolis—was the only one who went back to England, where he died. John, like young George, moved to Tarkastad, and, like Elizabeth, he never married. Sarah's two youngest daughters helped Elizabeth in her school, and both were married to ministers—Mary Ann to Rev. Johann Budler and Harriet to Rev. Jan du Plessis. And so, by a process of elimination, I could work out that since Edward had returned to England, leaving two daughters at the Cape, and since John hadn't married, it had to be Sarah's youngest son, George Nathaniel, who had passed down the Barker name to us in Africa.

George, the father of them all, was completely jarred off course when he lost Sarah. He resigned from Theopolis three years after Sarah died and went to minister in Paarl where Elizabeth kept house for him. After eight years—an unusually long time for that era—he was remarried to a woman named Hilletje Smuts. He had no children with her, and I can't help comparing that to Sarah's sixteen pregnancies. Twenty years after Sarah's death, George had to resign from the ministry. He had gone completely blind.

When Jane's descendent contacted me by email and she and I swapped information about our shared ancestry, she told me that Theopolis still exists as a farm. She had looked for it during a visit to the Eastern Cape but didn't have much time, or much cooperation from the local farmer, or a car that was happy on the dirt roads. She also mentioned—making my heart jump—that Sarah's grave was still hidden in the bush near Kasouga, and she gave me the name of a woman who might be able to take me to it.

So I made the pilgrimage. On a clear winter afternoon in June 2017, I drove south from Grahamstown, where I had been spending two precious days touching, reading, deciphering, paging through, and photographing the vellum-bound manuscript of George's original diaries in the

Cory Library. I headed towards the small coastal town of Port Alfred at the mouth of the Kowie River, just a little farther east along the coast from the beach where the Barker children had frolicked by the lagoon.

En route, I stopped at Salem. The Methodist Chapel where the children had gone to school still stands, surrounded by a low white wall and cypresses. To my surprise, the heavy metal doorknob yielded to my pressure, and I stepped into the quiet nave. The wooden pews and floor planks are perhaps just as they were when George used to preach there. I envisioned Sarah sitting in one of the back pews, and I thought of her children Elizabeth, Edward, and John taking refuge in there during the Sixth Frontier War.

In Port Alfred, I met up with my Theopolis guide, Joc Guest. She was of the no-nonsense, salt-of-the-earth brand of South African women. We climbed into her clapped-out, 1990s sedan—good for the dirt roads we'd have to negotiate, she said—and headed off towards Theopolis. Joc, who is of 1820 settler stock, grew up on the neighboring farm, and she knew the terrain well. After we made a turnoff and headed along a bumpy dirt road, we passed a small pickup truck coming in the opposite direction. Joc waved.

"That's Howson's *bakkie*," she said. Howson Long was the present owner of Theopolis Farm. "He'll be gone for the long weekend."

The next day was a public holiday, commemorating the day in 1975 when more than 20,000 pupils in Soweto began a protest march against the apartheid regime, and 700 hundred people, many of them youths, were killed.

"Howson said he will tie a rag to mark a tree so we know where to go in to find the grave," said Joc.

We drove through the farm gate, secured it behind us— and there we were, in that place where Sarah had made her home for nearly twenty years. We drove up the hill, stopped about halfway up at the farmhouse, and got out of the car to be greeted by the barking of a ferociously friendly, little black-and-white mongrel. I stood inhaling the air of the place, listening to the scuffle of the farm dog and to birds calling in the distance—but no hadeda ibis as I had expected, as I had hoped, since it is their piercing, honking call that I so strongly associate with Africa.

Down the slope, across the *veld*, I saw a clump of trees suggesting the curve of the Kasouga River. Somewhere in there, I thought, was Sarah's grave. But Joc turned, and led me in the other direction, farther up the hill toward a thicket of low trees and bushes. We were searching for the ruins—all that remained of the mission station after it was abandoned and its buildings burnt down during an 1851 rebellion. As we neared the summit, Joc pointed to an outcrop of large, fawn-colored stones. "Those are from the ruins," she said. When we reached the summit, we posted ourselves through a barbed-wire fence. It was completely overgrown up there, with knots of scrubby trees that all looked indistinguishable one from the other.

"We should split up to search," said Joc.

So then I was alone in this place where Sarah had walked. I wasn't at all sure what I was looking for, and I felt as if I was just walking around in circles, lost.

After about quarter of an hour, I heard Joc call, "Halloo!"

I followed her voice deep into a thicket. At first, I could see nothing, but then, as she pointed, I could make out some large, fawn stones through the undergrowth. I stooped and ducked as I edged closer and closer, my clothes catching on the thorns of *wag-'n-bietjie* bushes until, gradually, I could make out two long walls, about two feet thick, with a space between them where a wide door would have been. One of the walls had spurs that suggested buttressing, and it met another fragment of wall at a right angle. The structure was choked with vegetation, reminding me of the ancient Mayan settlement of Chichen Itza where the jungle would encroach and overtake it in a matter of a few years if it were not checked.

It broke my heart. George and the people of Theopolis labored—twice—to build the mission station. Now there was hardly anything to show for it. One of these years, there will be no trace of these last remaining remnants of the settlement. I am blessed to have seen it at all.

It had taken longer than we thought to find and explore the ruins, and we still had to search for Sarah's grave before the winter light started to fade, so we retraced our steps and walked down across the *veld* towards the Kasouga River. We scanned the line of trees masking the river, trying to find the rag that Howson Long had said he would tie up to mark our point of entry. We couldn't see it. It had been some years since Joc had visited the gravesite, but, working on instinct and failing the rag marker, she led us toward a natural opening in the trees that looked vaguely familiar to her.

In the murky shadow of the trees, the bank sloped steeply down towards the riverbed. We slithered down the side, walked across the riverbed—so bone-dry at the height of winter that it was hard for me to imagine it in devastating full spate—and scrabbled up the far side. Joc remembered from before that she came up from the riverbed onto a plateau, and the gravesite was right there. But it wasn't. Howson Long had told her that it was in a clump of tall trees and we fanned out trying to locate it, circling as we'd done to find the ruins, but, again, each knot of vegetation seemed indistinguishable from the other.

"We probably won't be lucky again," I heard Joc say.

"What do you mean?" I asked with a spasm of alarm.

"Well, we were lucky to find the ruins. We probably won't be so lucky twice."

But we couldn't *not* find it. I had come halfway around the world to be at Sarah's graveside. A loop started running through my head, "Please . . . please . . . please . . ." I didn't know if I was praying or if I was calling on the spirit of the place. I felt an ache starting at the back of my throat. After years of combing through diaries and archives and letters, this was the culmination of my search for Sarah. A hundred times I'd imagined standing at her graveside, feeling a sense of closure. I couldn't even begin to bear the thought that we wouldn't find it.

We decided to go back across the riverbed, to try again to find the elusive rag at the entry point. We slithered and slid down the bank, catching at branches that snapped off uselessly, my sneakers filling with dry sand. On the other side, we searched up and down the length of the trees. By now it was late afternoon and the light was beginning to fade.

My fast breathing had little to do with the exertion. I felt the adrenaline rising as I faced the probability that I was not going to find Sarah's grave. I'd come all this way, and I wasn't going to have that one tangible connection to her.

"There's Howson!" called Joc suddenly.

And there was his *bakkie*, winding along the farm track towards the farmhouse. I stood still, hope rising, as I watched Joc walk up to meet him. Their conversation drifted down to me.

"Did you tie up a rag up for us?"

"No, sorry, I forgot."

Just at that moment a flock of hadedas flew overhead, unleashing their haunting, throbbing cry. I couldn't have wished for a better omen.

The light was failing by the time Howsen Long joined us. He was a compact, weather-beaten man, and I guessed him to be in his sixties. He carried a long stick, shiny and smooth from use.

I reached out my hand, "Mr. Long, I'm the great-great-granddaughter of Sarah Barker."

"I'm Howson," he said.

Like Joc, Howson had the clipped Eastern Cape accent of my mother and her siblings, with flattened vowels and pronounced r's. As Howson led us toward the river, he told me that he was descended from the Sephton party of 1820 settlers.

And here was another of the serendipitous loops that had been so uncanny in my search for Sarah's story. That same party of settlers had also included a young couple named Christian and Ann Oschse. Christian George Oschse was a twenty-year-old furrier when he boarded the *Aurora* to immigrate to South Africa with his new wife, Ann Mundy. They had been married the previous October at St. Mary's in Islington, London—the same church where Sarah and George were married. Once in South Africa, Christian and Ann had twelve children, the youngest of whom was named Hester—and she married Sarah's youngest son, George, my great-grandfather.

And so I traced the circle of serendipity in my mind: Sarah and George had married at St. Mary's, where Christian and Ann Oschse married four years later; Sarah give birth to young George at Theopolis and he married Hester Oschse; Hester was the daughter of 1820 settlers from the Sephton party, and the Sephton party also included the ancestors of Howson Long, who now owned Theopolis. The symmetry of the interweaving seemed uncannily perfect.

Now, Howson led us to the opening in the trees where

Joc's instinct had taken us, through the dry riverbed, and up the other side.

"You were only twenty feet away," he said, pointing to our footprints. He walked around a clump of trees and stopped. "Shall I leave you to have a quiet moment on your own?"

It was in a shaded glen. The trees formed a circle around the grave, like a small chapel, and the evening light filtering in through the leaves formed the patterns of a stained-glass window. The tombstone, which George had brought over from England, is about four feet high and, curiously, the writing on it was facing me, away from the grave, which lay beyond it on the other side. George had engraved:

SARAH WILLIAMS

BELOVED WIFE OF

REV^D GEORGE BARKER

WHO DEPARTED THIS LIFE

20 DECEMBER 1836

AGED 46 YEARS

Underneath, are Sarah's dying words: "Amen. Even so, come, Lord Jesus."

I stood in this quiet, dappled place with my hand on the shoulder of Sarah's gravestone. Even though she never saw it or touched it, it is what I have of her. There are none of her letters; no diaries or artifacts. There are just the two signatures where she signed Elizabeth's marriage certificate and where she signed her own with the little underlining beneath the "W"; there are the two portraits, one in color, one black-and-white; and there is her gravestone.

I don't want to be fanciful or embellish the truth to say that I could feel Sarah's essence there, but I was aware of something. I was aware of reaching across time to this woman who was so real to me. I felt a sense of kinship, of shared experience, even a kind of intimacy. Perhaps it was just something as simple as love. In my long, haphazard, circling search for her, I had grown to love Sarah deeply. It was as if I had found a soul mate from two hundred years ago. I don't find it strange that I should love someone I have never known tangibly, any more than I find it strange that, even though she was born almost one hundred and seventy years before I was and I am older than she ever was, I feel somewhat of an age with her. I have come to know her, in all her sweetness and goodness, and struggle and humanity. She had planted me in Africa, our paths of immigration had intersected, and I had come back to find her.

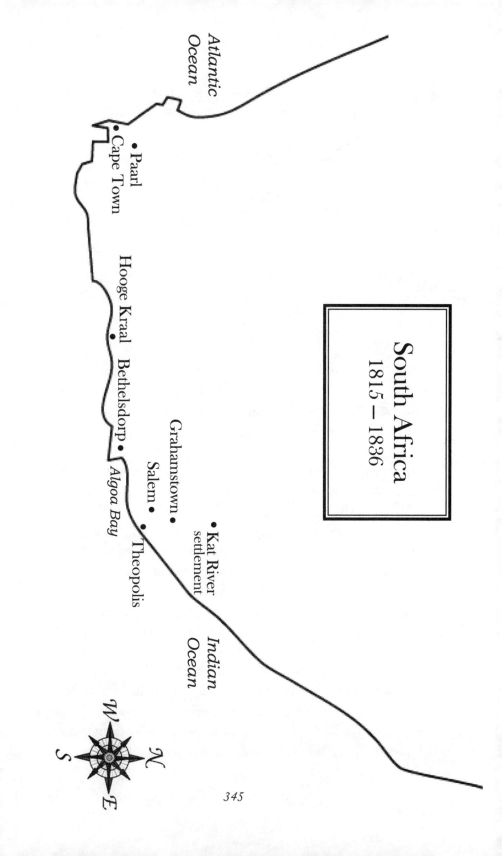

South Africa
1815 – 1836

Atlantic Ocean

• Paarl
• Cape Town

Hooge Kraal

• Bethelsdorp

Algoa Bay

Grahamstown •
Salem •
• Theopolis

• Kat River settlement

Indian Ocean

ACKNOWLEDGEMENTS

ALTHOUGH THIS BOOK took about three years to find its way onto the page, I have been writing it my whole life. It began with the often-told stories of my mother, Joan Krummeck née Barker, about our ancestors in the Eastern Cape. It continued with my brother, Peter, and his forty-part radio series, *Red George*—based on the diaries of our great-great-grandfather—which I directed for SAfm shortly before I emigrated. It developed still further when my sister, Anne, began to explore the church archives in Essex after she moved to England almost two hundred years after George and Sarah left. In part, I wanted to write the book so that our extended family—including Sarah's look-alike, Elspeth, and our cousins, David, Cathie, Martin, and Gerda—might have a record of our pioneering relatives.

I am grateful to my goodness-knows-how-many-times-removed cousin, Diana Hall Kelly, for reaching out to share her own personal connection to Sarah's extended family, and for passing along the name of Joc Guest, who would take me to Theopolis Farm. Thanks also to present-day farm owner, Howson Long, for guiding me to that poignant place.

I could not have wished for a more nurturing environment for my nascent writing career than *plork*—play+work—amongst the faculty and students of the Creative Writing & Publishing Arts MFA program at the University of Baltimore. Thanks especially to Kendra Kopelke, and also to Marion Winik and Jane Delury for their kind words and encouragement. A continuing gift of the program is that fellow student, Danielle Ariano, a courageously thoughtful writer, is now my writing partner; her probing insight and constant injunction to "dig deeper" gave me a perspective I wouldn't have unearthed on my own. The inspiration of another gifted writer, Tony Peake, also gave me a new perspective on how to approach the book, and I am grateful to him and to Peter Cartwright for their interest and generosity when I explored George and Sarah's history in England.

A huge part of this book is indebted to the detailed research and the transcription of sections of George's diaries by Marion Rose Curry for her master's thesis, *The History of Theopolis Mission, 1814–1851*. One of my sorrows is that I didn't have the opportunity to thank her in person before she died. It was heart-warming to discover such willingness—eagerness, almost—amongst researchers and research institutes to be of assistance. I am particularly grateful to Cornelius Thomas, Head, and Louisa Verwey, Librarian, at the Cory Library for Historical Research at Rhodes University for giving me access to the original manuscript of George's diary; Melanie Geustyn, Senior Librarian at the National Library of South Africa, who twice arranged for me to do research on a copy of George's diary and the original manuscripts of some of his personal letters; Fleur Way-Jones, Curator Emeritus at the Albany Museum, for going into their deep archives to show me the color portrait of Sarah; and Joanne Ichimura, Archivist at the School of Oriental and African Studies at the University of London, for helping me to negotiate the bewildering amount of research material relating to George in the London Missionary Archives.

Even though part of the process of working through this book was coming to the realization that I would not be able to pin down the exact provenance of Sarah, I am hugely grateful to Kristine Smets for her extensive genealogical research, including finding the marriage certificate of George and Sarah, and for her gentle patience in guiding me through the arcane methods of tracing ancestral histories. I'm grateful, too, to the Reverend Scott Bellows for helping me to understand some of the more esoteric biblical and religious references as they relate to missionary life.

The entire community of the When Words Count Retreat in Vermont has provided invaluable support along the way to this book being published. I am grateful to Green Writers Press and publisher, Dede Cummings, for believing in the book and for her exquisite design; to Sarah Ellis for her thoughtful story edits and her myriad copyedits to align my spelling, punctuation, and capitalization with standard American; and to Charlotte Williams for the final proofread. I want to give a special shout-out to marketer extraordinaire, Ben Tanzer, for helping me to get the word out, and to the generous writing community in Baltimore.

Finally, thanks to my early readers, Yvette Franklin and Björn Freter; to Sharyn Skeeter for her invaluable insight; and to Douglas Blackstone for his growing understanding of what it means to share the life of a writer.

BIBLIOGRAPHY

Anderson, Gerald H. "Van der Kemp, Johannes Theodorus (1747-1811)." *BU: School of Theology, History of Missiology* 1998. http://www.bu.edu/missiology/missionary-biography/t-u-v/van-der-kemp-johannes-theodorus-1747-1811/.

Barker, George. *Journal*. Grahamstown: Cory Library, Rhodes University, 1815-1828.

Beinhart, William and Luvuyo Wotshela. *Prickly Pear: The Social History of a Plant in the Eastern Cape*. Johannesburg: Wits University Press, 2012.

Brand South Africa. "The Origins of South African Music." April 4, 2002. https://www.brandsouthafrica.com/south-africa-fast-facts/arts-facts/origins-of-south-african-music.

Cape Town History. "Old Customs House: The Granary/Old Customs House 1809-1814." Accessed May 15, 2018. http://capetownhistory.com/?page_id=458.

Couzens, Tim. *Battles of South Africa*. Cape Town: David Philip, 2004.

Curry, Marion Rose. "The History of Theopolis Mission, 1814-1851." Master's thesis, Rhodes University, 1983.

CWM/LMS Council for World Mission Archive 1764-2017. "Papers of the London Missionary Society." Archives & Special Collections. SOAS Library, University of London, England.

Daily, Christopher. "Gosport Academy (1777–1826)." The Queen Mary Centre for Religion and Literature in English: Dissenting Academies Online. Accessed August 23, 2016.

https://dissacad.english.qmul.ac.uk/sample1.php?detail=achist& histid=64& acadid=61.

du Preez, Max. "Honour Khoisan by learning about them." IOL NEWS. December 16, 2014. https://www.iol.co.za/news/opinion/ honour-khoisan-by-learning-about-them-1796157.

Duncan, Paul. *Hidden Cape Town*. Cape Town: Penguin Random House South Africa, 2013.

Ehret, Christopher. "Sample Khoisan 100-Word Lists." *Social Science Division*, UCLA. Accessed March 3, 2018. http://www.sscnet.ucla. edu/ history/ehret/Khoisan100word.pdf.

Espenak, Fred. "Annular Solar Eclipse of 1824 Dec 20." EclipseWise. com. Last modified May 8, 2016. http://wwpw.eclipsewise.com/solar/ SEprime/1801-1900/SE1824Dec20Aprime .html.

Eve, Jeanette. *A Literary Guide to the Eastern Cape: Places and the Voices of Writers*. Cape Town: Double Story Books, 2003.

Grahamstown & Frontier Country. "Lord Charles Somerset, Governor at the Cape." Accessed January 8, 2017. http://www.grahamstown. co.za/page/lord_charles_somerset.

Hickey, William. *Memoirs of William Hickey*. Edited by Alfred Spencer. London: Hurst & Blackett, 1925.

Holt, Basil Fenelon. *Joseph Williams and the Pioneer Mission to the Southeastern Bantu*. Alice, South Africa: Lovedale Press, 1954.

Huigen, Siegfried, Jan L. De Jong, Elmer Kolfin editors. *The Dutch Trading Companies As Knowledge Networks*. Leiden: Brill, 2010.

Jeffries, F. "Marriages of Remarkable Persons." *Gentleman's Magazine and Historical Chronicle for the Year 1800*, 1800.

Keegan, Timothy. *Colonial South Africa and the Origins of Racial Order*. Cape Town: David Philip, 1996.

Kwa Zuzulwazi "Remedies of the Khoikhoi." January 13, 2014. http:// www.kwazuzulwazi.co.za/2014/01/13/remedies-of-the-khoikhoi/.

Lewis, Samuel. *The History and Topography of the Parish of Saint Mary, Islington, in the County of Middlesex*. London: J.H. Jackson, 1842.

London Metropolitan Archives, Register of Marriages, P83/MRY1, Item 1198. "London, England, Church of England Marriages and Banns, 1754-1921." Saint Mary, Islington.

Lovett, Richard. *The History of the London Missionary Society, 1795-1895*. Oxford: Oxford University Press Warehouse, 1899.

Mackay, Sue. "Obituary: Sarah Barker." *Grahamstown Journal*, January 5, 1837.

Macquarie University. "18th & Early 19th Century Sailing Vessels," Journeys in Time. 2009. https://www.mq.edu.au/macquariearchive/journeys/ships/vessels.html.

Malherbe, Vertrees Canby. "The Cape Khoisan in the Eastern Districts of The Colony Before and After Ordinance 50 of 1828." PhD thesis, University of Cape Town, 1997.

Manktelow, Emily. *Missionary Families: Race, Gender and Generation on the Spiritual Frontier (Studies in Imperialism MUP)*. Manchester: Manchester University Press, 2013.

McCallum, Graham Leslie. "The Cape-Wagon—Form Follows Function." July 14, 2016. https://grahamlesliemccallum.wordpress.com/2016/07/14/the-cape-wagon-function-follows-form/.

Miller, Russell, ed. *The East Indiamen*. New York: Time Life Education, 1980.

"Monthly Missionary Prayer-meeting, Bethelsdorp." *The Evangelical Magazine and Chronicle 1986*. London: Thomas Ward and Co., 1846.

"Monthly Missionary Prayer-meeting, Theopolis." *The Evangelical Magazine and Chronicle* 1986. London: Thomas Ward and Co., 1846.

Mundus: Gateway to missionary collections in the United Kingdom. "London Missionary Society." http://www.mundus.ac.uk/cats/4/251.htm.

Philip, John, D.D. *Researches in South Africa; Illustrating the Civil, Moral, and Religious Condition of the Native Tribes*. London: James Duncan, Paternoster-Row, 1828.

Ross, Robert. *The Borders of Race in Colonial South Africa, The Kat River Settlement, 1829–1856*. Cambridge: Cambridge University Press, 2013.

Sales, Jane M. *Mission Stations and the Coloured Communities of the Eastern Cape, 1800-1852*. Cape Town: Balkema, 1975.

South African History Online. "Lord Charles Somerset arrives in the Cape as Governor." May 14, 2012. http://www.sahistory.org.za/dated-event/lord-charles-somerset-arrives-cape-governor.

South African History Online. "Mission Stations—A-F." March 31, 2011. https://www.sahistory.org.za/article/mission-stations-f.

South African History Online. "Mission Stations—T-Z. March 31, 2011. https://www.sahistory.org.za/article/mission-stations-t-z.

South African History Online. "South Africa's Academic and Cultural Boycott – Timeline." February 3, 2017. https://www.sahistory.org.za/article/south-africas-academic-and-cultural-boycott-timeline.

South African History Online. "The Arrival of Jan Van Riebeeck in the Cape—6 April 1652." March 28, 2012. https://www.sahistory.org.za/article/arrival-jan-van-riebeeck-cape-6-april-1652.

South African History Online. "The fifth Frontier War: Sangoma Makana attacks Grahamstown under the patronage of Xhosa Chief Ndlambe, and is defeated." March 16, 2011. http://www.sahistory.org.za/dated-event/fifth-frontier-war-sangoma-makana-attacks-grahamstown-under-patronage-xhosa-chief-ndlamb.

South African History Online. "The San." March 24, 2011. https://www.sahistory.org.za/article/san.

Sutton, Jean. *Lords of the East: the East India Company and its Ships.* London: Conway Maritime Press, 1981.

Tanner-Tremaine, Paul. "Genealogies; Names; Parties; Ships; Miscellany," British 1820 Settlers to South Africa Accessed September 8, 2018. https://www.1820settlers.com.

The Great Karoo. "Colonel John Graham, founder of Grahamstown." Accessed August 21, 2017. http://www.thegreatkaroo.com/page/colonel_john_graham.

Whitehouse, John Owen. *A Register of Missionaries, Deputations, etc., From 1796 to 1885: Compiled for the Use of the Directors and Missionaries of the Society.* London: London Missionary Society, 1886.

XhosaCulture. "Makhanda Nxele—Warrior Of The 5th Frontier War." Last modified April 22, 2016. http://xhosaculture.co.za/makhanda-nxele-xhosa-warrior-of-the-5th-frontier-war-nxeles-war/.